IN THE COURSE OF A LIFETIME

In the Course
of a Lifetime

Tracing Religious Belief,
Practice, and Change

MICHELE DILLON AND PAUL WINK

UNIVERSITY OF CALIFORNIA PRESS   BERKELEY   LOS ANGELES   LONDON

University of California Press, one of the most
distinguished university presses in the United States,
enriches lives around the world by advancing
scholarship in the humanities, social sciences, and
natural sciences. Its activities are supported by the UC
Press Foundation and by philanthropic contributions
from individuals and institutions. For more
information, visit www.ucpress.edu.

University of California Press
Berkeley and Los Angeles, California

University of California Press, Ltd.
London, England

Library of Congress Cataloging-in-Publication Data

Dillon, Michele.
  In the course of a lifetime : tracing religious belief,
practice, and change / Michele Dillon and Paul Wink.
    p. cm.
  Includes bibliographical references and index.
  ISBN 978-0-520-24900-4 (cloth : alk. paper)
  ISBN 978-0-520-24901-1 (pbk. : alk. paper)
    1. United States—Religion.   2. Faith development.
I. Wink, Paul.   II. Title.
BL2525.D55 2007
200.1'9—dc22   2006021748

Manufactured in the United States of America

16   15   14   13   12   11   10   09   08   07
10   9   8   7   6   5   4   3   2   1

This book is printed on New Leaf EcoBook 50, a
100% recycled fiber of which 50% is de-inked post-
consumer waste, processed chlorine-free. EcoBook 50
is acid-free and meets the minimum requirements of
ANSI/ASTM D5634-01 (Permanence of Paper). ♾

To the women and men in this study
whose lives we have been privileged to know;
to Ravenna Helson and Jack Block,
shapers of the study of lives; and to
Michael and Andrew, whose lives
enrich us daily

Contents

Illustrations

TABLES

FIGURES

Preface

Many social scientists are indebted to people who are so generous of spirit that they willingly sit down and talk to interviewers, answering their intrusive and probing questions about all kinds of things going on in their lives. Our debt must be larger than most. The data we use in this book came from a longitudinal study of men and women born in Northern California in the 1920s; they were interviewed intensively in childhood and adolescence and four times in adulthood: in 1958, 1970, and 1982, and at the end of the 1990s. Again and again, these individuals, who came from a mix of social backgrounds, opened up their lives so that psychologists and sociologists might learn something about the human condition and how the interplay among the self, social relationships, and the American cultural context shapes people's experiences and life outcomes. We are deeply indebted to all the participants, and especially to the 184 individuals most recently interviewed in late adulthood, between 1997 and 2000. We are grateful to them for their remarkable commitment to participating in the study throughout their lives. Our debt to the study participants, though enormous, does not end with them, but extends to include their parents, many of whom were interviewed when the study participants were adolescents, and to the participants' spouses, who were interviewed at various times over the decades.

A long-term longitudinal study such as this is also clearly dependent on successive generations of researchers. We are extremely fortunate that, long before we were born, researchers at the Institute of Human Development (IHD) at the University of California, Berkeley, initiated this study in 1928, though at the time they did not intend it to go beyond six years! The remarkable legacy of the study's formative figures, most especially Jean Macfarlane, Marjorie Honzik, Harold and Mary Jones, and Judith Chaffey, clearly lives on; the legacy was sustained by countless researchers and interviewers who worked at the institute over the years and whose data gathering, analyses, and publications were supported by several federal and private foundations.

Although both of us received our PhDs at Berkeley, Dillon in sociology and Wink in personality psychology, neither of us had worked on the study while we were students there in the late 1980s. The study came to a pause for several years in the 1990s, until, quite serendipitously, Wink had the opportunity to reinitiate the study in 1997 when he received a grant from the Open Society Institute (the Soros Foundation). Over dinner one fall evening in 1995, while we were both on sabbatical in Berkeley, Jack Block and Gail Roberts encouraged Wink to embark on the IHD project. We are most appreciative of Carole Huffine's support of the late adulthood interviews and in facilitating our access to the IHD archives. With the permission of the study participants, Carole, who was in charge of the IHD archives, made their names and addresses available to Wink. This set in motion the first steps in contacting them and setting up personal face-to-face interviews, almost all of which were conducted by Wink and by Pamela Bradley, a personality psychologist and research archivist at the IHD. We are most grateful for Pamela's gentle style and probing empathy as an interviewer and for the rigorous attention to detail with which she maintains the IHD archives. We also thank Lillian Cartwright for interviewing some of the participants. The IHD director, Philip Cowan, has also been remarkably accommodating during Wink's several visits to the archives. We also thank the Henry Murray Center at Radcliffe College for making available to us the computerized portion of the IHD archives, and are especially indebted to Jackie James, who facilitated our access to the archives.

Our research using these data has been generously funded by many organizations. After the initial grant to Wink from the Open Society Institute, our collaborative research and writing were supported by grants from the Louisville Institute and the Institute for Research on Unlimited Love (part of the Fetzer Institute's initiative, Scientific

Research on Altruistic Love and Compassionate Love), and by small grants to Dillon from the Fichter Fund of the Association for the Sociology of Religion, and to Wink from Wellesley College faculty and Brachman-Hoffman research awards. We are particularly grateful to the John Templeton Foundation, which gave us generous support for the past three years. Many individuals associated with these organizations were particularly facilitative of our work. We acknowledge Susan Block, James Lewis, Lynne Underwood, and Richard Schwartz.

Our intellectual debt is not only to previous IHD researchers but also, more recently, to the several colleagues and friends who have commented on and critiqued various pieces of our work and to the many local, national, and international audiences who have responded to presentations on various aspects of our data. Among colleagues whose incisive comments and constructive suggestions have elevated the work in hand, we are particularly grateful to Nancy Ammerman, Robert Bellah, Jack Block, Lillian Cartwright, Glen Elder, Christopher Ellison, Ravenna Helson, Michael Hout, Michael McCullough, Stephen Post, Rhys Williams, and David Wulff. We are also appreciative of the helpful comments of our anonymous referees and of our statistical consultant, Allison Tracy. We thank Anne Fitzpatrick for her dedicated work in transcribing the late adulthood interviews. We have been ably assisted by several hardworking research assistants over the last few years. In particular, we acknowledge Laura Price, Kristen Fay, Britta Larsen, Janie Whitney, Adrienne Prettyman, Julia Scott, Lucia Ciciolla, Monica Garcia, Rebecca Cate, Tom Kressler, and Diana Dumais. At the University of California Press, we are much appreciative of the exceptional work of Reed Malcolm, Kalicia Pivirotto, Laura Harger, Bonita Hurd, and the production staff.

1

The Vibrancy of American Religion

"If I had had the sense then that I have now, I'd refuse to live in Texas." So declared Barbara Shaw when interviewed in 1958, at age thirty, five years after she had left Berkeley, California, with her young husband, an engineer who was returning to west Texas to work in his father's prosperous ranching business.[1] Becoming part of a well-established Texas family with a beautiful home might have struck those who knew Barbara as a perfect match for what researchers described as her "flamboyant and exuberant" personality. In adolescence, Barbara was socially ambitious and self-confident, a disposition encouraged by her mother, who believed "there was no reason [Barbara] couldn't be a member of Congress" and who repeatedly reminded Barbara to "always better" herself. Barbara's marriage certainly landed her in a well-to-do and socially prominent family. Unfortunately, Barbara's mother did not get to witness her daughter's accomplishment: she died, much to Barbara's sorrow, when Barbara was just twenty-three.

Barbara's passions for socializing, politics, and public speaking found no shortage of opportunities in Texas. The girl who as a high school senior in Berkeley was president of the Associated Women Students and who in college had enjoyed an exciting social life was easily drawn into the civic and social activities of her husband's family. But Texas was a very different place from California. And Barbara had very little sense of what to expect, though her father had grown up in Texas before moving to the Bay Area to work in a successful law practice. The difference of place was crystallized especially in the religious atmosphere that dominated everyday life in west Texas. "It's a Baptist town," Barbara explained, "where you can't smoke, drink, or tell an off-color story."

It wasn't that Barbara was not herself religious. While growing up in Berkeley, she had in fact been very active in the Congregational Church's Winthrop Club and Pilgrim Fellowship, and had "thoroughly enjoyed" the church's local activities and regional conferences during high school and college. Indeed, in 1944, when she was sixteen, she told the interviewer from the Institute of Human Development that the man she would marry "must be religious and ambitious," characteristics that mirrored her own sense of self. But she was keenly aware in her 1958 interview that being a Congregationalist was very different from being a Southern Baptist, and especially so in the 1950s, when Baptists were renowned for their separateness from other denominations (see Marty 1996: 448–49). Barbara pointed to the very different hold exercised by the two churches over their members: "Church didn't have the same meaning to my family. You went to church and then you came home, or you were active in the various groups. But these people live their religion. Every member of the family is a good Baptist and lives it. They are self-disciplined, they give 10 percent of their income—every member does—to the church each year. I've learned to give my tithe too, out of my allowance. My husband's whole family is involved heavily and lives by all its Christian tenets."

Barbara's husband and father-in-law were deacons, her mother-in-law was the church organist and music director for local religious radio and television programs, and her children, according to Barbara, had been "going to Sunday school since they were a month old." With all the time and energy that Barbara's family were contributing to the church, it is not surprising that Barbara too became highly involved. She longed for California but embraced the social and cultural demands of her new environs. She and her husband were members of a religious film discussion group and, to her surprise, "Even *I* teach Sunday school classes" (emphasis hers). For her Texas Baptist family, "religion is their life," and Barbara was making it her life too. Yet she envisaged a future life outside Texas and back in California.

Interviewed twelve years later, in 1970, Barbara was still living in Texas, now in Dallas, and was enjoying her marriage and five growing children. Her husband continued to be a "devoted Baptist" and highly involved in church affairs, taking the lead, for example, in planning the building of a new church. But Barbara, though still attending weekly church services, was significantly less involved in the congregation's other activities. Throughout the interview she spoke a great deal about personal change and her growing maturity and independence. She had gained much of this newfound autonomy by carving out greater independence from her husband's and the community's straight-laced Baptist values. The change in Barbara's attitude may have been influenced by the increased media visibility of the women's movement and the do-your-own-thing cultural mantra of the 1960s. In any case, one of her rebellious joys was driving around her affluent neighborhood loudly playing Janis Joplin in her open-roof car. She was also somewhat resistant to the extensive demands of her church, commenting: "I used to do everything at church. . . . I was [a devoted Baptist] for fifteen years, and now I'm sort of out of the stage of 'living for' anyone else. I kind of do my own thing. And now I've all but given up. I just go to services and get my kids there. I go every Sunday, but I'm not real involved [in the church's other programs]. I might be again, one day. But I'm not real involved right now" (age forty-two, 1970).

Although now doing more of her "own thing," Barbara had not become socially withdrawn. She was still entertaining a lot, and among her diverse activities she organized programs for various women's groups, such as lawyers' wives, and she did some substitute teaching. Barbara had also resumed one of her earlier avocations—journalistic writing—and had started doing book reviews for reading groups. Her busyness now, however, seemed motivated more by her own interests than by her obligations as the wife of a socially prominent man in a culturally conservative city. Consequently, Barbara seemed more at ease and accepting of herself: "I guess I was concerned about the impression I made on others at one time. But now it's really glorious. There's no one I want to impress. I have a few, intimate good friends that I like. . . . I no longer try and impress anybody. I'm me."

When interviewed in 1982, Barbara, now in her midfifties, spoke with a "noticeable Texas accent," betraying her tacit acknowledgment that she would, of course, never leave Texas. But she still longed to return to California and buy a house so that she could spend an extended time there every year. Although fulfilled in her marriage and content in her Texas life, she confided, "I always wanted to live in California. That's been a big shadow." Despite this disappointment, Barbara led a full life, continuing to be involved in women's groups and in reading projects, and she had also become an avid gardener like her father, who had tended a beautiful garden at their Berkeley home when she was growing up.

Barbara's husband's extensive religious and civic commitments continued, and they frequently used their spacious home and grounds to host Baptist events. All their five children—with the youngest now seventeen—were active in the church, and indeed Barbara herself was much more comfortable with the current religious services than with those she had first encountered in west Texas in the mid-1950s. As she recalled of that time, "People there wanted to know 'if I'd been saved in the Baptist Church.' And the biggest thing in town was the church. And dancing was sin. Cards were sin. And it still is dry. No liquor stores. No bars. . . . And the little rural Baptist churches, I don't think I could sit through so many of their tough sermons any more."

Barbara's experience of church in the 1980s was very different— the result not only of the fact that she had moved from rural west Texas to Dallas but also because the particular Baptist congregation she was attending was a more welcoming place: "We're in a beautiful big cathedral-type Baptist church, with a very enlightened preacher who is a good friend of mine with a good sense of humor. It's a warm, loving, wonderful church. And I'm very grateful for it." Barbara's sense of gratitude and affection for the church continued to grow, such that when interviewed sixteen years later (in 1998), she was highly involved in church and church-related activities. Turning seventy and enjoying excellent health, Barbara was attending services every Sunday and Bible study every Thursday, and some weeks she participated in additional church discussion groups and committee meetings. Summarizing the gradual evolution of her sincere commitment to the Baptists, she stated: "We are dedicated. That is something we do and we love. It is a part of our life and it is just great." Barbara acknowledged that she had not always felt so close to the Baptists. Recalling her adolescent involvement in the Congregational Church, she commented, "I loved my church; and my preacher, when I told him I was marrying a Southern Baptist—that was considered unusual—he said, 'I hope we have raised you to be of service to any church you join.' It took me a while, but it is a very good religion, and I have loved the people I have met in it." Although Barbara had journeyed far, from Berkeley to Texas, she was sufficiently grounded in church and in religion that, as so presciently predicted by her Congregational pastor, she was able not only to adapt but to become genuinely committed to the Southern Baptist culture in which she was destined to live her adult life.

Barbara's accommodation of the Baptists and Texas culture did not, however, come at the price of self-denial. She continued to be the socially outgoing person that she had been in adolescence, and she managed to use her skills in an entrepreneurial way that allowed her to flourish in her new family and social context. In late adulthood, one of Barbara's main church-related activities was organizing fifty chapters of Mothers-of-Preschoolers that were funded by, and which met at, local churches. Barbara was very proud of her volunteer work with this nondenominational organization, and she said the idea behind the project was for older women to play a central role in helping and supporting young mothers. An accomplished public speaker, Barbara regularly addressed different chapters of the group, visiting Baptist, Catholic, Assemblies of God, Nazarene, Methodist, Presbyterian, and other churches all around Texas to talk about parenting and marriage. She was thus at the forefront of a local program that contributed to the nationwide interdenominational ties that have been forged among conservative Protestants and Catholics since the 1980s as they have tried to steer America toward more steadfastly moral "family values" (cf. Dillon 1995).

As might be expected, given Christian teaching on the sanctity of marriage and the renewed attention paid to family values in political activism, Barbara's speeches concentrated on strategies to maintain an intact and fulfilling marriage. One of the values she emphasized was the importance of young mothers staying at home when their children were very young. She also exhorted the young mothers to "honor and respect" their husbands, to "know their needs," and to tell them how grateful they were for all the material and emotional things their husbands contributed to the marriage. Barbara's message may seem jarring in a society where the equality of men and women is taken for granted though not always evident. But she insisted that what she was "trying to do is make the women stronger and more loving, because I think that—especially in a city like Dallas, where men go to work—there is always someone [else] looking good." Just as Barbara had managed to bend to a cultural environment that was alien to her cosmopolitan background, she wanted the young women she counseled to be pragmatic in adjusting to marriage and motherhood and to the competitive demands of the local culture.

AMERICAN RELIGION

We open our book with Barbara because her life illuminates the strong social presence of religion in America and its vibrancy in anchoring individuals and families over time as they encounter life course and cultural change. This is a narrative of American lived religion that is captured in our study's longitudinal data, gathered from Barbara and close to two hundred other women and men in interviews from adolescence through late adulthood. At one level, Barbara's religious behavior is straightforward. If we were to apply any of the standardized self-report scales that characterize much of the research on religion, assessing either frequency of church attendance or the importance of religion in everyday life, Barbara would get a consistently high rating on both scales during adolescence and throughout adulthood. Since her teens she had attended church services every week and had consistently devoted a considerable amount of time and energy to church-related activities. Yet we can see from her interview material that Barbara did not exhibit the sort of piousness, certainty of doctrinal belief, and unreflective conformity that some readers might associate with highly religious individuals.

In fact, Barbara's high rating on a religiousness scale, though an accurate indicator of her frequency of church attendance and of the important place religion held in her life, is at the same time deceptively superficial. It would give us no hint of the dynamism surrounding her lifelong religious involvement. It would give no clue that Barbara switched religions, moving from the Congregational to the Baptist tradition; it would give no hint that how religion is lived varies from one community and time to another; it would provide no suggestion that the meaning of religion changed for Barbara over time, from being primarily a social outlet in adolescence right through middle adulthood to being a more fully internalized attachment in late-middle and late adulthood; and it would tell us nothing of the fact that, over her lifetime of weekly church attendance, religion itself changed in tandem with other social, demographic, economic, and cultural changes.

The extensive interview data we have documenting Barbara's life show four relatively distinct phases in her religious commitment and in the place of church in her life. Her adolescence was a formative time of extensive socialization, and church activities gave her a religious identity while simultaneously providing an outlet for other social activities with her peers. We can think of Barbara's early adulthood—when she moved to west Texas and started a family—as a phase of social compliance. Her forties, in contrast, were a time of rebellion—she was still attending church every week but was openly challenging its behavioral strictures and focusing on her own needs rather than conforming to social expectations. Finally, in the fourth phase, in late adulthood, we see a more integrated melding of Barbara's inner religious feelings with her everyday social activities.

Each of these phases underscores the fact that religion—what it is, how it is expressed, and what it means—cannot be abstracted from other aspects of an individual's everyday life and the broader culture. Rather, religious involvement intertwines with personality, family, work (whether paid or unpaid), and other everyday commitments, as well as with social and institutional change. It is more than just a co-incidence that Barbara was socially compliant in the 1950s, that she was rebellious in the late 1960s, and that she was at ease with herself and her pro-family activism during the post-Reagan-era of political attention to traditional family values. Because religion interpenetrates everyday life, its obligations and rhythms invariably mesh with the cultural mood and with the individual's routines. On the one hand, the cultural demands of religion can be such that daily habits have to be stretched, as understood by Barbara, who worked to allow the church to blend into her life as intensely as it had for her Baptist husband and in-laws. On the other hand, for some in our study, family transitions and cultural shifts nudged them to diminish their commitment to the church.

Yet we should not be surprised that Barbara, a confident, outgoing, and sociable woman, was able to carve a niche in a conservative church that frowned upon partying and other social temptations. Religion—as it is lived—is malleable and responsive to individuals' and religious institutions' negotiation of their environment. Religion is about faith beliefs and doctrines, but it is also about social interaction. Going to church is itself a social activity, and teaching Sunday school, organizing fund-raising parties and events, and mentoring young mothers are but some of the many routine social activities that churches encourage. Such activities fitted well with Barbara's personality and social status, enabling her to fully express her organizational and leadership qualities. In short, there is a sociobiographical and cultural logic to religion that shapes how it is construed and practiced, and this invariably means that how religion is construed and practiced is highly contingent on the pragmatic considerations and resources of everyday life.

Now let us consider a different representation of religion as lived by Jane Bell, another of the participants in our longitudinal study. Jane too was born in 1928; she had two older brothers and a younger, adopted sister. Both her parents were college graduates and were economically well-off. Jane's father was socially reserved—he preferred to spend his spare time reading rather than in social activities—but her mother was active in politics and community affairs, especially the League of Women Voters. Smart, independent, and athletic, from an early age Jane shared her father's intellectual interests and reserve more than her mother's outgoingness. Jane especially liked the outdoors—hiking and horseback riding—and at age sixteen, when asked what she wished she could have, responded, "What I daydream about is a large farm with stock on it and horses to ride, hilly country, and my horse at full gallop with the wind whistling through my hair."

Jane's father was an inactive Jew from a strictly Orthodox household, and her mother was an inactive Protestant. Jane herself was interested in religion and, during adolescence, attended informal church meetings and religious discussion groups, mostly at the Episcopal Church. Commenting on her religious interests, she said at age sixteen,

> Oh, I'm very different from both my parents—they're atheists. I think about God a lot. I read the Bible quite a bit—that is, largely out of historical interest. And I'm not quite sure [of] what I believe, but I feel there is something in religion that is important even if I don't know just what or why. But I'm not an atheist as they are. . . . It seems to me that religion, and religious feelings and beliefs, could not have been so important throughout the course of history unless [religion] stood for something and meant something that was really fundamental.

Jane met and married her husband, a Catholic, while in college, and they subsequently had four children. When interviewed at age thirty (in 1958), Jane described her late twenties as the "absolute low" of her life because of the death of her father, her "steady rock," to whom she had been very close. His death, moreover, occurred at the same time that one of her children was diagnosed with a serious illness. To deal with her despair, Jane sought psychiatric counseling, and during the 1958 interview, she was somewhat optimistic: "I feel I'm on the way to some sort of solution and understanding of [the depression]. . . . I have to accept my life as it is." At the same time, Jane was wistful that she did not share her husband's strong Catholic convictions, something that she felt anchored him in ways that she was not. Although involved in their children's religious education, Jane said she was unable to bring herself to adopt such beliefs. For Jane, God was "some nebulous force behind the universe," and as she commented, she did "not feel responsible to a God."

Pursuing her need to accept "life as it is," Jane went into psychotherapy in the late 1960s. She also started participating in one of the many encounter groups that were gaining popularity in California during this time. Illustrating how sociocultural change and the new resources it injects into everyday life can effect individual change, Jane emphasized how important therapy had been in advancing her self-understanding. During her midlife interview (at age forty-two, in 1970), she commented: "I feel that my life has just completely changed—my feelings about myself, like about what I'm doing here on earth. And I'm still growing. I don't think it will ever stop now. . . . I've never felt better about myself. I'm more confident, and I feel my identity very strongly. I feel I can do pretty much what I want to do. . . . I feel I'm worth something." Further reflecting the therapeutic culture taking hold in America in the 1970s (see Bellah et al. 1985: 120–23), and her belief in inner awareness as a pathway to personal growth, Jane, when asked about future goals for her children, said she would like to teach them "to be in touch with themselves and their feelings."

Paralleling her experiences in psychotherapy and encounter groups, Jane developed a sharper spiritual awareness. In the mid-1970s she grew interested in Eastern meditation practices that at the time were still relatively new to American society, having been ushered in as part of the post-1960s expanded spiritual marketplace that made non-Christian and non-Western religious traditions more accessible to the public (see Roof 1999). Jane's journey illustrates the cultural intertwining of spiritual and therapeutic interests. It began with her attendance at a lecture for mental health professionals given by an Indian guru. Jane described her response to the lecture: "Something happened the first time I walked into that place, into the ashram. It's an indescribable something, but I felt a real internal shift inside me. Something profound was happening, and I didn't understand it, but I knew it felt really good" (age fifty-four, 1982). She experienced "the same joyous feeling" when she went to a friend's wedding there, and after a few more return visits to the ashram, Jane embarked on learning meditative practices and subsequently began to engage in intensive meditation. One of the meditation rituals required the meditating person to bow and leave a fruit offering for the master, or guru. But as Jane explained, "You're not bowing to him, because he's only a representation of the self. It's a sign of recognition of and respect for one's own self." Engaging in these meditation practices had a hugely strengthening effect on Jane: "I was having some very pro-found experiences in meditation. I was experiencing a strength and a peacefulness and a protection that I had never before experienced, and it was all coming from inside me. I felt there was very little that I was afraid of, or that I couldn't do. I felt somehow protected. My whole attitude toward life became very upbeat, very positive, very cheerful, very altruistic; very little dismayed me." Jane continued to practice intensive meditation and to experience its emotional and self-affirming flow, and almost twenty years later, in her early seventies (at the time of her 1999 interview), meditation and other spiritual rituals continued to be a regular and highly meaningful part of her life.

One of the motivations behind Jane's attendance at that first Eastern spirituality lecture was that she herself had trained as a family therapist in the early 1970s. For Jane, being a clinician was rewarding not just because she was helping others but also because she found it helpful in understanding her own family dynamics, and it was integral to her own growth. At the time of the 1982 interview, she was doing group therapy with families. She was enjoying the work immensely and, importantly for her, also found it to be "part of [her] own healing."

At the same time, despite her preoccupation with her own inner healing, Jane's spiritual and therapeutic experiences also helped her to achieve a broader concern for others and their well-being as she aged. She carved out a productive career training other therapists, and she traveled extensively across the United States giving psychotherapy workshops until she retired in the early 1990s. Following her retirement, Jane became more involved in her long-standing artistic pursuits, especially working in her garden, where she had created some natural shrines, spaces that she regularly used for meditation. She also spent a lot of time writing poetry, painting, and sculpting. Importantly, she had also become an active volunteer. Prior to her husband's cancer and subsequent death in the mid-1990s, Jane had taught English to immigrants, had worked with undereducated adult prisoners, and had run a caregivers' group for families of Alzheimer's patients. Jane was proud that her work contributed to others' well-being. Additionally, as she noted in 1999, she took pride in how it reflected and increased her own growth: "I think the [family counseling] I did when I was working was terribly important. . . . I feel really good about that, and about the people I helped along the way. And then it's who I have become that I feel proud of too. . . . I have come to a greater depth of understanding and forgiveness. I'm in a whole different place because of it."

Just as Barbara's life highlights the strong hold of established religion in American society and its authority in anchoring individuals, families, and communities, Jane represents another important, though less visible, strand in American history and culture: the autonomous spiritual seeking of individuals who look for the sacred outside churches and who push the boundaries of personal and spiritual growth (cf. Fuller 2001; Roof 1999; Schmidt 2005; Wuthnow 1998). Jane was able to use emotionally painful personal experiences to push herself forward in her journey toward self-insight and spiritual engagement. And just as personality plays a role in influencing who is and who is not religious, it is also important in accounting for who favors a less church-centered spiritual path. Jane, as we saw from her comments in adolescence, had seeker tendencies from an early age. But even as introspective and psychologically minded as she was, it would be hard to imagine that she could have embarked on a fruitful spiritual quest were it not for the cultural changes of the 1960s and the rise of the therapeutic ethos. Demonstrating the way that religious and spiritual vocabularies and habits are critically shaped by the cultural mood, Jane was able to avail herself of newly accessible Eastern philosophies and practices as well as to tap into the increased popularity of psychotherapy. The fact that she was living in California, the wellspring of experimentation with alternative lifestyles and ways of being, no doubt further enhanced both the legitimacy of her personal quest and the range of resources from which she could profitably draw in order to meet her personal needs.

Although Barbara's religious origins were Protestant and Jane was from a nonreligious mixed marriage, they otherwise shared a relatively similar sociodemographic profile: they were two women born in California in the late 1920s to middle-class parents. Both women went to college, married successful men, had children, maintained cohesive families, and were active outside the home, one in voluntary work and one for pay. Yet they present two different, almost "ideal typical" ways of being religious. Barbara exemplifies commitment to an institutionalized or church-centered religiousness, and Jane demonstrates commitment to a non-church-centered spiritual seeking. In this book we give a lot of attention to comparing these two different, though overlapping, ways of being religious, and we are especially attentive to their implications for everyday social and psychological functioning.

The main point we want to make here is that, despite the differences between Barbara and Jane, both illustrate a critical dynamic of American religion: Religion as it is interpreted and lived in everyday life is not rigidly concretized in ways that leave little scope for individual autonomy. The nature, place, and meaning of religion are highly contingent on the specific sociobiographical, cultural, and historical contexts in which lives unfold. Both Barbara and Jane illustrate that Americans are pragmatic in deciding whether and how to be religious. In making these choices, they find many supporting motifs and resources within American culture and its long history of religious vibrancy, resources that in turn help individuals construct meaningful and purposeful lives. As our data from the 1930s through the 1990s show, there is much autonomy in how Americans construe religion, church, and the sacred. At the same time, though it is not heavy-handed, religion matters a great deal in many people's lives, adding texture and meaning to their everyday reality, anchoring their personal and social commitments, and buffering them in times of adversity.

THE IHD LONGITUDINAL STUDY

We have a lot of firsthand, detailed personal information about Barbara and Jane because they are participants in one of the longest-running (and still active) longitudinal social science studies. The study combines individuals from the renowned Berkeley Guidance and Oakland Growth studies established by researchers at the Institute of Human Development (IHD) at the University of California, Berkeley, in the 1920s. In 1928, as the spirit of scientific progress and modern culture enveloped America, Jean Macfarlane embarked on the Berkeley Guidance Study (GS) of child development, drawing a community sample of infants born in Berkeley in 1928 and 1929.[2] A couple of years later, her colleagues Harold Jones and Herbert Stolz initiated the Oakland Growth Study (OGS). They recruited a sample of preteens, born in 1920 and 1921, from five elementary schools in east Oakland close to its border with Berkeley. The OGS participants were studied intensively by means of a range of standardized interview, observation, and self-reporting methods until they graduated from high school in 1938–39, and participants in the Berkeley Guidance Study were similarly studied until they graduated from high school in 1946–47.[3] The initial samples were equally divided by gender.

The men and women of the two studies were first interviewed in adulthood in 1958, when they were in their thirties. Shortly after the first adult interview, the samples from the two studies were merged into a single IHD longitudinal study (Block 1971), and its participants were

TABLE 1. DESIGN OF THE
IHD LONGITUDINAL STUDY

	Older Cohort			Younger Cohort			Total
Age Periods	Interview Year	Age	N	Interview Year	Age	N	N
Adolescence	1934–38	14–18	160	1943–46	14–18	159	319
Early adulthood	1958	37–38	99	1958	30–31	138	237
Middle adulthood	1970	49–50	97	1970	41–42	136	233
Late-middle adulthood	1982	61–62	91	1982	53–54	149	240
Late adulthood	1997–2000	76–79	63	1997–2000	68–70	121	184

NOTE: Older cohort = Oakland Growth Study (born 1920–21); younger cohort = Berkeley Guidance Study (born 1928–29).

interviewed in 1970, 1982, and 1997–2000 (see table 1 for the study's time line). At each adulthood assessment, the participants were interviewed in depth about all major aspects of their lives, and they also completed lengthy, structured questionnaires. The study therefore has an enormous amount of data across multiple decades and encompasses a wide range of social and psychological topics, with detailed material on religion; family life and personal relationships; work, leisure, and volunteer activities; political attitudes and activities; and physical and psychological health. Today the IHD study is composed of close to two hundred women and men who have been tracked through intimate, in-depth personal interviews across their entire lives, from early adolescence through late adulthood.[4]

The progression of our study participants' lives spans the major social changes of the twentieth century (Elder 1981). Their childhood coincided with the Great Depression; they were adolescents in the 1940s, an era shadowed by the country's mobilization for World War II; they established families and careers during the 1950s, at the height of the postwar suburban boom; they encountered midlife—and their own teenage children—during the cultural turmoil of the 1960s and 1970s; they witnessed the conservative resurgence of the Reagan era in the 1980s; and at the turn of the twenty-first century they were living in a high-tech, multicultural society whose hallmarks were global trade, Internet communication, and a host of geopolitical and militaristic tensions.

We are particularly fortunate to have access to these individuals' lives and to the unprecedented opportunities for social science research afforded by the historical longevity and ethnographic breadth of the data contained in this long-term study. An additional unique feature of the study is that many of the participants' parents were also interviewed in-depth in the 1930s and 1940s. The parents' data thus provide an important anchoring perspective on the participants' childhood and adolescence and on the family atmosphere in which the participants grew up. Moreover, the parents' data are of further value in their own right. They offer a detailed historical portrait of adult lives in the 1930s and 1940s and, through retrospective accounts of their own upbringing, provide us with a window into everyday life in America reaching back to the turn of the twentieth century.

The study participants represent one particularly interesting slice of American society rather than being representative of the larger population of Americans nationwide. They were born in Berkeley or Oakland in the 1920s, either in 1921–22 or in 1928–29.[5] The older cohort, therefore, are members of the exemplary "Greatest Generation" (so labeled by Tom Brokaw [1998]); they grew up experiencing some degree of economic deprivation due to the Great Depression, and they subsequently participated in military and war-related operations during World War II. The members of the younger cohort (born in 1928–29) were too young to remember firsthand the worst effects of the Great Depression and, as high school students, were too young to participate in World War II. Similarly, during the tumultuous 1960s and 1970s, the older cohort would have had a more settled adult identity and consequently were less likely to have been influenced by the social and cultural changes of that era. Nonetheless, though the formative impact of major historical events such as World War II differed in their lives (Elder 1981), both cohorts are members of the long civic generation of Americans, with the younger cohort making up the core of communally involved Americans—those who join more groups and associations, vote more regularly, and have greater trust in political and social institutions (Putnam 2000: 254).[6] Almost all were White. Over half came from middle-class families and over a third from working-class families, and the participants themselves went on to secure higher levels of educational and occupational attainment than other Americans of their generation (Eichorn 1981: 41; Eichorn et al. 1981: 412). Though there continued to be socioeconomic variation among our study participants, their comparative socioeconomic advantages persisted throughout their lives; as we discovered, most of the participants were economically secure, in good health, and enjoying highly satisfying lives in late adulthood (see chapter 8).

The majority (63 percent) of the study participants grew up in mainline Protestant families, especially Presbyterian, Methodist, Episcopalian, and Congregational. Testifying to the denominational diversity so characteristic of American religious history as a whole, approximately 10 percent came from nonmainline sectarian Protestant traditions that included Christian Scientists, Mormons, Seventh-day Adventists, Swedenborgians, and Nazarenes. Sixteen percent of the participants grew up Catholic, 5 percent came from mixed-religious households (e.g., Catholic-Protestant or Protestant-Jewish), and 6 percent came from nonreligious families. In late adulthood, 24 percent of the participants were not church members, and another group, representing about 15 percent of the participants, did not actively identify with a denominational tradition. Thirty-four percent were mainline and 9 percent were nonmainline Protestants, 16 percent were Catholic, and 2 percent were Jewish.

The proportional distribution of Protestants and Catholics in our study approximates national data. Three-quarters of Americans born in the 1920s identify as Protestant and 19 percent as Catholic (Gallup and Lindsay 1999: 17). The dominance of mainline Protestants in our study, though representative of the Berkeley-Oakland community in which they were born in the 1920s, is not typical, however, for the United States as a whole today. The main difference in denominational membership between now and the 1920s is not in the ratio of Protestants to Catholics, but in the trends within Protestantism. There has been a steady decline in the membership of mainline Protestant denominations, and a corresponding increase in evangelical membership.[7] Our longitudinal data captures some of this change; we discuss in chapter 6 the small number of individuals in our study who had a postmidlife religious transformation in the 1970s and 1980s, nearly all of whom embraced an evangelical tradition.

Although our sample—with its predominance of mainline Protestants and a proportionate number of Catholics—does not fully reflect the more variegated religious diversity currently apparent in America, it nonetheless allows us an in-depth look into the lives of individuals whose religious traditions are squarely located in the center of American culture and society. Even though there are far fewer mainline Protestants today than a generation ago, they continue to wield substantial economic, political, and cultural influence in contemporary American society (see, e.g., Ammerman 2005: 4–5; Wuthnow and Evans 2002). The use of the term *mainline* is itself an acknowledgment of the central place that the various mainline denominations occupy in the American religious establishment (Roof and McKinney 1987: 236). To a large extent, mainline Protestant theology, with its affirmation of individual authority, religious freedom, social responsibility, and the autonomy of church and state, captures the core values in American culture.[8] Mainline Protestants are thus well suited to represent the broadly defined middle-class culture that permeates American life and to show how private lives and public institutions fit together (cf. Bellah et al. 1985: viii–ix). At the same time, the presence of nonmainline Protestants in our study, though they are few in number, allows us to note how they differ from and are similar to their Catholic and mainline neighbors.

We should also point out that, although this is a California sample, its men and women present very much as culturally mainstream Americans, notwithstanding the image of California as avant-garde. After all, these men and women were born in the 1920s, and they came of age before the culturally turbulent 1960s and 1970s. When last interviewed in late adulthood (1997–2000), they looked a lot like same-age Americans nationwide. For example, 81 percent of the study participants said that religion was currently important or very important in their lives; 49 percent of the participants self-identified as Republican, 30 percent as Democrat, and 21 percent as independent. These patterns closely approximate those of national opinion polls.[9]

THE PURPOSE OF THIS BOOK

The IHD study has led to numerous publications, including books by Glen Elder (1974) on the effects of the Great Depression on the study participants' transition from childhood to early adulthood, Jack Block (1971) on personality change from adolescence to early adulthood, and John Clausen (1993) on the life-span implications of planful competence, as well as a volume edited by Dorothy Eichorn and colleagues (1981) on life in middle adulthood, and many peer-reviewed journal articles. The IHD data has also been used by Arlene Skolnick (1981, 1991) in her writings on the changing American family, and Erik Erikson drew on his involvement in the study to derive his influential theory of identity (Erikson 1951) and, much later, used data from the study participants' parents to write about vital involvement in old age (Erikson, Erikson, and Kivnick 1986). Despite the breadth of topics in the books published from the IHD study, however, none of the researchers gave attention to religion, the focus of the present volume.

The purpose of this book is to document the dynamic intertwining of religion with everyday life over time. We use our extensive longitudinal data, gathered over sixty years of individual life-course and cultural change, to highlight the vibrancy of American religion; individuals' autonomy in how they understand and practice it; its adaptability to changing individual, social, historical, and cultural circumstances; and its positive role in everyday social and psychological functioning. We embark on this errand with attentiveness to the social and cultural context in which religion is construed and practiced. We recognize the many transformations in American religion over time and are cognizant of the changes that have occurred in the post-1960s era. But we also attend to the historical continuities and to the continuities in individual lives in how religion is understood.[10] In sum, because our data span much of the twentieth century and the major cultural and social changes that it spawned, our research findings allow us to see the continuities as well as the discontinuities in religion during this time. (We outline the religion questions in the appendix.)

The study's long time frame allows us to heed Philip Gorski's call for scholars to avoid truncating history in their assessment of changes in religion (2003). He argues that social scientists should use a long-term, rather than a short-term, historical perspective in assessing any evidence indicating support for or against secularization. Secularization, the idea that the significance of religion progressively declines with modernization and urbanization, is generally seen as following a linear and undifferentiated fashion.[11] Gorski argues for greater attentiveness to the fact that religion ebbs and flows over time. Any upward or downward trend at any given time may, over a longer span, he says, be cyclical rather than linear and irreversible. He also argues for greater attentiveness to the actual historical and sociocultural context in which religious behavior occurs, because (as his own research on Christianity in medieval Europe shows) the hold of religion is rarely all-encompassing.

Attention to the links between present and earlier times is hampered by the paucity of data available about the place of religion in individual lives and in families in earlier eras. Our study, in contrast, has data from the 1930s (and further back, given the parents' accounts) through the end of the 1990s and thus provides a relatively long view on religion. This time frame is particularly significant because it means we are not confined to simply comparing the current moment with, for example, the fabled 1950s, a decade that saw remarkably high levels of church involvement (see, e.g., Wuthnow 1988). Instead we are able to capture the ebb and flow that existed before and after the 1950s and, by having this longer perspective, to make a more nuanced assessment of the ways in which the meaning and significance of religion changed over the twentieth century. By the same token, having access to sixty years of life course data for the same people means that we can document the continuities and discontinuities in individual lives over time. Our data thus allow us to attend to the dynamic nature of religion and to recognize that, while for some, such as Barbara, religion may be a lifelong presence, for others it may ebb and flow over time, and in either case—as exemplified by both Barbara and Jane—the salience, characteristics, and implications of religious engagement may take on different hues in different social and biographical circumstances.

Our book uses statistical and qualitative thematic data and individual case studies to accomplish three related objectives: (1) to document religious beliefs and practices across the cultural and life course changes taking place during the lives of our study participants; (2) to identify the similarities and differences between church-centered religiousness and a more individually negotiated spiritual seeking; and (3) to document the links among religiousness, spiritual seeking, and social and psychological functioning in late adulthood.

The first segment of our book provides a historical context by examining the everyday salience of religion in the 1930s, 1940s, and 1950s, before the cultural upheavals associated with the 1960s brought about significant changes in Americans' religious beliefs, attitudes, and practices. We use our data to present a cultural snapshot of the variation that characterized religion in California in the 1930s and 1940s (chapter 2), and then focus on documenting the religious habits and attitudes of our adolescents in those decades and how their church activities fitted with the routines of school and the expanding consumer society (chapter 3). Of further historical and cultural relevance, we next explore (in chapter 4, based on interviews conducted in 1958) the extent to which a vocabulary of religious choice and autonomy was evident among our participants prior to the 1960s—when they themselves were young parents in their thirties and living through the 1950s, the height of American religiosity.

The three subsequent chapters (chapters 5, 6, and 7) capitalize on the study's longitudinal life course data to show how patterns of religious commitment and the meanings of religion change over the course of the life cycle from adolescence through late adulthood. We first examine the life course patterns of church-centered religiousness in the sample as a whole and identify how they vary by gender, cohort, and denomination, paying particular attention to how changes in social roles (e.g., empty nest and old age) and institutional events (e.g., Vatican II) may determine levels of religiousness (chapter 5). We then move to consider the extent to which individual stability in religiousness, rather than radical shifts, characterize the participants across the life course, and we also explore whether the meanings attached to religious commitment vary from early to late adulthood (chapter 6).

Chapter 7 introduces a different type of religious engagement by examining evidence of spiritual seeking among our study participants. After we briefly review the meanings associated with spiritual seeking, we focus on the study participants' patterns of spiritual seeking across adulthood and discuss the early life-course antecedents that are conducive to spiritual seeking in late adulthood.[12] (See appendix.)

The detail in the IHD interviews on religion is matched by the breadth of the nonreligious topics included at each interview time, providing an unprecedented opportunity to investigate the relation between religion and wide-ranging aspects of everyday social and psychological functioning. Because of the increased aging of the American population and the growing attention that scholars and policy makers are paying to the aging process, we focus, in particular, on the late adulthood phase of the life course. Thus in chapters 8, 9, and 10, we investigate the links between religion and the everyday functioning of our participants as older adults. As we go about this task, we also engage more specific, theoretically interesting issues in regard to ongoing cultural debates about religion. We examine how religiousness and spiritual seeking map onto the personalities and activities of our study participants and onto their social attitudes (chapter 8). We also disentangle the purported association between self-absorption and spiritual seeking and examine the links among religiousness, spiritual seeking, and concern for others (chapter 9). We conclude the presentation of our findings by asking whether religious commitment helps individuals negotiate the challenges of late adulthood (chapter 10). In particular, we examine whether religiousness and spiritual seeking are related to physical and psychological health and fear of death.

Focusing on the relation between religion and these various dimensions of everyday functioning in late adulthood enables us to identify the ways in which religiousness and spiritual seeking may enhance positive aging. Further, with late adulthood as the outcome, we also investigate the long-term power of religion in adolescence and in early and middle adulthood to predict social and psychological functioning in old age. Thus, as we document the links among religiousness, spiritual seeking, and psychosocial functioning in late adulthood, we also examine whether similar patterns can be predicted from the data on religiousness and spiritual seeking gathered at earlier times in the life course. We complete the book in chapter 11 by discussing our findings in light of American culture and by looking forward to the evolving contours of religion as the aging baby boom generation moves toward old age.

In sum, the purpose of this book is to shed light on the dynamic nature of religion as it is lived across time and adapted to changing life course and cultural contexts, and we do so by drawing on longitudinal, in-depth interview data from close to two hundred individuals (as well as using interview data from many study participants' parents). These data provide a window into individual lives and into the multilayered social, historical, and cultural settings through which those lives moved across time. The background limitations of our data—the fact that all but a few of the study participants were White, they were born in Northern California, most continued to live in the West, and most came from mainline Protestant or Catholic families—mean of course that we cannot capture the multilayered experiences of Americans more generally. Nonetheless, the breadth and depth of the IHD study make it an amazingly fertile furrow in which to unearth the riches that lie deep in the everyday lives of ordinary people. It allows us to follow these lives, to see how and why they may have changed over time or maintained continuity with habits of heart and mind that, in some cases, may have been in place as early as adolescence or young adulthood. Despite our instinct, as Robert Bellah and his coauthors observe, to think of individual lives as isolated and arbitrary personal narratives, lives are lived and yield meaning in shared familial, communal, and historical contexts (1985: 81–83). Lives intertwine with other lives and with a social history that is, in part, crafted by people getting on with their ordinary everyday activities.

We chose to anchor this study by focusing on the place of religion in individual lives. But as we move through successive chapters, it will become clear that a focus on this domain of activity necessarily illuminates much detail about the broader sociobiographical and cultural milieu in which lives are lived. In short, by studying religion in American lives, we learn a lot about not only religion but also American culture and the interplay of individual lives and social processes more generally.

2

Meet the Parents

The Family Context Shaping Religious Socialization in the 1930s and 1940s

The recency of California's White settlement is such that "in 1850, the West 'Coast' was not along the shores of the Pacific . . . [but] was lapped by the waters of the Mississippi" (Finke and Stark 1992: 66). In their extensive historical mapping of religious adherents in America, Roger Finke and Rodney Stark note that the "Far West," including Mormon Utah, was essentially unsettled in 1850, and that across the Mississippi the only states "having any substantial population" were Iowa, Arkansas, Missouri, and Texas (66). As a result of the gold rush, California's population increased from 93,000 people in 1850 to 380,000 by 1860; yet by 1890, Berkeley, the site of the University of California since 1866, had a population of only 5,000, and Oakland, always bigger, had fewer than 50,000 people.[1] It is hard to imagine it, given their cultural significance today, but the Bay Area cities that provide the geographical context of our study were incorporated not much more than 150 years ago—San Francisco in 1850, four months before California was admitted to the Union, Oakland in 1852, and Berkeley in 1878.[2]

The relative recency of California's population settlement and its religious composition were apparent in the family histories of our study participants. Over one-third of the study participants' grandparents were foreign born, and of those born within the United States, most came from outside California.[3] Most of the participants' mothers (84 percent) and fathers (84 percent) were born in America around the turn of the twentieth century (1889–1905). Among the parents born outside the country, most came from Europe, either from another English-speaking country such as Great Britain or Ireland or from Italy and Scandinavia; a small number came from Canada. Forty-four percent of American-born mothers and fathers came from within California; the regional origins of the non-California-born parents represented a broad swath of America, but New York, the midwestern states of Minnesota, Illinois, Indiana, Iowa, Ohio, Missouri, and neighboring western states such as Colorado, Nebraska, and Washington provided the most settlers.

California's gold rush culture certainly encouraged much revelry among its rapidly expanding population. Less widely documented, however, is the fact that this population also proved to be a fertile ground for religious evangelization efforts. The mid–nineteenth-century missions were spearheaded by the well-organized efforts of New England Congregational and Presbyterian pastors sent by their home churches, who were concerned about the moral laxity of the much fabled forty-niner miners; their vision was "to bring to Pacific shores a Puritan commonwealth" (Starr 1973: 85–87). But though it certainly did not become Puritan or evangelical, Northern California buzzed with religious activity. By the 1860s, San Francisco's religious vibrancy and ecclesiastical culture were such that it was described as a "city of spires" (75, 107). The Methodists, renowned for their frontier religion, constituted the largest denomination in California. Newly arriving Irish and Italian Catholics, however, added to the already established presence of Hispanic Catholics, and their increasing political and cultural power resulted in the dedication of Old Saint Mary's Cathedral in 1854. Similarly, Episcopalians built a vibrant congregation around Grace Cathedral, founded in 1850, the same year that the first service was preached at the First Unitarian Church in San Francisco, then the only Unitarian church west of Saint Louis (97).[4]

Across the bay, Berkeley and Oakland, the communities in which our study participants were born, also saw the construction of several different denominational churches. The religious climate was further enhanced by the establishment of theological schools in tandem with the expansion of the University of California, and the Berkeley area became a major western base for several Protestant denominational seminaries: Congregationalist (1866), Presbyterian (1871), American Baptist (1871), Episcopalian (1911), Evangelical Lutheran, and Unitarian (1904), as well as for Catholic seminaries, with the presence of Franciscans, Dominicans, and Jesuits.

Therefore, although frontiers historically are "deficient in churches" (Finke and Stark 1992: 66), and although California and the West today have lower rates of religiously affiliated people than other regions in the United States do,[5] this should not blur the fact that Northern California offered a vibrant and relatively diverse religious environment to its residents. In the 1930s and 1940s, Berkeley and Oakland were far smaller and more homogeneous places than they are today.[6] Nonetheless, their city directories from that era each list several centrally located churches. Thus, for example, in the 1930s, while Berkeley had only two movie theaters, it had many different Protestant churches, including Lutheran, Presbyterian, Episcopal, Congregational, Unitarian, Free Methodist, Mormon, Plymouth Brethren, Evangelical, Christian Science, Apostolic, and Seventh-day Adventist, as well as Catholic and Russian Orthodox Churches; a Unity Center; and Hebrew Orthodox, Reihaisho Hershinto, and Buddhist temples.

VARIATION IN PARENTAL RELIGIOUSNESS

The interviews with the parents of the study participants provide a rare window into the family religious atmosphere of ordinary Americans in the 1930s and 1940s. These valuable data illuminate the religious attitudes and habits of an earlier generation of parents and their approach to children's religious socialization. The parents' interviews are of further value because so little is known about the religious beliefs and habits of Americans in the 1930s and 1940s. Reliable national survey data on religion are available only from the late 1930s onward, and, because in the 1950s religion had a strong presence in American society, there is a general tendency to assume that the patterns evident for the 1950s extended back to earlier decades too. The paucity of studies from the first decades of the twentieth century further encourages the historical presumption that earlier generations of Americans were uniformly serious about religion and uniformly similar in their religious habits.[7]

What emerges from the parents' interviews, however, is a nuanced and differentiated portrait of the relevance of religion in everyday life. In the 1930s and 1940s, when the study participants were experiencing adolescence, 27 percent of the parents had high levels of religiousness: they attended church services or other church-related programs on a regular weekly or almost weekly basis, and religion was important in their daily lives. Forty-two percent of the parents were moderately religious—they generally confined their participation in church activities to once or twice a month, and religion was somewhat important in their daily lives—and 31 percent were not religious: these parents might attend church on special occasions such as Christmas and Easter or for weddings and funerals, but religion did not figure in their daily lives.[8] Catholic and nonmainline Protestant parents showed higher levels of religiousness than the mainline Protestants.[9] Furthermore, in keeping with a long tradition of parental unity in regard to church (see, e.g., Bendroth 2002), mothers' and fathers' self-reported religious involvement was highly intercorrelated, and this was the case for both Catholics and Protestants.[10] In other words, highly religious mothers tended to be married to men who were more religious than other men, even if the religiousness of these men was not as strong as their wives'.

The power of parents' religiousness in determining the atmosphere and routines in the family home is exemplified across several of the study's families. When Ann Gibson's mother, the oldest daughter in a family of eight children, was growing up on a farm in Utah, her social life revolved around the Mormon Church, and Ann's mother and father maintained a similar church-centered home in Berkeley. All in the family were devout members of the church, though the family considered the father, an accountant, least devout because he drank a small amount of alcohol when meeting with clients. The parents spent a considerable amount of time at church services and activities. The mother belonged to a church sewing group, and both parents were active in church clubs and attended church dances. They also exchanged dinners with church friends, and they used their home to host some of the church's social activities.

In one Presbyterian family, both parents and their two preteen daughters attended services every week, and the father, a skilled carpenter who hoped to own his own business, also taught their children's Sunday school class. They were described by institute researchers as an "easygoing family unit," and the parents' church participation fitted well with their commitment to being good parents. Both parents liked quiet evenings at home reading, but they pushed themselves to be active in their children's school: the mother attended parent-education classes and was involved in the PTA, and the father joined the "Dads'

Club" at the school. In another working-class family, the mother had taught Sunday school at their Baptist Church when the children were in elementary school, and although they were not regular churchgoers in 1941, the family read the Bible at home together several evenings a week and discussed its meanings.

The everyday religiosity of one upper-class Lutheran family was such that, although the father had a very successful business, the family lived "thriftily in order to put profits back into the business." Both parents and their only son were devout members of the church, and, typifying the enduring cultural power of the Calvinist ethic described by the social theorist Max Weber (1904–05/1976), work and self-discipline pervaded their daily lives. This atmosphere was captured in the remarks of our study participant's mother, who, when asked whether her son was ever moody, said, "He's not moody. Neither his father nor I am moody either. We don't have time to be moody. We work all day, and we're too tired to have any effort left to be moody at night. . . . We have no time for moods."

In a middle-class Catholic family where the father was a convert from a Swedish mission church, everyone attended weekly Mass without fail. Additionally, the mother oriented much of her social activity to the church. She was active in the Catholic Ladies' Aid, helped with church fund-raising dinners, and was involved with her son's Boy Scout group. Unlike this mother, the parents of a lower-class Italian Catholic boy confined their church activity to weekly Mass attendance, but the Church's moral code pervaded their daily lives, an ethos which meant, for example, that the parents would send their children only to parochial schools.

In contrast to these families, in which parental religious involvement anchored family routines, religion in some of the other households occupied a marginal position. This is illustrated by one father whose account of the hindrances to his and his family's church involvement could easily be mistaken for that of someone interviewed in 2003 rather than in 1943:

> My father's father was a minister, and the religious influence was always
> very strong in my family. Dad seldom got to church, but only because he felt
> he had to work seven days a week. He was actually a very religious man. I
> pretty much grew up in the Methodist Church in Redding, and when I went
> to college I somehow just gravitated over to Trinity Methodist and was very
> active in the young people's organization. That's where I met my wife. When
> we were up in Sacramento, we all went to church regularly; and when we

came back, the children attended church every Sunday as long as we lived in Berkeley. There hasn't been much churchgoing, however, since we moved out to Lafayette. There seems to be so much that needs doing around the place, and Sunday has been the best working day, especially while we've been building the house. Also, it's harder to get to church out there than it was in Berkeley. . . . Mrs. J. and I have been somewhat worried that the children are so uninterested in religion, and she's inclined to feel that it's my fault that there isn't more religious influence in the family, because I set an example of being more interested in things to do around the place.

The upwardly mobile mother of another study participant was more succinct about the lapse in her family's churchgoing: she commented that she and her husband were "always out late on Saturday night and did not get up on Sunday for church." In one family at the opposite end of the socioeconomic spectrum, no one attended church, because the parents could not afford the tithe. In another family, where the father was a skilled laborer who worked two different jobs, nobody went to church, because they "didn't have time to go."

For other parents, it was geographical mobility that loosened the hold of ingrained religious habits. One father, a Finnish immigrant, spoke of the impact of this transition on him and his young family's religious behavior: "In Finland, most people are Lutheran. My parents were very religious, and I had to go to church as a boy. But we don't ever get to church here, except once in a while when they have some doings at the church [and Eleanor, the daughter] happens to be going at the time and asks us to go. Churches are one thing we just let go around here." Another girl's mother simply said, "When I came to this country [from Denmark], I was too busy to think of religion."

Although geographical mobility can also provide new opportunities for church participation, old attitudes and habits die hard for some. Julie Ash's mother said that her family did not emphasize religion, because, when she was growing up on a coastal farm in Washington State, they didn't have a church in her community. The wide range of churches available in Berkeley in the 1930s and 1940s, however, did not motivate her to attend any; to the contrary, religion continued to be of no importance to her throughout adulthood. Similarly, a Scandinavian father explained that he brought his skepticism of churches with him when he emigrated from Sweden: "My father was one of a group of farmers who felt the Lutherans were too worldly, and [these farmers] formed a little independent group of their own. They didn't even have a church. They just met in the schoolhouse. The Lutheran is the established church in

Sweden, and my folks felt they were too proud. Also, the Lutherans used to come around to collect taxes, since they were the established church, and my folks felt that they robbed the poor farmers." This man believed in the value of religion and in God and an afterlife but was highly critical of churches even in the voluntary and more pluralistic religious environment of the United States, reiterating his complaint that all churches were "money grabbing."

Hearing what the parents of our study participants had to say about church and about their own religious involvement makes us aware that there was much variation in parental religiousness in the 1930s and 1940s. The variation we document is not an aberration. Rather, the pattern of parental religiousness evident in the IHD data is in line with the patterns in the few other historical studies that exist. These studies indicate that religious involvement in the 1930s and 1940s was varied and lacked the intensity of church participation of the 1950s. For example, Robert and Helen Lynd's landmark community studies of "Middletown," Indiana, in the 1920s and 1930s showed that religion had less of a hold on individuals and on family and community life than might be anticipated for that time. They concluded that "although the tradition is that 'every one goes to church,'" a survey of actual church attendance contradicts this assumption. Similarly, they commented, while "in theory, religious beliefs dominate all other activities in Middletown, large regions of Middletown's life appear uncontrolled by them" (1929: 358, 406). At the broader, national level, Gallup survey data confirm that Americans expressed lower levels of religious interest and commitment at the end of the 1930s than in the 1950s. Whereas one in two attended church in the 1950s, only two in five attended in the late 1930s (Gallup and Lindsay 1999: 15). These findings further highlight the fact that the high level of American religiousness seen in the 1950s was not typical of the first half of the twentieth century.[11]

GENDER DIFFERENCES IN PARENTAL RELIGIOUS ACTIVITY

The long historical association between women and church activity (see, e.g., Bendroth and Brereton 2002; Douglas 1977) was evident in our study: the participants' mothers were religiously involved more than the fathers. According to the 1934 interviews, when the older cohort were in their teens, their mothers (48 percent) were more likely than their fathers (33 percent) to be moderately or highly involved in church; and at the opposite end of the spectrum, more fathers (30 percent) than mothers (21 percent) had little interest in church. The cultural expectation that mothers have primary responsibility for religious activity and children's religious socialization was underlined by one father, a semiskilled, nonchurchgoing Catholic who became widowed when his son was seven. He lightheartedly commented that "church is mostly for women and children," a view he attributed to his own nonchurchgoing father.

Other fathers echoed this view and indicated that they found recreational alternatives to church more appealing. One middle-class father who had been raised in a strict Lutheran family recalled that as a youth he hadn't cared much for the Lutheran Church. He elaborated:

> I went to another church, a Presbyterian one, where there were more young people and where they had a basketball team, which is probably what I was interested in. I had a pretty good time at this church and even sang in the choir, but I've been less religious since I've gotten older. . . . [My wife] and the children have joined a church here in Berkeley, but I never got around to joining. I like to play golf on Sundays, and I have a lot of other things to do anyhow, so I could never see much point in formally joining. I probably go to church about three times a year, mostly to please my wife. I'm not averse to going, but there are other things that, I feel, give me more pleasure.

Similarly, Cynthia Stone's father commented, "My wife and Cynthia get [to church] perhaps once a month. They usually invite me, but I'm a lot more likely to stay home and put in a morning down in the basement varnishing my fishing pole."

Another father, a Catholic, said he preferred Sundays for "family recreation." A Presbyterian man who was an occasional churchgoer said that he always told his wife "that the welfare of the family comes first and the considerations of heaven and hell are secondary." A financially successful Protestant man who himself was not interested in church nonetheless commented on the inability of churches to counteract the appeal of new leisure activities: "The automobile has done a terrible thing to the church, and I'd like to see the tendency for people to go for a Sunday ride, instead of to church, corrected." The comments of another father suggested that this lack of preference for church was not a newly emerging cultural phenomenon in the 1940s: in recounting his own childhood religious activity, he said that, although he was sent to Sunday school, he "was not forced to go. It was just considered the thing to do, but whenever a picnic or something else came up, it was understood [I] would skip Sunday school."

Many fathers, of course, were religious—approximately 70 percent had at least some involvement in church. One Swedenborgian father took church very seriously, participated in all religious activities organized at the church, and was described by the IHD interviewer as having "a strong religious streak." Another father was highly involved with the Christian Missionary Alliance, and yet another was a religious seeker committed to finding "philosophic answers." This man, a low-income farmer, was active for various periods of time with Nazarenes, Theosophists, Rosicrucians, and Spiritualists and was even interested in making his farm a Theosophy center. One highly religious father sang in the choir at the Presbyterian Church every week, and another was on the Presbyterian Vestry Board. The high religiousness of some other fathers testified to the long-standing significance of religion in helping individuals cope with personal tragedy. One Catholic father continued to go to church every week even though his lapsed Catholic wife did not attend; this father got a great deal of comfort from his faith following the death of one of his older sons, who was killed in military action. And in a Presbyterian family, both parents, but especially the father, got heavily involved in the church after our study participant's sibling died; the father became a Ruling Elder and was regarded as being stricter than the minister about "un-church behavior."

Even though many of the fathers were religious, fathers were more likely than mothers to have hobbies and other non-church-based social activities that dampened the personal appeal of church for them. Many of the mothers, on the other hand, spontaneously spoke of the religious fulfillment they found in prayer and in church. A Greek Orthodox mother in a conflict-ridden marriage said she got "a great deal of comfort out of prayer." This woman, who had a positive view of God as a helper—as a God whom "you ask things of, and who makes an effort to give them to you"—said she didn't know what she would have done "without [my] religious beliefs these past twenty years." Another mother explained that, even though her "total absorption" with the Nazarene Church and its strict rules pitted her against her nonreligious husband and their only child, Deborah, she felt that she could not cope without its religious rituals. The church helped her, she said, to be "honest with herself," and it also became her "source of support. . . . When I was low and discouraged, it was the one sustaining thing in my life. And because the church had meant so much to me, I subscribed to its doctrines, which are very strict. It disapproves of dancing and movies, which has probably been a trial both to my husband and to Deborah, but I simply had to have the support it gave me."

And unlike their husbands, mothers tended to explicitly mention their appreciation for the recreational and social outlet that church provided them. One mother fondly recalled that the church had provided "her entire social life" during her college years, and she continued to be active in the Presbyterian Church and a church social group with other parents. A Baptist mother explained, "Religion has always been more of a social outlet to me than a religious outlet. It wouldn't make much difference to me what church I went to. I like the music; I like the rituals; I like meeting friends there. At times it's been the only escape I had. It was the one thing my husband didn't object to my doing." A Presbyterian mother who attended church infrequently said that, when she went to church, she did so "for the social end of it." One Methodist mother who had converted to Catholicism upon marrying talked of her difficulties with some of the church's teaching; yet she enjoyed the family's social relations with the priests. She commented, "I really don't think I had any inner disturbance about becoming a Catholic. Of course, I've never been as good a Catholic as my husband. But the thing I have most trouble with is confession, because many of the things that the Catholic Church considers sins, I don't agree with. I don't think they are sins. And so, while I still go to confession, I find myself very uneasy about it in my own mind. . . . One part of the religion that has been very satisfying to all of us has been our social contact with the priests in our church."

Men were not immune to the social appeal of church, but it did not emerge as a prominent theme when they spoke about church. A non-religious mother who was raised by strict Dunker (Protestant pietist) grandparents commented that, although her grandfather was a devout farmer-preacher, she felt that he was "mellow and a good mixer," and that he liked being a preacher for "the social life and the contacts." The social impetus for church attendance was also highlighted by an upper-class mother who recalled the significance of church in her husband's courting of her: "Religion wasn't important to my husband. He used to go riding with his father on Sunday as [his father] went to see his patients, but when he started paying attention to me, he started going to our church, the Baptist Church then. That's the way he won my mother over completely—because he regularly attended the Baptist Church and went with us each Sunday. Even in those periods when I much preferred other boys, he was always at the house, walking to church with us, and coming home to Sunday dinner."

In sum, our data suggest that women's greater tendency to be involved in church was partly driven by the expectation of mothers' greater responsibility for children's religious socialization. But women's participation was also enhanced by the meaningful role of faith in women's lives and by the fact that many found church itself an attractive social and recreational outlet, an appeal that was not as salient for men.

VARIATION IN MOTHERS' CHURCH INVOLVEMENT

Not all mothers, however, were equally committed to church. Many, in fact, had little interest in religion (21 percent), and one-third of mothers of members of the older cohort were not attending church at the time of the interview in 1934, during their children's early adolescence. Catholic mothers (87 percent), reflecting the Catholic obligation to attend weekly Mass, were more likely than Protestant mothers (63 percent) to be frequent churchgoers. In terms of overall religious interest and involvement, however, Catholic and Protestant mothers did not differ significantly.[12]

Among Protestant mothers, those with higher education and who were married to highly educated men were more likely than less-educated mothers to be religiously involved. This finding supports the well-documented historical association between mainline Protestantism, social status, and civic and church involvement (see, e.g., Roof and McKinney 1987; Wuthnow and Evans 2002). It may also, of course, reflect the possibility that the effects of the Depression on everyday life made it more difficult for Protestant mothers of lower socioeconomic status to be attentive to church in 1934, even though our data did not indicate a significant association between a mother's religious involvement and the economic deprivation felt by the family due to the Depression. Among Catholic mothers, on the other hand, there was no association between education and religious involvement,[13] a result that reflects the overarching traditional emphasis on church attendance for Catholics irrespective of social class. The larger point, however, is that, denominational and socioeconomic status influences apart, several mothers showed little evidence of religious commitment during their children's adolescence, a finding highlighting the variation in mothers' interpretations of the obligations associated with children's religious socialization.

The differences in mothers' religious behavior may have resulted to some extent from the increased professionalization of Sunday school that was occurring during that era, especially for Protestants. As documented by Coble (2002), church-based young people's societies proliferated from the end of the nineteenth century and throughout the first decades of the twentieth century as churches sought to invigorate religious socialization in the face of increased societal change. One of the results of this shift was that "mothers no longer controlled the key moments of religious formation but yielded responsibility for that task to 'experts,'" mainly pastors, lay leaders, and even young people themselves (80). For some mothers at least, and fathers too, transferring this responsibility to church experts presumably freed them from having to be exemplary church-attending, or otherwise religiously involved, role models for their children.

It was also discernible from parents' interviews that some mothers and fathers had long distanced themselves from church because of their own negative experiences while growing up in what they perceived as excessively strict religious households.[14] One nonreligious mother raised in a devout Catholic family said that from an early age she had disliked a lot of things about the church, and had rejected it as soon as she left home. Another mother stated while recalling her religious upbringing: "My family was Methodist—no card playing, no dancing, and everything very strict. My father took it very seriously. He sat there and said 'Amen' with the best of them, and sang hymns with enthusiasm, and then he'd come home and blow the family sky high. My mother didn't go to church. It bored her. . . . I went as a matter of habit, but I hated it. I hated to think of the cross. I went to Sunday school and church until I left home."

Christina Lucas's mother spoke of her own mother, saying that she was "a devout, stern, intolerant Lutheran [who] believed her husband and her children would go to hell if they didn't believe everything the Lutheran Church said." Her father was not so interested in church, "although in his later years, when he got older, he went to church to please his wife, since he hated to have her die thinking he was doomed to hell." Mrs. Lucas said that, from around the time she was twelve, she couldn't swallow the Lutheran tenets. She wouldn't go to confirmation, because she didn't believe what she would have to say there, and she was "horribly humiliated" that her mother "used to get the Lutheran ministers to work on" her. Mrs. Lucas poignantly elaborated on the lasting impact of her Lutheran upbringing, commenting that her life continued to be "dominated by Lutheran puritanical ideas, and still shows the effects of it"—she felt inadequate, she said, in relation to others and, unlike her husband, found it difficult to be humorous.

Such experiences are not women's alone. Some fathers similarly spoke of rejecting church as soon as they left home. Jane Bell's father, as noted in chapter 1, was raised in a strictly Orthodox Jewish family, and he was an atheist by his late teens. Another father, whose own father was a Methodist minister, was raised in a "prudish atmosphere where ordinary pleasures were called vices." Explaining why he himself didn't "have any religion at all," this man said that hearing his father preach, "and then seeing him at home being terribly mean to his wife, strongly impressed" him. Similarly, Kate Ward's father described his father as "a fear-of-God Lutheran" who had been a tyrannical "martinet" with his children. Both of Kate's parents were nonreligious. Another father said that his parents had been "strict Lutherans who discouraged cards, dancing, and dating." He elaborated: "My father was very much interested in religion and quite an influential member of the church. . . . I was always very much interested in church groups and in church activities when I was in my early twenties, but I gradually came to realize that very few people who pretended to be extremely religious practiced what they preached. I gradually caught on to the fact that there was an awful lot of hypocrisy in it. This wasn't, however, a sudden loss of faith, but a gradual process of catching on." Clearly, then, even had Sunday school not been professionalized, some mothers and fathers likely would not have attended church when their children were young precisely because of their own negative experiences with or perceptions of religion during their youth.

Although religiously strict churches are effective in attracting and maintaining new members (see, e.g., Finke and Stark 1992), our data suggest that the aggregate logic behind this does not necessarily persuade all individuals, nor is it transmitted intact across generations. As documented by Wade Clark Roof for his sample of baby boomers (born between 1946 and 1952), rigidly religious family backgrounds can produce very different, alternate types of religious engagement in adulthood (1999: 231–32).[15] The fact that some of our study participants' parents, the *grandparents* of the baby boom generation, reacted negatively to church because of their early negative experiences of religion underscores the idea that, irrespective of generation and any specific theology, a strict religious family atmosphere can contribute to suppressing rather than fostering religious participation. Although the meaning of religious strictness can certainly vary across time and culture, some people, as one father raised by strict Presbyterian parents said of himself, can get "too much religion as a youth to have any later."

The parents in our study who had rebelled against church, many of whom were migrants to California, may have had more of a rebellious streak than others who stayed settled elsewhere. Nevertheless, their rejection of their parents' religion reminds us that intergenerational differences in religion, something we hear a lot about these days, are not a new phenomenon. To the contrary, intergenerational religious differences in this country extend back to the early Puritans and were highlighted by the dilemmas they encountered in ensuring that their children and grandchildren would remain within the church.[16] Further, while members of the baby boom generation are especially renowned for their rejection of traditional religious authority (Roof 1993, 1999; Wuthnow 1998), our findings signal the importance of acknowledging that such rebelliousness was not unheard-of in their grandparents' generation. From a life course perspective, youthful rebelliousness is a normal part of the transition to adulthood, as members of each new generation carve out a separate identity and worldview, although the nature of this rebelliousness tends to differ across social and historical eras. Despite such difference, the historical continuity in the extent to which *religion* is a locus of intergenerational influence and countermovement is impressive.

THE CULTURAL ROUTINIZATION OF RELIGIOUS SOCIALIZATION

The cultural importance of religious socialization in American society, and the venerable status of Sunday school in American history (Brown 1901; Boylan 1988), is evident in the fact that 90 percent of the study participants' parents sent their children to church or Sunday school. This figure is remarkable given that many of the parents were not highly religious themselves and some had rejected their own religious upbringing. Most of them construed their children's religious education as a normative part of child socialization, an expectation that continues to be strongly apparent among current cohorts of Americans.[17] The study participants' parents voiced a positive regard for religious training similar to that of one Lutheran mother who commented, "Church is a good experience for children. There's nothing bad in it, and it's good training for later life." Another mother remarked, "It can't possibly do the children harm to learn the Bible stories and the Ten Commandments." A working-class mother who was not very religious herself nonetheless "thought it was a good idea for children to go to Sunday school," and she made sure "that the youngsters' clothes were ready so that they could go."

Parents' regard for their children's religious socialization motivated some who had not been active churchgoers to attend church more frequently, like many parents with school-age children today who increase their church participation for the same reason (see, e.g., Chaves 1991; Edgell 2006; Stolzenberg, Blair-Loy, and Waite 1995). Bill Stevens's father recounted, when interviewed in 1943, "We didn't either of us go to church for a long time after we were married, but when [Bill] was eight or ten, my wife went around to all the different churches in Berkeley and decided that the Christian Science Church was the best. So we entered him in their Sunday school. We don't belong to the church ourselves, but we have always gone since then. I think some religious training is good for the children, and our going is partly a matter of backing the kids."

Similarly, an upper-class mother who had started going to the Congregational Church after several years of not attending any church explained, "All of us joined the Congregational Church two years ago. We did it, I think, because our daughter was interested. . . . I went with her, and eventually my husband went. Our daughter simply loves Dr. Stewart's sermons, and I think they were very helpful to her in giving her security at a time when she was a little awkward and insecure."

But while almost all parents sent their children to Sunday school, some did not insist on or encourage attendance too strongly. The attitudes of some parents toward Sunday school illuminated the extent to which religious participation in America has historically been seen as the result of an individual's voluntary decision (see, e.g., Ahlstrom 1972; Warner 1993). This attitude was typified by one Lutheran father who commented, "I think religion, like a lot of other things in life, probably does somewhat more good than harm, and if the children want to go, I'll encourage them, but I wouldn't make an issue of it." Christina Lucas's parents similarly felt that they "should never coerce the youngsters; they should be allowed to go to Sunday school and church of any denomination they choose." As summarized by the Finnish-born father of another girl: "We never stop her [from] going to church, but we never coax her to go either."

A mother who herself had not attended church or Sunday school as a child pointed out that she "tried halfheartedly to get the children interested in Sunday school. But they didn't have any good luck with their

Sunday school teacher, and I felt I couldn't force it on them—it would defeat what one was after." A father who as a youngster had sung in the Episcopalian Church choir, but who was a "poor churchgoer" in adulthood, commented, "We encouraged [the children] very strongly to go to Sunday school, though we didn't ever tell them flatly they had to." Even some Catholic parents were lenient about their children's church attendance; one mother, for example, said she "wouldn't force religion on any child."

The cultural tension between Americans' esteem for religious socialization and their simultaneous regard for individual religious choice and responsibility was evident in Ted McRae's upbringing. Ted's churchgoing Catholic mother died when he was seven years old, and his policeman father was an active Mason who "was never deeply bitten by religion" despite the centrality of the church in the Lutheran-Methodist community in which he grew up. Ted's father remarried, and his second wife was a Methodist who regularly attended the Methodist Church. The only point of friction between Ted's father and his Catholic grandparents was the children's religious training. Ted's stepmother, a considerate woman, dealt with this by occasionally taking the children to Catholic Mass. But, as she explained,

> their father has a feeling that the children should not join a church until they are old enough to decide what they want. On the other hand, while his first wife was alive she took them to the Catholic Church regularly and he didn't object. . . . He knows [his first wife's parents] would be happy if the children went to church regularly, but he sees to it that life is made very entertaining for them on Sunday, with many activities going on, and [so] they go to church infrequently. However, it is perfectly clear that both [children] are attached to the Catholic religion, and I think it is highly probable that they will become good Catholics in time. I am on the spot, since their father feels one way about religion and the grandparents feel another way. I take them to church on Easter, Christmas, and a few other Sundays of the year so that their grandparents won't be antagonized, but for the rest of it I leave it up to them. I have told them many times: if they want to go, I will drive them in.

Other parents, largely as a result of their distance from or criticisms of religion, thwarted their children's religious socialization. Not surprisingly, some agnostic parents chose not to send their children to church or Sunday school, because, as one father said, "We felt we didn't want to have a lot of stuff put into their heads that we didn't believe." Another nonchurchgoing father elaborated on the evasive approach to religious socialization that he inherited from his own father, stating,

My mother was slightly religious, but it was one of the old man's famous theories: it isn't right to drum anything into a kid's head. He felt that they should be allowed to grow up without any influence like that and then make up their own minds, and none of us ever went to church much. [Our daughter] got interested in church for a time and went to the Lutheran Church, but it didn't last very long. My wife may be a little more religious because of her upbringing, but I think she agrees with me; and I agree with my father that you shouldn't drum it into a kid's head. Neither one of us ever goes to church. If somebody gets married, we'll sit there and watch them, but that's the only time we go.

The father of one of the girls in our study, a politically involved labor supporter, was noticeably more strident in explaining his strong opposition to children's religious socialization:

I regard religion with very serious doubts, largely because people don't practice what they preach, . . . or they get full of conflict and anxiety because they don't practice it. Neither one is good. The trouble is that religion is removed from realities, is too divorced from life. People set up one standard to talk about and pay lip service to, and [have] another set of standards to live by. . . . The children have had periods when I could see them getting wrapped up in religion. I didn't think it was healthy, and I offered counterattractions to keep them from church. It's just too easy for people to go to church, and sit hopelessly waiting for God to come to their rescue, instead of taking their own responsibilities. I think religious beliefs divorced from reality are a handicap, and I didn't want my children handicapped that way. So I blunted the edge of their enthusiasm, and successfully too, I think, without upsetting them.

Nevertheless, despite these few sharply voiced objections to church and to children's religious socialization, almost all the parents sent their children to church or Sunday school, embracing the idea that churches teach children positive values and provide them with security and a sense of belonging.

RELIGIOUS VARIATION

Our study participants' parents established their families in Berkeley and Oakland in the 1920s, and brought their children up in the 1930s and 1940s amid a vibrant religious landscape characterized by diverse denominational choices. Most of the parents had some degree of religious involvement, and approximately one-third were highly religious. The variation in religious commitment among the study participants' parents adds nuance to the assumption that religion had a uniformly strong presence in the routines of earlier generations of American families. Our data come from a region of the country known for its comparatively lower levels of church participation. Nevertheless, the more differentiated picture of religious commitment that we uncovered fits with the findings of other community studies (e.g., Lynd and Lynd 1929, 1937) and with national data for Americans (see, e.g., Gallup and Lindsay 1999) at the end of the 1930s.

We found that, continuing a long gendered tradition, mothers tended to be more active religiously than fathers, though mothers too varied in their degree of religious involvement. And although there was differentiation in levels of religious commitment within as well as between families, it was generally the case that a family's church-related routine fitted well with their other family and social routines, rather than being a compartmentalized task. Uniting parents across different levels of religious commitment, and underscoring the esteemed place occupied by Sunday school in American culture, almost all the parents sent their children to church or Sunday school, though some had reservations about doing so. The lasting imprint of our study participants' family contexts will be evident throughout this book as we follow their lives and their religious engagement over the twentieth century.

3

Adolescent Religion
in the 1930s and 1940s

We've tried to give her everything she wanted—trips, parties.
She's had swimming lessons, diving lessons, dancing lessons,
art lessons, has gone horseback riding. We've explored all the
areas around San Francisco . . . [we've taken] car trips up and
down the coast, and on the riverboat to Sacramento.

Mother of Melissa White, 1943

From this opening quote, we might well presume that Mrs. White
was summarizing the social activities of a teenager in today's era
of the overscheduled child. But she was referring to the recreational activities of her fifteen-year-old daughter, Melissa, in Berkeley
in the early 1940s. Not all families had the economic resources and
social ambitions of Melissa's upper-class parents. But many of our
participants as adolescent boys and girls kept hectic schedules—studying several subjects in school; taking piano, guitar, and public-speaking lessons; participating in high school social and service clubs; and
undertaking various sports and hobbies. It was evident that, by the
mid-1930s and 1940s, many families, and adolescents in particular,
were taking advantage of the expanding social and recreational activities becoming increasingly available during this era in America.
Eight out of ten adolescents reported going for car rides with their
families, and two out of three liked browsing in the area's department
stores. A common weekend routine for adolescents was to go ice-skating at a local rink and to movies, dances, and ball games.[1] And like
teenagers today, some also had part-time jobs, working weekends or
for a few hours after school in Woolworth's or other stores or offices,
or they had daily paper routes. One friendly and very responsible boy

held several seasonal jobs while in high school—he sold Christmas trees, worked for a fruit market, and parked cars and sold programs at baseball games.

Along with school and friends, church was a vibrant part of adolescent life in the 1930s and 1940s. Attendance at religious services and Sunday school, and participation in church-based youth groups and events, was routine in the lives of many of our adolescents. A quarter of the participants had high levels of religiousness (24 percent), an additional one-third were moderately religious (31 percent), another one-third were somewhat religious (32 percent), and just over one in ten (13 percent) were not religious.[2] If we combine those who received a high or a moderate score on our religiousness scale, the results mean that, in adolescence, religion played a salient role in the lives of 55 percent of our participants. This figure corresponds closely to rates of religious involvement among today's teenagers. A recent nationwide study of thirteen- to seventeen-year-old American adolescents found that the majority, 52 percent, attend religious services at least twice a month, 29 percent do so occasionally, and 18 percent never attend church (Smith and Denton 2005: 37). Similarly, 51 percent of contemporary adolescents say that religious faith is very or extremely important in shaping their daily lives, 31 percent see it as somewhat important, and for 18 percent it is not very or not important (Smith and Denton 2005: 40).

It is clear from the interview transcripts that many of the IHD adolescents took religion seriously. One highly religious girl attended morning services and the Christian Endeavor program at the United Presbyterian Church every Sunday and also participated in "Singspiration" once a week at someone's home. One highly religious boy went to Sunday school at the Baptist Church every week and read a couple of verses from the Bible every night. He also went to the church's social hour every Sunday afternoon and participated in some of the church's periodic skiing trips. Another boy, Karl Harper, had been attending Sunday school at the Lutheran Church since he was six, was confirmed there, and continued regular attendance right through adolescence. Karl liked the preacher at his church because he was calm and "never shouts when he preaches." Though Karl didn't care much for reading, when he was at home sick with the mumps before confirmation, he read *Boy's Life* and memorized the books of the Bible. At seventeen, he enjoyed being the organist for the church's choir practices.

For the majority who were religious, it was also evident that church activities blended smoothly into schedules that accommodated school-work, extracurricular interests, and other social activities. One upper-class Presbyterian girl who went to church every week was on the high school honor roll, was a pledged member of one of its coed clubs, and was involved in drama, public speaking, and the young people's symphony orchestra. One Lutheran girl described her typical weekend: On Saturdays "a crowd of boys and girls" would come to her house in the morning; they frequently went to a show in the afternoon and came back to her house after supper to dance. On Sundays, she went to Sunday school in the morning, attended a movie with friends in the afternoon, and listened to radio plays with her family in the evening. A Catholic girl who came from a very sociable and strongly religious family attended an all-girl Catholic high school but had a mixed group of friends. She and her friends all went to weekend dances together and returned to her house afterward for hot chocolate.

It was generally the case that the adolescents liked going to church or Sunday school or that, at least, church was "all right."[3] A Baptist girl who liked Sunday school a lot said she missed it only "if I've been out real late [and] I don't get up in time." A Presbyterian girl who attended the youth forum on Sunday evenings said: "I think the thing that appeals to me about the church is the wonderful feeling of closeness it gives you." A Catholic girl who enjoyed going to Mass every Sunday with her mother and brother said she "wouldn't miss church for anything." Another Catholic girl said she liked to go to Mass and went to confession once a week, but she pointed out that "you only *have* to go once a year." She liked confessing to a young priest at her church; she told the interviewer that she could tell this priest things she worried about or felt bad about and "ask him how to act if I am not sure." Afterward, she said, she always felt relieved. A Protestant girl who attended Sunday school every week and liked it said that, even though her mother sometimes didn't want her to go, she went anyway. Reflecting a stricter family and denominational attitude, a Catholic boy said that, although he liked Sunday school, "liking it is irrelevant" because his parents and the church required him to go every week. When he was twelve, one Presbyterian boy said that Sunday school was "O.K." and that he liked the sermons. Similarly, a Congregational girl, said she got "a lot out of the sermons," and that going to church gave her "a good feeling. It gets a load off your mind." A Presbyterian boy who had a positive attitude toward Sunday school was nonetheless aware, like some of the fathers quoted in the previous chapter, of the recreational alternatives to church. He remarked, "You feel better when you go to church, but when you are getting ready to go, you'd just as soon go on a picnic instead."

It was also apparent that some of the study participants went to church or Sunday school primarily because their parents required them to go, and several who went were indifferent about their attendance. Many of our adolescents (28 percent), especially boys, mentioned that they disliked or were bored by church and Sunday school. One Protestant boy said it was "too much trouble" to go to Sunday school, since he had to walk a mile to the church. A Catholic boy whose mother was irritated by his attitude toward church said, "I'd rather sleep than go to church. Every Sunday I have to [go]. They can't force me to do anything I don't want to, but they say no shows or anything else I want to do, so I find myself at church. It bores me." Several other boys mentioned that they, too, preferred to sleep late or to listen to the radio. One boy commented that he gets "tired of sitting still, listening to the old preacher, and I get hungry." Another Protestant boy complained that he "never *learned* anything there." A girl from a high-status Catholic family whose members were lax in their church attendance took an even more critical view: "None of us are terribly religious. We don't go to church very often. We should, I guess. Religion is what one feels in one's own mind, really. It's not just going to church, paying a fine for your sins and praying. I can't see Catholicism as being built on anything real."

Although, according to our findings, rates of adolescent religious participation in the 1930s and 1940s are remarkably similar to those of today, there are also differences. Unlike today, when Catholic and mainline Protestant teenagers have similar levels of church attendance,[4] denominational differences were apparent among our study's adolescents. Well over twenty years before Vatican II allowed Catholics to more loosely interpret the obligations associated with being Catholic, two-thirds (66 percent) of the Catholic adolescents, compared to over half (57 percent) of the Protestants, were moderately or highly religious, a difference reflecting the significance of weekly Mass attendance for Catholics. Among Protestants—who today experience quite a lot of variation between mainline and nonmainline traditions—we found that religiousness did not vary according to whether the participant was affiliated with a mainline or a nonmainline church: in our study, 56 percent of mainline and 58 percent of nonmainline Protestant adolescents were moderately or highly religious.[5]

Significantly, although most of the study participants went to a church or Sunday school of the denomination with which one or both parents were affiliated, a sizable number (15 percent) regularly went to services at churches with which their parents were not affiliated. This finding pointing to intrafamily variation in church habits suggests that family religion before the 1950s showed less uniformity than is sometimes assumed.[6] One boy, for example, went to the Christian Science Church with his grandmother, his parents attended the Lutheran Church every week, and his siblings attended the Presbyterian Sunday school. In one family, our study participant attended the Congregational Church, her sister joined the Episcopal Church, and their mother attended a nondenominational Protestant community church. A boy who "loathed" the Greek Orthodox Church that his parents attended refused to go; after trying out several different churches, he decided he preferred the Catholic Church, which he then attended regularly with a neighbor, a girl his own age with whom he was friendly. One girl attended the Presbyterian Church even though her mother regularly went to the Episcopal Church; this girl commented, "I went to the Episcopal Church two or three times, but I didn't like it. It's a lot like the Catholic Church, isn't it? You just spend your time getting up and down."

Not surprisingly, in view of the fact that churchgoing tends to have a family rhythm (see, e.g., Myers 1996), parental religious involvement was positively related to the religiousness of adolescents. For the sample as a whole, irrespective of denominational background, adolescent religious involvement was very strongly related to parental religiousness.[7] Based on analyses for a subsample composed of participants in the older cohort (born in 1920–21), adolescent religiousness was positively and independently associated with the mother's and father's religious involvement. In fact, the father's religious involvement had a stronger relation to adolescent religiousness than the mother's involvement had. This finding suggests that, because fathers are less likely than mothers to be religiously active (see chapter 2), when fathers are involved their example can be more powerful (cf. Roof 1999: 225). A boy who went to the Episcopalian Church only for Easter and Christmas services commented at age sixteen, "I only go because my father goes, not because I feel better for it or anything." The reverse effect is captured in a story told by a father who did not attend church. He recounted how he sometimes tried to encourage his adolescent son to go to services more frequently; his son, however, not missing a beat, would quickly end the conversation by retorting, "Why don't *you?*"

Our data further revealed that the well-documented gender differences in religious involvement are established fairly early in life. Already during childhood, there was a tendency for girls to be more regular churchgoers than boys, and this gender difference in religious involvement was considerably more pronounced in adolescence. Whereas almost two-thirds of adolescent girls (62 percent) were moderately or highly religious, this was true of less than half the boys (46 percent).[8] Similar gender differences are apparent among contemporary American teens; 56 percent of girls compared to 49 percent of boys attend religious services at least twice a month (Smith and Denton 2005: 279).

Apart from gender and denomination, there were no other sources of social variation in the adolescent religiousness of the study participants. Among a subsample of participants (from both cohorts) for whom we had data on the quality of family relations in adolescence, there was no evidence of an association between family cohesion or warmth and adolescent religiousness. This means that in our study the adolescents who were highly involved in church did not tend to come from more cohesive or well-functioning families than those who were not religiously active. It is also noteworthy that, irrespective of differences in the educational and social-class backgrounds of parents, our adolescents participated in church services and in other church-related activities with much the same regularity. Furthermore, among the older-cohort adolescents interviewed in 1934, we found no evidence that the economic deprivation which families experienced as a result of the Great Depression had an effect on adolescents' religiousness.[9] The insignificance of parental education to adolescent religiosity is similarly apparent among today's youth (Smith and Denton 2005: 277).

The fact that variation in parental educational background does not produce differences in the religious commitments of adolescents further underscores the broad cultural emphasis in America on religious socialization and the expectation that children and adolescents will be involved in church. Indeed, confirming parents' reports of sending their children to church or Sunday school, the vast majority of adolescents specifically reported that they had gone to church or Sunday school: 84 percent went when they were six to ten years old; 81 percent attended between the ages of eleven and fifteen.[10] These figures are of additional relevance because they further highlight the cultural normativeness of our particular sample; a similar proportion (81 percent) of Americans in the same age category as our study participants (age sixty-five or over in 1998) reported having had religious training in childhood (Gallup and Lindsay 1999: 61).

In sum, the majority (55 percent) of the participants were moderately or highly religious during adolescence. Of particular note, and underscoring yet another historical continuity in American religion, the variation in levels of adolescent religious involvement in the 1930s and 1940s closely parallels studies of religiousness among adolescents today. Girls were more religiously involved than boys, and, regardless of gender, adolescents were more likely to be highly religious if their parents were religiously active.

ADOLESCENTS' RELIGIOUS BELIEFS AND INTERESTS

While the various levels of religious activity among our adolescents in the 1930s and 1940s closely resemble the trends for today's youth, one might well wonder whether our participants were more intrinsically devout in their faith. After all, a third of our study participants are members of the highly renowned Greatest Generation (Brokaw 1998), and all of them are part of the long pre–World War II civic generation of Americans highly involved in community activities (Putnam 2000). Thus they are cohorts known for their subjugation of self-interest to the common good. Was this selflessness evident in the nature of their adolescent religious beliefs?

In their study of religion among youth today, Christian Smith and Melinda Denton were surprised to find that, although 80 percent of their interviewees prayed on a regular basis, the content of their prayer was dominated by a self-focused desire to feel good and solve personal problems. What Smith and Denton found distinctly lacking was an emphasis on fulfilling God's wishes and a desire to obey God's message "regardless of personal consequences or rewards" (2005: 149). Like today's youth, approximately 80 percent of our adolescents prayed.[11] But unlike the participants in Smith and Denton's study, who held a highly instrumental view of God, construing God as "something like a cosmic therapist" who helps people do what they want (148), our adolescents' prayers were largely devoid of self-orientation. In our study, the most frequently endorsed reason for prayer was to "ask God to help those who need him" (39 percent), as exemplified by a boy who used the Bible to pray at length for his mother's recovery from a major illness. The next most frequently endorsed reasons for prayer were to "thank God for all he has done for me" (36 percent), "have God help us to do good things" (16 percent), "feel closer to God" (16 percent), and "do as my parents taught me" (16 percent). Showing an unselfish strain, and in stark contrast to the participants in Smith and Denton's study, none of the boys and girls in our study endorsed statements indicating that they prayed in order to "get what I want" or to "cause God to change his plans." Moreover, a mere 10 percent indicated that they prayed to "ask Jesus to help me."

The view of God as a helper to those in need was so pervasive among our study participants that it was reflected even in the comments of the minority, mostly boys, who didn't pray. Giving voice to the self-reliant individualism embedded in American culture (see, e.g., Bellah et al. 1985), one boy said, "The family as a whole—well, none of us go to church, but personally I think that, unless a person has a need for God's help, the church is a waste of time. You ought to be able to help yourself." Relying on God for help was also scorned by a girl who, like her humanist father, had "no belief in God." She felt that "religion [was] dangerous because it kept people from feeling personally responsible to make a better world."

The image of God endorsed by most of our adolescents affirmed the core Christian belief in God as the creator (51 percent) and in Jesus as the savior of humankind (25 percent). An oppositional view was offered by one nonreligious boy, who commented dismissively, "I don't know exactly what I think. I suppose I think there is a God, but where or what he is I don't know, and I am not particularly interested." Other adolescents, nonetheless, affirmed beliefs that underscored God's goodness. Several endorsed a view of God as "one who makes us want to do good things" (21 percent) and "a beautiful thought to make us live better" (24 percent), and by the same token they affirmed Jesus as the one who "taught us to do right" (26 percent) and as "a great example" (17 percent). One highly religious Presbyterian girl who said she "tells God about things" rather than saying formal prayers also said that what was important about Jesus was not his "appearance" but the fact that he "knows all and forgives all." Very few of the boys and girls thought of God in concrete terms such as "Ruler and King of Heaven" (five people) or "a person in the sky" (one person)

Similarly, adolescent beliefs about the afterlife and about hell did not suggest a fearsome God. The most frequently endorsed view of the afterlife was that it entailed "everlasting sleep" (33 percent). Pointing again to the appealing goodness of God, some adolescents thought of the afterlife in terms of everyone being "rewarded for the good they have done" (17 percent) and being reconnected with their loved ones (15 percent). None of the participants thought that "the dead stay in their graves until judgment day." Some said, "Only those who really believe in God go to Heaven" (15 percent), and others said the dead live on only in people's memories (15 percent). Remarkably, only five of our adolescents believed that "nothing happens" after death; this exceptional view was unequivocally stated by a boy who occasionally attended the Methodist Church and who was described by researchers as being generally pessimistic. He commented, "I think when you're dead, you're dead." Overall, our findings on belief in afterlife parallel today's attitudes: approximately eight in ten Americans, including teenagers, currently believe in an afterlife (Greeley and Hout 1999; Smith and Denton 2005).

Just over half of the adolescents (53 percent) regarded the Bible literally as "God's own words to man." Others were more likely to regard it as a less awesome document—more simply as useful knowledge (27 percent) and as history (15 percent). American attitudes toward the Bible provide a good example of the ebb and flow in the popularity of particular religious beliefs over time. The literal view of the Bible was endorsed by fewer of our adolescents in 1934 than in national surveys of teenagers in the late 1950s (62 percent), but by more than in national surveys in the early 1990s (39 percent; Gallup and Lindsay 1999: 160). The most frequently cited source from which the adolescents said they got their idea of God was Sunday school or church (58 percent), thus affirming the cultural expectation that Sunday school is necessary for children's religious socialization. Fewer specifically mentioned their parents (27 percent), a finding supporting the presumption that religious instruction is the professional domain of churches and not primarily the duty of parents. A handful of adolescents evoked a more self-directed sensibility, saying they got their ideas from thinking about God for themselves, from "nature," or from "experiencing or feeling near to God." Highlighting the limits of peer conversations and adolescent reading habits, none of the adolescents said they got their idea of God from talking with their friends or from reading general fiction or nonfiction literature.

From their prayers and their views of God, Jesus, the afterlife, and the Bible, it is evident that our adolescents embraced a relatively benign theology. And, since most of them got their views from church, Sunday school, and parents, we can infer that this theology—representing God as a positive resource rather than a negative, commanding authority—was already in place in America in the 1930s. Indeed, none of the participants agreed with the statement that God "sends pain to those who do not believe in Him," a finding that anticipates the benign-accepting, religious relativism so strongly associated with post-1960s America.

Lest anyone begin to think that a fire-and-brimstone theology had no presence among Californian Depression-era youth, there was evidence that a judgmental God lurked in the minds of some. A minority saw God as a judge who punishes or rewards people (23 percent), as did a boy from a highly religious Swedenborgian family, a Boy Scout who spontaneously mentioned that he believed in a "punishing God." Some regarded hell in vividly punitive terms (31 percent). These adolescents envisioned hell as "a place where people pay for all the bad they've done on earth" (17 percent), "a place of never-ending torture" (8 percent), and a "fiery place below the earth where the devil rules" (6 percent). Catholics in our study were the most likely to endorse condemnatory images of hell, a finding that reflects the intensely judgmental pre–Vatican II theology that so tightly gripped the faithful during that era, and which is so vividly rendered in James Joyce's fictional account of Catholic Stephen Dedalus's upbringing (1916: 108 ff).[12] But, in keeping with the relatively optimistic theology that generally characterized adolescent beliefs, a majority (52 percent) of the study participants endorsed a metaphorical rather than a biblical-literalistic image of hell. Whereas some of these adolescents thought of hell as "a feeling of great misery within oneself" (15 percent), others thought of hell simply as an idea: an idea that "exists only in people's minds" and, for some, a "foolish" idea.

The fiery view of hell notwithstanding, it was evident overall that most of the study participants had a respectful though relatively undemanding and compassionate theology in adolescence. It was further apparent from their remarks made during interviews that a substantial minority were interested in the more intrinsically religious or spiritual aspects of church.[13] These adolescents spontaneously commented on their interest in church sermons, the way that a pastor or Sunday school teacher made theological points understandable, and the enjoyment they got in discussing particular points from the Bible. A Presbyterian boy who with his family went to church about once a month said that he was interested in religion and specifically in arguments about the Bible. Although another boy's Methodist parents and siblings were, like him, not regular churchgoers, they all frequently discussed meanings of passages in the Bible, because, as he pointed out to the interviewer, "it is a very contradictory book." A girl who attended a nondenominational Protestant Sunday school liked studying the Bible because her Sunday school teacher, continuing a long American tradition of giving incentives and prizes to children to attend Sunday school (Boylan 1988: 156–60), gave five cents every week to the student who got the top score on the group's Bible worksheet, and this girl wanted to maintain her winning record.

Incentives aside, some adolescents emphasized the pleasure they got from listening to hymns or of singing in the choir, and they generally commented approvingly about the discussions organized at church. Jane Bell, whose parents were not religious and who did not herself attend religious services (see chapter 1), was drawn to the many interesting intellectual opportunities at the local Episcopalian Church. She stated, "There are informal meetings, music, sometimes outside speakers, sometimes reading poetry. You can attend or not, as you wish. Then there are discussions on religion and one discussion group on comparative religion, which I took last year." Another participant, a boy who was active in the Presbyterian young people's group, pointed out that, though he didn't like church rituals, he liked church discussions.

RELIGION'S SOCIAL OPPORTUNITIES

The sincerity of our adolescents' faith and their interest in the intellectual and spiritual content of religion were complemented by the vibrant social role that the church played in their lives. Underscoring the fact that religion is constituted by far more than just piety, prayer, and biblical exegesis, many spoke of the social world that church provides. Our adolescents clearly appreciated the social opportunities for interacting with their peers that church allowed and, in fact, encouraged. Contemporary commentators have made much of the idea that church is an important resource in developing social relationships (e.g., Putnam 2000), but this would not have been news to church leaders a century ago. In the late nineteenth and early twentieth centuries, Protestant church leaders in particular were dedicated to creating youth-centered social spaces in which adolescent boys' and girls' religious formation would be enhanced by their praying, working, and playing together (Coble 2002: 80–81). There were strong expectations that young people would not simply attend Sunday school classes but would also actively participate and assume social and leadership responsibilities in mixed-gender young people's societies.

The remarks of many of our adolescents suggest that these initiatives were effective in making the church a social center for youth. During semistructured interviews conducted while they were junior high and high school students, a majority (55 percent) spontaneously commented on the social dimensions of their church involvement.[14] Girls (57 percent) were more likely than boys (31 percent) to comment on the social aspects. One girl said she enjoyed "the social contacts in Christian Endeavor," and several others noted that they enjoyed participating in their church's club meetings and social hours on Sunday evenings. One boy, an only child who was friendly, popular, and independent, said that his "happiest social times" during high school were in the Methodist Church; he was very active and held official positions in the young people's group. His parents were not religious, and he got involved initially because the boy he shared a locker with in junior high school attended the group. Highly committed to the church, this boy said that, if he had ten thousand dollars to spend, he would pay his way through college, and "then I'd help my church build the gymnasium—we have a tennis court and we have the grounds for the gymnasium, but we haven't got the money raised yet and I'd like to help."

Another boy particularly liked his Baptist church's social hour because the man in charge owned an ice cream shop in Berkeley and the whole class went there for free ice cream every Sunday afternoon. A Catholic boy who had stopped attending his own church "was active in a Protestant church for social reasons." A boy who went to the Presbyterian Sunday school every week said he liked going on camping trips with his church; a Swedenborgian girl emphasized how much she enjoyed her church's summer camps. Although the Catholic Church offered fewer social opportunities, one girl who attended a parochial school and who went to Mass every week with her parents, enjoyed spending the summers with her school friends at a Catholic camp in the Santa Cruz Mountains.

Lillian Sinnott used to go to the First Christian Church with her parents but stopped going because it had no youth group. She then became very active in the Presbyterian Church, and through its various social activities, including the regular dinners it provided to visiting servicemen, she first got the sense that she was popular and could entertain an "audience." Another girl, who was closely involved in the Presbyterian Church, said, with a "very pious expression," that "religion was quite important" to her. She taught Sunday school, had been a delegate to church conferences, and had taken church courses in stewardship and community problems. But what was important to her was the church's social aspects—"church suppers and friends in church." When the interviewer asked more specifically how she felt about God, "she was sort of taken aback and said that 'of course she believed in God.' She said apologetically that she didn't pray very often but felt that she got comfort and help when she did." Another girl, a Mormon who said she planned to go on an evangelizing mission while in college, explained that, although she fully believed all of the church's dogma, the main reason she wanted to do the mission was so that she could meet lots of new people.

A girl whose father's family was Unitarian and whose mother's family was Jewish attended a Congregational church for a while but then switched to a Catholic church because, she said, "the best-looking boy goes there." Another girl used to go to a Methodist church but then started attending a Presbyterian church because her "friends go there." Like her parents, she felt that "one church is as good as another." A girl who had been attending an Episcopalian church got friendly with two Christian Science girls who were "very cheerful and happy," and so she started going to their church. Similarly, Suzanne Carter and her siblings "switched around churches" for social reasons, going to the Baptist and then to the Presbyterian for a while. Suzanne had joined one church because "there was lots of excitement and a friendly young minister." The mother of another girl recounted a similar socially driven pattern for her adolescent daughter: "She liked the youngsters that went to the Northbrae Community Church; so it was no hardship on her. And then when we moved to San Francisco, of her own volition she went to the Community Episcopal Church. . . . And then when she had a boyfriend that belonged to the young people's group at the Congregational Church, she went there regularly."

Given that interreligious and interdenominational tensions are part of the story of American religious pluralism (cf. McGreevy 2003), it is not surprising that such tensions surfaced in some teenagers' accounts of their church sociability habits. One girl whose parents were strong Presbyterians longed to go to other churches. She said, "I would like to go around and visit other churches. I have a friend who belongs to the Catholic Church, and she has visited our church with me. I'd like to go to her church [but my parents are opposed to the idea]." By contrast, another girl's father, a hardworking carpenter from an immigrant Finnish Lutheran family, commented favorably that his daughter "has gone to all the churches in Berkeley, even Catholic."

Like the ex-Lutheran father we quoted in chapter 2 who as a youth was attracted by the Presbyterian Church's basketball program, some of the teenagers unabashedly went to church or Sunday school because it was one of the main social activities available, and it provided a chance to be with their friends. Thus one boy who went to an Episcopalian church twice a month commented, "I only go because other kids go." Another said, "There isn't anything else to do," and another remarked, "We have a lot of fun on the way home [from Sunday school]."

Parents strongly approved of the social opportunities that church provided adolescents. Largely because one girl's parents pushed her to go to church for social reasons, she resisted joining. She explained,

> I think that you can be really religious—have your own religion—and that you don't have to go to church to show it off, but my father just doesn't see it that way. He thinks you have to go to church to be religious. We had sort of a bad time about that on Easter. We went to church Easter morning, and on the way home they asked my sister and [me] to join the church. And they sort of sprung it on us, and I didn't want to join the church. Part of the trouble is that they say, "Go to church and meet boys—meet some boys"—I hate their pushing.

Another girl's "status-driven" mother, who felt that her "children should choose the religion of their own choice," said she was glad that her daughter picked the Episcopalian Church because "a better class of people go to the Episcopal Church—and to Saint Stephen's particularly. I am hoping she will take an active part in the various clubs and groups there." Another mother, who was anxious because her shy daughter was not a member of any of the social clubs in high school, said that for social reasons it was "a pity the children did not like church." Mrs. Davis, a working-class, nonreligious Methodist mother, regretted that she had "not seen to it that the children went to a church they enjoyed. I feel that's one of my big faults in raising them, that they didn't have religious education of a forward-looking sort, rather than a dogmatic sort, since I feel that it would have given them moral support, especially during adolescence. And also it could have been a social center that would have given them a feeling of having some social group to belong to."

As it turned out, however, her son Fred (our study participant) became involved in the Quaker Church in adolescence. An outgoing and popular boy whose favorite hobby was bowling with friends, Fred was also a good singer and sang in a school quartet, though, to his disappointment, he did not get admitted to one of the high school's high-status music clubs. Interested in "looking good," Fred used the money he earned working two hours a day as a houseboy in an apartment building to buy some of his clothes. Fred's involvement in church, though it stemmed from his singing, was largely contingent on, he said, "social contacts." He explained, "I think a lot about religion right now. I'm in the choir at the Friends' Church. . . . My vocal teacher is director there, and I got roped in. I don't know how long I can stick [with] it. . . . Last Sunday I looked over the church from where I was sitting, and you know, I couldn't find a decent-looking girl there."

In sum, it was evident that many of the adolescents regarded church as an attractive social opportunity, as did their parents, especially mothers (see also chapter 2), and they viewed religious activity very much in terms of the sociability it provided. Moreover, these church activities were widely regarded for their ability to "keep the kids out of trouble," as one girl who went every Sunday to church and to the social evenings at the Baptist Young People's Union commented. Others similarly endorsed the view that religious organizations were "keeping people from being bad" (24 percent) and "doing more for people now than even before" (18 percent).[15] This positive view was echoed by Ann Gibson, one of the Mormon girls in the study, who, though she came from a devout family (see chapter 2), was allowed by her parents to date non-Mormon boys. Appearing "audacious" to the interviewer, Ann confided that, at a friend's house not long before, she had had some punch spiked with tea and she had also taken a drink of Coca-Cola, though caffeine was prohibited by her religion. When asked what benefit she had derived from her religion, Ann responded "very seriously" that she "might actually have become a juvenile delinquent" had it not been for her religion. According to Ann, when she was thirteen or fourteen she had had friends who were "really rough"—one girl drank, smoked, and hung out with boys. Ann felt that her own morality was jeopardized by associating with this girl, but that her church's teachings had kept her safe.

Like most adults, adolescents do not necessarily draw distinctions among the reasons and motivations for their churchgoing. For most people, religious involvement is driven by multiple considerations. Lillian Sinnott's comments captured both the social and the spiritual dimensions of church participation. A girl who, according to her mother, "liked to be the center of attention," Lillian told the interviewer in June 1944 that the most important event in her life during the previous six months had been "taking my stand for Christ. It changed my whole life—it was at the young people's meeting of all the Presbyterian churches in Oakland. Now I am happy. Mother used to wonder whether I could be happy, but now I have changed completely and am happy—I have the same skin and the same body and the same abilities, but all the rest is different." One year later, however, at age seventeen, after she had transferred to a different high school and found new friends, Lillian lost most of her interest in church. She reflected on her earlier church commitment, commenting tersely that she simply "needed something at that time to hold on to." Yet, further underscoring the emotional support religion provides many individuals in times of loneliness or distress (cf. Ellison and George 1994), she conceded that whenever she felt down she still wanted "to rush back to church."

MULTIPURPOSE RELIGION

Our data show that church and religious activity played a substantial part in the lives of adolescents in the 1930s and 1940s. The majority had moderate or high levels of religious involvement and readily incorporated Sunday school and church activities into well-packed schedules that stretched to accommodate school obligations, family chores, part-time jobs, and wide-ranging extracurricular activities, sports, and hobbies. Although our adolescents were members of a generation distinguished for their civic seriousness, their religious beliefs did not bear the mark of a heavy-handed or punitive theology. Most expressed beliefs and attitudes that suggested a relatively benign and nonintimidating view of God, a worldview that focused more on God as helper than as judge, and a view of the afterlife as a time of reward rather than as punishment. Moreover, while several of the participants clearly appreciated the liturgical and spiritual aspects of church, it was religion's social contacts and opportunities that loomed large in the lives of many of the adolescents.

Church involvement among the adolescents was strongly related to the religiousness of parents and the religious atmosphere at home. It was also evident, however, that as a matter of practice, if not of spoken acknowledgment, the adolescents more or less determined the level of their own religious involvement. Although some went to church or Sunday school against their own impulses, most of those who went enjoyed going and being involved in the church's various activities. For most, church involvement was not overly burdensome; its routines blended with the adolescents' other activities rather than soberly constraining them. Today's churches have greatly extended the definition of church to include an array of nonreligious services (see, e.g., Ammerman 2005; Chaves 2004; Edgell 2006), but even in the 1930s and 1940s religious socialization and participation were understood in relatively broad terms. Reflecting the views of early religious leaders (cf. Boylan 1988; Coble 2002), church involvement was regarded as a truly wholesome social experience. Church participation provided not only devotional opportunities and biblical or doctrinal education during the formative years of childhood and adolescence but also affirming and welcoming social outlets for peer interaction, especially in the church's young people's groups and meetings. Moreover, the fact that so much of adolescents' religious involvement took place in separate, age-segregated spaces most likely enhanced its appeal for the adolescents as well as conferred on them the freedom to determine the nature and extent of their participation.

Our data on the religious beliefs, practices, and church experiences of the study participants as adolescents in the 1930s and 1940s adds to a growing but still relatively narrow body of research on the place of religion in adolescent life. We are impressed by several crucial findings from the data. Our adolescents' geographical origins are important: They grew up in Northern California, a region of the country known for its comparatively lower levels of religious activity. Yet clearly church was well entrenched in the routines of many young people in the area as they went about their lives. This is historically interesting in its own right, and it reminds us that the portraits painted by large-scale population surveys, while correct in the outlines, obscure the details of religion as incorporated into everyday life. Attention to these details expands our ability to see the localized relevance of religion in daily life.

The timing of our participants' adolescence is especially critical. The study participants came of age in the decades prior to the 1950s, the era of high religiosity in America and the benchmark against which the subsequent decline of religion is typically measured. Our pre-1950s data complicate the pervasive assumption that there is an "increasing secularization of youth" (Gallup and Lindsay 1999: 160).[16] Our findings show that adolescents in the 1930s and 1940s had various levels of religious involvement, and the patterns we uncovered essentially parallel the variation evident among American teenagers today. Not all youth were uniformly religious in the 1930s and 1940s, and the proportion of American teens who are highly religious today is fairly similar to what we found to be the case in Berkeley and Oakland in those decades. We are cautious not to overgeneralize from the findings of our particular study. Nevertheless, we cannot help but be impressed at how a longer historical view, one that extends even a little further back than the 1950s, points to certain continuities in American religion and thus tempers the tendency to emphasize a story of decline without giving considered attention to the nuances that challenge such a narrative.

In their report on a recent national study of youth and religion, Smith and Denton are particularly critical of the substance of contemporary adolescent religiosity. Although the authors present data indicating relatively high levels of religious engagement on a broad range of activities and beliefs, they are dismissive of its theological depth and argue that the therapeutic and instrumental use of religion sharply distinguishes contemporary religion from commitment in past eras (2005: 147–48). Contemporary teenage religion might well be characterized as instrumental and undemanding. Adding an edge to Smith and Denton's assessment, however, is their presumption that religion in earlier eras had substantially more depth.[17]

Our findings offer partial support to Smith and Denton's conclusions in that we document a more other-oriented and a less instrumental view of the meaning of prayer. Not only did our adolescents shy away from praying for personal gratification, but even the choices given to them concerning the reasons for praying indicate that the IHD researchers in the 1930s had a limited awareness of the therapeutic use of religion. Nonetheless, a closer look at how adolescents in the 1930s and 1940s incorporated religion in their lives clearly reveals a wide range of attitudes and practices, ranging from serious devotion to a focus on the mainly social and pragmatic aspects of church involvement. This should not be surprising, because even the seventeenth-century Puritan settler generation found that "halfway covenants" were necessary in order to maintain their less-devout grandchildren's church involvement (cf. Noll 1992). In more recent eras, we are familiar with eighteenth- and nineteenth-century devotional revolutions and awakenings, initiatives aimed at drumming up the lax religious commitment of nominal believers (Finke and Stark 1992: 87–88). Moreover, despite the heightened religious fervor of the 1950s, cultural observers found that it too was superficial and instrumental. Will Herberg argues that religion in the 1950s was nontheological, focused on a this-worldly ethic of good behavior rather than on transcendental questions, and that it provided adherents with a sense of social belonging rather than a purposive link to the divine (1955: 96). Similarly, Peter Berger (1961) states that middle-class Protestantism was theologically benign and lacked prophetic and transcendent dimensions. And as our data from the 1930s and 1940s show, adolescent religion then had its instrumental purposes—especially evident in the social function of church, a social objective that was even explicitly intended by late-nineteenth-century church leaders.

While we do not doubt that adolescent religion changes in tandem with the social and cultural context in which it exists, we believe it is important for researchers to recognize that everyday religion in previous eras also had its functional and instrumental, as well as spiritual, purposes. The transgenerational continuity in religion that fuses different motives is captured in the remarks of Sarah Jackson's father. A high-status, economically successful Ivy League graduate who came from a solid Protestant family, Mr. Jackson built a large ranch house with a swimming pool and other conveniences for his young family in the 1930s. We close this chapter with his narrative, an account reminding us that religious habits, though they may vary from one generation to the next, invariably meld the spiritual and the social and are always intertwined with pragmatic considerations:

> My father's family were Congregationalists and my mother's were Presbyterians. . . . In my father's family they were very religious—had prayers every morning and that sort of thing. My grandfather . . . was a strict disciplinarian, and insisting upon regular church attendance was one aspect of this. . . . My own father was in YMCA work and became very active in the church in Boston. After we were living in Berkeley, he again became a leader in the church. My mother's family had gone around the Horn to Hawaii as Presbyterian missionaries. Her father was one of the authors of the first translation of the Bible into . . . [language]. He was a minister and a leader in the church, and his daughter—my mother—was active in the church also, not rabid on religion but always very active. . . . I joined the Presbyterian Church in the East but joined the Congregational Church here [in Berkeley] and went to Sunday school and was active in church groups. It's funny, though, with a rather religious background on both sides, that once you get married you don't go to church any more. For one thing, you have a garden to take care of, and then the children come along, and there are lots of things to do, and you find that, [even] with the best intentions, you just never quite get there. We did decide that the children ought to have some religious training, so we sent the girls to the Congregational Sunday school, where they won various Bibles. . . . Nowadays [they] are usually over at the tennis club playing, and have the standard alibi that they never have time to go [to church]. I'd say that they're just as well equipped to meet a spiritual emergency as my mother and father were with all their strict religious training. I won't concede that those girls are a

bit worse off in that sense. Religion for their [devout] grandparents was a social medium and a business medium. The Centennial Union Church was where the majority of the businessmen in Honolulu got their start. Old Mr. N. watched the young fellows coming along, and they knew that if they did well in church they'd be noticed. As far as the spiritual side, my girls know more about it than would appear from the relatively slight exposure they've had, and I know they'd be equal to a spiritual crisis even though we don't have prayers every morning and don't say grace at the table. (Sarah Jackson's father, June 13, 1947)

4

The Imprint of Individual Autonomy
on Everyday Religion in the 1950s

My father was an agnostic but never talked about it much.
He was a very practical man and liked to reason things out
for himself, and once he'd reached his own conclusions,
nobody else's opinions made the slightest difference to him.

Michael Perry's father, talking in 1943
about Michael's grandfather

Religious freedom is a staple of American culture, most visibly
evident in the many religious denominations present in America,
the free expression clause of the Constitution, and the formal
separation of church and state (cf. Ahlstrom 1972; Warner 1993). The
freedom of individuals to define their religious identity and to exercise
their own authority in regard to religion became especially pronounced
in the 1960s (see, e.g., Greeley 1985; Roof 1993; Wuthnow 1998). The
1960s, as is well documented, was a time of cultural upheaval and was
characterized in particular by the assertion of individual freedom. It was
a time, in short, when "the nature of freedom itself was contested and
redefined" (Wuthnow 1998: 53–54). This expansion of individual freedom extended to religion, with the effect that the 1960s and 1970s are
widely seen as transformative, as marking a "turning point in American
religious life" (Roof and McKinney 1987: 11), and even signaling the
emergence of post-Puritan America (Ahlstrom 1972: 967–68).

Of course, the freedom of Americans like Michael Perry's grandfather to make up their own minds about church, faith, and morality is
long-standing. As Nathan Hatch's important study of the "democratization of Christianity" underscores, the early nineteenth century was
renowned for its emphasis on individual autonomy. It was a time when

individual conscience and the common sense of ordinary people took priority over the dictates of religious elites. Hatch's observations about that period could be applied to the 1960s:

> The American Revolution and the beliefs flowing from it created a cultural ferment over the meaning of freedom. Turmoil swirled around the crucial issues of authority, organization, and leadership. Above all the Revolution dramatically expanded the circle of people who considered themselves capable of thinking for themselves about issues of freedom, equality, sovereignty, and representation. Respect for authority, tradition, station, and education eroded. Ordinary people moved toward these new horizons aided by a powerful new vocabulary, a rhetoric of liberty that would not have occurred to them were it not for the Revolution. . . . The correct solution to any institutional problem, political, legal, or religious, would have to appear to be the people's choice. (1989: 6)

Therefore, while studies today rightly emphasize the autonomy with which Americans regard religion, it is worthwhile to keep in mind that earlier generations also used a rhetoric of liberty, and some took a highly individual approach to religion. It should be acknowledged, however, that, prior to the 1960s, religious freedom was primarily construed in terms of the Christian tradition, and Protestantism in particular. The story of Lucy Smith, the mother of Joseph Smith who founded the Mormons, illustrates this autonomy particularly well. As recounted by Hatch, Lucy Smith, who grew up in northern New England in the latter part of the eighteenth century, "wrestled interminably with the problems of competing denominations." She eventually concluded that she would take her cues from the Bible rather than any church and "sealed this individualization of conscience by finding a minister who would agree to baptize her as a solitary Christian without attachment to any congregation" (1989: 43).[1]

In light of the tendency to draw a sharp distinction between the post-1960s and previous historical periods, we were particularly interested in using our interview data to explore whether the accented religious freedom ushered in by the 1960s already had some currency among ordinary Americans in the 1950s. The 1950s offer a particularly useful counterpoint to the 1960s. Just as we consider the 1960s to be the decade of cultural turmoil and social protest, we know the 1950s as the decade of cultural conformity and consensus, of the acquiescent "organization man" (Whyte 1956) and deference to institutional authority. The cold war politics of the era made religious affiliation and church attendance a badge of American patriotism and offered a richly symbolic contrast to the godlessness of communism (see, e.g., Herberg 1955). Not coincidentally, church attendance, belief in God, and confidence in churches and religious institutions were at a historical peak. In the 1950s, one out of every two American adults (49 percent) was attending weekly religious services, and close to 80 percent said that religion was very important in their own lives, and that it provided relevant answers to all or most of the era's problems (Gallup and Lindsay 1999: 10, 15, 20).[2] It was also a time of peak fertility as Americans settled comfortably into the suburban affluence that had been created by postwar social and economic developments (Hine 1999; Hudnut-Buemler 1994). It is not accidental that Norman Rockwell, the "people's painter," painted *Walking to Church,* with its well-groomed family of five piously walking in lockstep to church, for the cover of the *Saturday Evening Post* in 1953.[3]

Our study participants' first interviews as adults occurred in 1958. They were then in their thirties, and almost all were married and had young children.[4] They were consequently poised—both as parents of school-age children and as good citizens—to be attentive churchgoers. We were intrigued to find out whether the vocabulary of individual freedom associated with post-1960s religion would already be evident in how they talked about their religious habits and attitudes in 1958, just a few years before the riotous 1960s challenged the cultural deference to the institutional authority of religion.

Studies discussing the changes in post-1960s religion emphasize three overarching characteristics that distinguish it from religion of the past. First, there is the perception that post-1960s religion is highly individualized, a change abetted by the development of a consumer marketplace where choices about religion are not so different from other lifestyle choices (see, e.g., Roof 1999; Warner 1993; Wuthnow 1998). In this view, rather than being constrained by the externally imposed authority of a theological tradition or of a religious institutional identity, people feel entitled to shop around for a church that suits their particular needs and preferences, just as they would shop around for a car, a psychotherapist, or a retirement community. Second, this new freedom contributes to the propagation of the idea that individuals can adhere to religious or spiritual beliefs without affiliating with a religious tradition or participating in church, a trend increasingly evident in national data (see, e.g., Hout and Fischer 2002; Roof 1999). A third characteristic is the marked tendency of religiously involved and nonreligious individuals alike to describe their moral values in nonsectarian or nontheological terms, typically summarized by the Golden Rule: "Do unto others as you would have them do unto you" (see, e.g., Ammerman 1997; Hoge, Johnson, and Luidens 1994; Hunter 1991; Wolfe 1998). In our analyses of the interviews from 1958, therefore, we elected to focus on these three themes in order to see whether the premises so salient in post-1960s religion had some presence in how our study participants talked of religion prior to the cultural impact of the 1960s.

FREEDOM OF RELIGIOUS CHOICE

Our study participants' talk indicated that a majority of them (54 percent) construed decisions about church and religion in terms of choice.[5] Individuals who invoked choice talked about religion in terms of preferences not beliefs, and about shopping around for a church that satisfied them—about going to different churches because they offered different conveniences. Or conversely, they did so because the services provided were basically interchangeable and so they regarded the specific church chosen as irrelevant. Protestants (63 percent) were significantly more likely than the Catholics (38 percent) to invoke a language of religious choice, a difference that fits well with the Protestant theological emphasis on religious freedom more generally. Other than denomination, however, there was no significant variation among our participants in their invocation of choice. Men (58 percent) and women (51 percent), interviewees in the older (58 percent) and younger (51 percent) cohort, and those of high (57 percent) as much as those of low (48 percent) socioeconomic status were equally likely to invoke choice.[6] Whether someone was highly religious or only marginally so, either at the time of the interview (age thirties), or during adolescence, also did not influence their likelihood of using a vocabulary of choice.[7] In sum, our findings suggest that the idea of religion as an individual choice was not uncommon in the 1950s, a time when the adulthood religious involvement of our participants was relatively high (see chapter 5). Rather than reflecting a casual approach to religion, choice appeared to be part and parcel of how a good many ordinary Americans, the religiously involved as well as the nonchurchgoing, thought about church.

That there should be a direct link between church shopping and religious commitment was assumed by one man in our study, who, although not religious himself in his thirties, commended his wife's friend for her deliberative approach to church shopping. Perhaps his daily experiences as a shoe salesman made this man, Bob Mears, emphasize how important it was for people to choose a religion that fits with their individual needs and interests. He said the friend "investigated many faiths, selected the one she wants, and is actually practicing and living up to this faith. There's a person who is actually religious—since she found the faith that fit her own ideas. She goes to church with a definite purpose that a lot of people don't seem to have who go regularly. Maybe I don't know enough. I talk to them about religion, and it doesn't seem to mean any more than going shopping." Apparently it was not shopping for a church per se that Bob disapproved of, but shoppers who do not systematically search for a church that suits them.

Others in the study exemplified the deliberative approach favored by Bob. A woman married to a nonpracticing Catholic who was the father of two children from a previous marriage recounted her deliberations in choosing a church. As a child, she had gone to a nondenominational community church more or less on her own, and in early adulthood had joined the Presbyterian Church. Before joining, she and her husband, a mill worker, had talked to several different ministers in their town northeast of San Francisco. They "had almost joined the Episcopal Church" but thought it was "too close to the Catholic"—an unfavorable option, given that her husband's divorce put him at odds with the church and gave him a bad feeling about Catholicism. On one occasion she had asked the Presbyterian minister to drop by, and they had all liked him. It was this visit, she said, that settled the question of which church they should join. An accountant who had gone to a Lutheran church as a boy also switched to the Presbyterian Church after he and his wife, a Christian Scientist who had strong faith in God, moved to a new town. They chose the Presbyterian Church because it had an "outstanding pastor." He commented that, for the first few weeks he attended, a time when he was having problems at work, he had felt the sermon had been written just for him.

The process involved in thinking about different churches was also illustrated by the comments of George Webster's wife, Lucy. She was brought up as a Congregationalist and had attended church, but her family was not devout. Her parents, she said, "were religious, but there was no grace or family worship." Both George and Lucy were schoolteachers, and although George was active in Presbyterian Church groups as an adolescent, he no longer attended services but was involved in the church's ancillary music activities. Lucy summarized their churchgoing situation in 1958:

We're not members of any church right now. Nancy [our daughter] does belong to a Sunday school; it's Baptist. It's close by, and George is working with the church orchestra. But with his working every weekend [with the church orchestra], we just don't get to church. There are only two Congregationalist churches, and it's five or ten miles to them. . . . We don't care for the Presbyterian Church, the kind of people who happen to go there. We did like the Baptist Church, although you can imagine how different that is [from] the Congregationalist Church. . . . But it was mainly that we liked the pastor, and he's leaving. I guess we should try the Methodist Church.

George was one of the more highly religious boys in our study in adolescence, and even then he was well versed in church shopping. When he was interviewed in 1943, he had recently left the Presbyterian Church, where he had been very active, including having been president of its young people's group. He had had a falling out with some of the other members, and had started going to Christian Endeavor at a different Presbyterian church. At seventeen he had said that this church was "informal and friendly," that he enjoyed it very much, and that most of the group stayed on for the evening service. He had gone "to the Baptist Church but found the group there mostly college age," and he had "plans to visit the First Congregational group."

Lillian Sinnott, the attention-seeking adolescent girl who enjoyed helping out at the Presbyterian Church's dinners for servicemen, was, in 1958, a middle-class, married mother of three daughters and engaged in a wide range of social and artistic activities. She recounted that she had attended the First Christian Church with her parents and siblings until adolescence, and then, with her parents' blessing, had shopped—or as she said, "hunted"—among a variety of churches:

We always went as a family until [I was] thirteen, and then my parents said we could go to anyplace we wanted and choose. So my older brother quit, and my sister tapered off, and I went hunting. I went to the Presbyterian Church for a while because of the youth group, and then, during the war, a very Fundamentalist soul-saving church and a youth center there—I worked as hostess. Then I tried the Catholic Church for a while and learned as much as I could. In college [I] had a friend who was a reformed Jew, and I went a lot with her. When it came time for [my husband and me] to marry, we picked, on the basis of the right-sized chapel, Episcopalian. Then I got acquainted with the Unitarian and liked it, and since then we have either gone to that or to First Christian, which I was raised in.

Lillian's narrative of her intrepid church hunting might lead us to expect that, after some years at the Unitarian Church, she might have tired of it and searched for new alternatives. This was not the case. Underscoring our study's broader findings that church shopping is not necessarily either reflective of, or antecedent to, a weakened religious commitment, Lillian remained an actively participating Unitarian throughout adulthood. When interviewed at age seventy, she was, in fact, one of the most highly involved religious and spiritual individuals in our study.

One of the positive consequences of construing religion in terms of choice rather than unswerving commitment is that in some contexts the freedom to choose increases the likelihood that individuals with only marginal interest or little background in religion can become active church participants. Similarly, regular churchgoers who become dissatisfied with a specific church can nonetheless maintain their religious interests by exploring other churches. The freedom to choose a church or to change one's preferences makes religious participation an open and inviting option. One middle-class suburban woman living in the Northwest had not "been at all religious" even as a child, but had become highly involved with the Presbyterian Church in the early 1950s after her husband and their children attended a church dinner. "Ever since," she said, their lives were "just turned right side up." She became a weekly churchgoer, served on many church committees, and participated in various church groups, including a couples' club. She had several inspirational religious poems pinned to the curtains on both sides of her kitchen sink window and, in her conversation about her philosophy of life, emphasized that "the most important thing [in life] is to have a right association with God. After that, everything else just comes along very easily." But though she was heavily involved with the Presbyterians she nonetheless had sent her daughters "to whichever Sunday school was the closest."

Another upper-class woman, Diane Pierce, found solace in the church after her firstborn son died from cancer when he was only eight and, tragically, her young daughter was killed in a car accident five years later. When her son had become ill, Diane had become active in the Presbyterian Church; she attended weekly and had been a church elder for a few years. Convenience and social contact figured prominently in her decision to choose the Presbyterian Church; it was, she said, "the nearest one to them when they lived in [a previous city] and they were friendly with the minister."

The significance of the minister as the point man attracting people to a particular church was also underlined by Allison Foley. She attended the Methodist Church about once a month, but held out the possibility that she and her husband might go more frequently if they were able to find a church, and more specifically a minister, that would satisfy their needs. She explained,

> The minister might change it. [We] go more often when we have a good minister, as we do now. Before, the minister was undoubtedly a fine man and a fine minister but the poorest speaker in the world. He couldn't get over what he was trying to say. We go to the Methodist Church, but we don't belong—although the minister said he thought we were members because we were more involved than a lot of members in church activities. We were baptized by the navy chaplain when [my husband] was baptized, but we haven't felt ready to join any specific church. Back in Alameda [where we lived previously], I think the minister was the determining factor . . . [that persuaded us to choose] the Presbyterian Church. I have a preference for it, and my husband for the Methodist Church.[8]

Allison's ability to sort through her preferences was something she learned as an adolescent, when, as she recalled, she and her friends "went to each other's churches quite a bit." One friend was a Mormon (they had "swell parties," and it was "a fine place for young people to get together"), another sang in the Baptist Church choir, another was a Lutheran, and Allison herself was Presbyterian. Allison was just one of several study participants who were active shoppers as adolescents; in particular, the social aspects of church prompted some to switch from one church to another (see chapter 3). As one of Allison's classmates told the interviewer back then, although he didn't "go to any church, he had "tried a lot of 'em out."

Roger Davis was another inveterate church shopper. In childhood he had gone to the Presbyterian Church with his parents and siblings, and his mother had played the church organ. But, highlighting how church habits are contingent on family routines, after his father died when Roger was only eight, Roger's church participation declined. His widowed mother started working as a real estate agent to help pay the family bills, and, as Roger explained, because Sunday was a busy day for showing houses and meeting potential buyers, they stopped going to church. Later, in junior high school, Roger went to the Baptist Church with one of his friends, then returned to the Presbyterian until he went to college and started attending the Congregational Church with another friend. During the war, he "didn't go much," but after he met his Catholic wife, he began accompanying her to the Catholic Church about once a month. Roger commented, "I have nothing against going, and sometimes I even enjoy it. . . . I do get a certain spiritual feeling myself."

Although Roger would not score high on standardized scales measuring church attendance or religiousness, he was nonetheless able to maintain a religious and spiritual connection because of the freedom that allows Americans to go to whatever church they please and whenever it suits them. A cessation in an individual's church attendance, therefore, is not necessarily irreversible (see chapter 5), and the potential for it to be reversed depends much on the multiplicity of churches available and on the cultural acceptance that picking and switching among them is fine. For some Americans, religious choice is a taken-for-granted component of everyday life, so much so that one interviewee, when asked about his parents-in-law's religious affiliation, answered without any apparent hint of irony, that they were "Methodist *at the moment*" (emphasis ours).

Like shoppers in the consumer marketplace, some individuals, such as Lucy Webster, made clear distinctions among denominations. Others, by contrast, focused on the interchangeability of denominations that the freedom to choose confirmed. Notwithstanding R. J. Neal's and his wife's allegiance to the Presbyterian Church, R. J., an electrical engineer, expressed an inclusive and nondiscriminatory view of religious differences. When interviewed at age thirty, in 1958, he commented: "Just as there are all sorts of roads leading to Berkeley, there are all sorts of ways to get to the same place." He believed that churches, regardless of their differences, all had "essentially the same goal." In this logic, one that R. J. attributed to his own grandmother, people should go to "the church of their choice," because it doesn't really matter which specific church is chosen.

When there is a range of choices, freedom to choose a church can also, of course, lead to indecisiveness or inactivity, as it did for some of our respondents. One professional couple had gone occasionally to different churches but had not actually joined any because they hadn't "been able to agree about which one." A divorced man, a construction laborer, was so indifferent to religious boundaries that he wasn't even sure—when interviewed in 1958 at age thirty—what church he was married in. He described himself as "pretty much nondenominational. . . . I've gone back and forth, and I've never really pinned down the church I like." Finally, as in weighing other choices, some interviewees commented on the perceived time and opportunity costs involved in church attendance (cf. Iannaccone 1995). One man said he would go to church more often except for the fact that "it's not just enough to go to church; they also want you to actively participate in the church's activities." Another man complained that the obligation of church attendance itself was far too time consuming. He had to have his children at Sunday school by nine o'clock in the morning, pick them up at ten-thirty, and be back for services at eleven that didn't get out until twelve-thirty. As he lamented, all of Sunday morning was taken up with church, leaving no time for other activities.

In sum, we found that a language of individual choice characterized how a substantial number of our study participants talked about religion when interviewed in 1958. Underscoring the fact that how people talk about church is not independent of the social settings in which individuals move, Protestants were significantly more likely than Catholics to invoke choice, a disposition in tune with the Protestant theological emphasis on individual self-determination. Because context matters, we recognize that the theme of choice might not have emerged with such prominence had our study's Protestant participants lived in regions of the country characterized by a lower incidence of religious pluralism, such as Minnesota or Iowa, which are dominated by Lutherans, or Tennessee or Georgia, where Southern Baptists predominate. Clearly, the relative recency of California's settlement and the relative diversity contained in its migratory and religious history may make Californian Protestants more prone than their coreligionists elsewhere to discard the yoke of tradition and thus to be remarkably unconstrained in their church attitudes and preferences. Not all of them, of course, invoked a language of religious choice. It is important to keep in mind that close to half our sample—not only Catholics but also a large number of Protestants—did not talk about religion in terms of individual choice. This highlights the variability that inevitably characterizes how religion is construed in any social milieu.

In any case, our data show that in the 1950s, well before the 1960s' emphasis on individual freedom, many Californian Protestants, and some Catholics too, felt entitled to choose a church based on their individual needs rather than on doctrinal tradition or theology. In American society, with its multiplicity of religious traditions, the invocation of choice does not necessarily presuppose a consumer choice logic—the same logic of personal preference, taste, and convenience that typically characterizes the choices we make in the economic marketplace. A vocabulary of choice, rather, can reflect a deliberative, comparative process of evaluating the "truth value" of different theological and denominational traditions. Our participants, however, spoke of choice in ways reminiscent of consumer choice; they used market language rather than speaking of choices among alternative moral or theological traditions. It may well be that many interviewees thought about religious choices in terms of theology, but their talk of religion in response to questions about their beliefs and practices did not indicate this. Rather, the language our study participants used in discussing religious options stressed pragmatism, satisfaction, and convenience rather than theological content, moral claims, or denominational identity. For many, their religious activity was contingent on the range of available churches, their convenience, the amenability of the pastor, the degree to which a church's religious and social activities were satisfying, and the extent to which other activities competed with church for the individual's time. We are not concluding that our study participants thought of religion in the same way that they thought of economic choices; they may or may not have. What interests us is not whether religious choice is equivalent to economic choice but that Americans in the 1950s (and earlier) felt entitled to talk about church in ways that affirmed the religious autonomy of the individual.

THE UNCOUPLING OF RELIGIOUS BELIEF AND CHURCH PARTICIPATION

A recent study of changes in American religion uncovered a substantial increase in the proportion of Americans who shun church participation while nonetheless continuing to believe in core tenets of religious faith (Hout and Fischer 2002). These "unchurched believers" may well be distancing themselves from the increased identification of churches with political conservatism as Hout and Fischer's analyses suggest (175). But even apart from any specific political motivations, the uncoupling of faith from church membership and attendance has long had a precedent in American society. Already in the 1940s, the parents of some of our study participants readily disentangled their Christian beliefs from their church and denomination. Ann Martin's hard-charging Baptist father spoke of the arbitrariness of denominational church boundaries and offered a view of faith that was independent of such divisions. He explained,

> I have never felt that particular denominations were really very important. I believe that there is only one real church, and Christ is its head. All the disagreements between different denominations have to do with man and not God. My religion is all summed up in the Lord's Prayer and in the Sermon on the Mount [recites both from memory and with considerable emotion]. Religion has been very important in my life, because it has

taught me to be more tranquil. I think there is good in every denomination. I think the Lord gathers souls wherever they are, and you'll find good people in every sect. I don't think the features of any particular denomination are important, but I do think that Christ is necessary for salvation. (January 12, 1947)

The idea that belief in or feelings of closeness to God are not tied to church participation was expressed in various ways by our study participants when they were interviewed in 1958. Close to one-third (30 percent) talked about religion in ways suggesting that faith and beliefs are, or can be, independent of church affiliation or participation. Once again, this view was professed by the highly religious as often as it was by those not religiously involved. And it was unrelated to sociodemographic characteristics such as denomination, gender, and adolescent religiousness.[9] Stephen Goss, the father of two adopted children who had his own insurance business, was highly religious. He and his wife attended the Presbyterian Church every week, and he was an officer in the church's youth group. Yet he said he didn't think that it was necessary to go to church to be religious, or that churchgoing was a vital part of religion.

One woman who was not attending church in the 1950s but who had attended a Protestant community church as a teenager said, "I can live my religion inside of me, so I don't need to go to church." A divorced and remarried woman who had attended the Christian Science Church as a child but who had not done so in adulthood said, "I'm a great believer in God, but I don't go to church. I believe with all my heart in God, but I think people can go overboard. . . . I think God is with you all the time and knows whether you are truly sorry about [things]. . . . And if you really are sorry, you don't have to tell anyone." Similarly, a Presbyterian woman born in 1921, and who by 1958 was in her third marriage after two divorces from alcoholic husbands, went to church "quite often," but not every Sunday. She said that people should not be fanatical about religion; she thought you could believe in God and read the Bible at home, but she also felt that "it is a fine thing to go to church."

An extension of the view that religion can exist independently from church attendance or a specific denominational tradition is the belief that religion is diffuse in everyday life—an idea that tends to be associated with the spiritual seeking of current times but which clearly has earlier roots in American consciousness (see, e.g., Miller 1956/1964; Schmidt 2005). Allison Foley, who attended services at the Methodist

Church about once a month, described herself in early adulthood as loving "everything that has to do with nature." Throughout the interview in 1958, she frequently alluded to the coincidental or synchronous nature of events in her life, commenting, for instance, that she would not have met her husband had it not been for the war. She had married a paratrooper in 1944 who was from the South and who happened to be stationed for a time at Oakland Port, where she was working in the blood bank. Talking of the place of religion in her life, Allison said,

> I think your whole life actually is based on religion, even though you might not realize it. And then too, just like we've often said, we feel closer to God when we're out on the beach or up in the mountains, looking at the wonderful things God has created, than when we're actually in church. But you have to have a certain amount of religious training. I think all religions are good; it doesn't matter which one. I think in one way or another, everyone on the face of the earth—whether worshipping Buddha or Mohammed—whatever they call him, they are worshipping the same Supreme Being, although maybe in different ways. If you want an example, it's like people all over the world climbing up a hill: some are backsliding, some traverse it, but all are reaching for the same goal in one way or another.

The diffuseness of the sacred beyond church walls was also emphasized by Martha Wilson, an upper-middle-class mother of three. Martha was highly involved in the Presbyterian Church. Commenting that church "has always been a very big part of our lives," she said in 1958 that the whole family was attending services every week and both she and her husband taught Sunday school. Martha spent several hours each week preparing the lesson, and during the week was in the habit of visiting any of the children who had been sick and missed class. She was also an elder in the Presbyterian Church, on the Board of Deaconesses, secretary of the young married couples' group, and on the church's executive board. Martha described herself as "deeply religious," saying, "If not for my beliefs, I couldn't exist. Religion plays a real part of my everyday life. I often pray, especially when I'm in trouble." But although she was heavily committed to the church, her sense of the sacred transcended the church. Martha told the interviewer she had "faith in a God, but he has no face," and that she thought of God "on every occasion." Martha gave as an example the day before the interview: when she was outside with her children and talking about the clouds, she had commented to them, "Isn't it wonderful that God gave us these beautiful clouds?"

A consequence of the uncoupling of religious beliefs from church participation is that church participation itself is no guarantee of the wholesale embrace of specific faith beliefs. One woman in our study was actively involved in a nondenominational Protestant church. A mother of four who felt that America's greatest problem was "too much accent on materialism," she went to church services and to the church's discussion group every week. But she confided, "I can't accept the biblical story of Jesus. I can reason to God but not to Christ. Of course, I don't tell my children this. . . . I go to both Sunday school and church every week. The point of Sunday school is discussion. It is very interesting. That is how we happened to start going to church, because these discussions were so interesting. A person can express his doubts about God and argue with the minister about the question."

In sum, American faith-believers today may be more deliberate than previous generations about distancing themselves from organized religion for political and other reasons (Hout and Fischer 2002). Nevertheless, the idea that one can be an unchurched believer has long been part of American culture. It is particularly instructive that this uncoupling was mentioned by a sizable number of our participants when interviewed in 1958, a time in American society when churches and institutionalized religion enjoyed an accentuated political and cultural legitimacy.

THE AUTONOMY OF MORALITY FROM SECTARIAN THEOLOGY: THE GOLDEN RULE

The American sociologist Talcott Parsons has argued that the enduring effect of the Protestant (Calvinist) ethic on American culture was to make decency in everyday life the criterion of moral behavior. This means that Americans do not confine their religion simply to church but extend it to the everyday secular world, which becomes a "field of Christian opportunity" for living a moral life in which one treats others with kindness and respect (1967: 403).[10] This generalized, nonsectarian ethos, summarized in the Golden Rule as "Do unto others as you would have them do unto you," is squarely inscribed within Christian theology, but its basic premise can also be found in other religious traditions as well as in secular philosophies and popular culture.[11]

For many churchgoing Americans today, an action-based everyday morality that stresses "deeds not creeds" is important (Ammerman 1997). Thus even when this morality is related in some way to church, or to religious codes such as the Ten Commandments, it is generally devoid of theological content, as Hoge, Johnson, and Luidens found in regard to the Golden Rule values of the Presbyterian baby boomers they studied (1994: 111–13). Yet, the appeal of the Golden Rule has long had salience in American culture and was evident in our data. The parents of the study participants made frequent allusions to the Golden Rule when interviewed in the 1930s and 1940s. In one nonreligious family, the mother told the interviewer that she had taught her daughter that the Golden Rule was the central idea of religion, and that she tried to live by it herself. Another mother, a Methodist, felt that "religion consisted of the Golden Rule, that if everyone followed the principles of love and kindliness, consideration and generosity, then religion as such would not be necessary." A Swedenborgian father commented, "Personally I don't know what 'loving the Lord' means. If we would love our neighbors, perhaps we would understand what 'loving the Lord' means." Other parents expressed similar views, summarized by one Presbyterian mother who believed, she said, in "deeds not creeds."

The idea that a Golden Rule morality can intertwine with church and biblical teachings and yet at the same time be independent of church was evoked by an upper-class Congregational mother. In 1934, talking about her own parents' lives, she said, "Religion . . . was very important to my mother. Her whole life was wound up with it. She lived it, and it was important to her to have the church and the minister be an intimate part of her life. My father . . . was less engrossed. On the other hand, his kindness to people, his unselfishness, meant that he lived his religion fully without the need of church."

In 1958, when the study participants themselves were first interviewed as adults (age thirties), close to a third (29 percent) used Golden Rule language in talking about their religious habits and attitudes. Protestants (31 percent) were significantly more likely than Catholics (13 percent) to make reference to the Golden Rule. And again, as with the themes of religious choice and unchurched belief, its invocation was independent of the individual's degree of religious involvement and other demographic characteristics, with the exception of cohort.[12] Our study participants' affinity for the Golden Rule was not an aberration. Will Herberg, the renowned observer of American religion of the 1950s, argued at the time that the tendency of Americans to assert their practical commitment to following the Golden Rule "would seem to offer a better insight into the basic religion of the American people than any figures as to their formal beliefs can provide" (1955: 95).

Joan Sweeney, a religiously active Episcopalian mother of five, explained that her moral philosophy was "to try and help other people. I think perhaps the adage 'One reaps what one sows' is the starting point. From there on, to be friendly, to be helpful and kind to other people. . . . Kind and helpful and thoughtful boils down to leading a good Christian life." Although her father did not go to church, Joan said that "no one followed the Ten Commandments closer. . . . A lot of people think they can lead a good Christian life without attending church. I guess I always thought that my folks did." And although Joan herself believed in the importance of "corporate worship," she nonetheless emphasized that to her the essence of the Christian life was "following the Golden Rule and the Ten Commandments."

The Golden Rule was also Martha Wilson's moral philosophy: "Love thy neighbor as thyself." Martha elaborated on these words, saying that if "people were more aware of other people, perhaps there would be less difficulty"—in such ordinary things as driving on the road, where "people don't have common courtesy"—and similarly in regard to bigger issues such as racial and ethnic prejudice. It was her view that "people want to live in peace—races and nations," although she also pointed out that she herself sometimes had negative ideas about people from different backgrounds, such as her fundamentalist sister-in-law and Jehovah's Witnesses. A Methodist woman who came from a poor, nonreligious family, and who, in early adulthood, was a happily married mother of three children, spoke of her moral philosophy using similar language. She said it was "just to try to be kind to people, and to put my trust in God, and then everything will work out. Try to treat people like you would like to be treated. And even if things get dark, there's always a challenge to face tomorrow, to see what happens." She wanted her children "to learn the Golden Rule in regard to other children" and several times during the interview spoke about her desire to teach her children not to be prejudiced, commenting that her parents had been prejudiced when she was growing up and still were prejudiced against Black people and Catholics.[13]

The greater importance of living out a morality in everyday actions, and not simply professing a Christian belief or simply attending church, was also emphasized by Patrick Jones, a truck driver who came from a mixed marriage. His mother was Catholic and his father Protestant; he had married a Lutheran and their children were attending a Lutheran Sunday school. Patrick said, "Just so long as you are decent to other people and accept them as they are, what difference [does it make] what church you go to—or none, if you want it that way?" Another man said, "I don't care what religion anyone has, [I just care] how they act." Underscoring the widely shared assumption apparent among our study participants that churchgoing in itself was no guarantor of ethical behavior in daily life, a woman who willingly converted from Presbyterianism to Catholicism to marry commented, "We're religious in our everyday life, but we don't go to church. We know many people who are just the reverse—devout churchgoers who aren't religious in their daily life."

Ray Tatum, who had recently been deserted by his wife, and who had stopped attending church after adolescence, explained that he had retained the basic things he had learned at his Quaker Sunday school: "honesty and integrity." When interviewed in early adulthood, he said that he tried to practice Christianity "as far as being ethical goes, and getting along with human beings." Roger Davis, the research scientist whose father died when Roger was eight, described himself as "in general, a Protestant." Highly committed to his wife and their three young children, Roger attended the Catholic Church about once a month with his family. He articulated his view of religiousness as essentially entailing "being a decent person, enjoying life, getting happiness from life but not shirking responsibilities, doing what is best for the family but not sacrificing oneself completely. . . . Basically religion comes down to being a good person and doing the right thing." An upper-class man who, as a child, had attended either the Episcopalian or the Presbyterian Church fairly regularly and had ceased churchgoing by early adulthood explained the place of religion in his life, stating, "I'm religious to the point of believing in God, but there are questions once in a while that pop into my mind. I think I believe in God, but I don't attend church regularly, in fact very irregularly. I think I live a type of religious philosophy." When asked by the interviewer what this was, he said, "Trying to understand others, being kind and so on. I don't always do this, but this is what I try."

Bob Mears elaborated on his philosophy that he should treat all people well, even those who wronged him (including a close friend who had betrayed a confidence):

> I guess the crux of it would be the old Golden Rule: try to treat the other person as you would like to be treated. I've tried a long period of years to do the best I could in my job, to give them the best I could do. Since I've been in the Masonic Order, I've more actively attempted to exemplify the idea of brotherhood and good feeling among fellow men, not only in our Order but with all people I've come in contact with. It's been a very steady influence, [encouraging me] to attempt to act as our principles set forth.

Bob referred to the multiple sources of moral authority that can inform everyday life, citing the Bible, the Ten Commandments, the Masonic

Order's principles, and Billy Graham in trying to explain his "honest attempt" to live morally.

> I believe in God and in a hereafter. [very thoughtful, frowning] I'm afraid I fall short in several of the teachings. At times at least, I try to do better and follow the Ten Commandments, and I believe that an honest attempt to live by these teachings is the main theme of religion, for me. I know that the Masonic Order has basic religious feelings. . . . Since joining the Masonic Order, I have tried to lead the better life. I've enjoyed the Billy Graham shows; [they] brought out my own ideas of right and wrong. I disapprove of the hypocrite who attends church and thinks he is right in the eyes of the Lord but doesn't practice his principles. It's more important to have your principles than to go to church.

The integrated link between religious commitment and everyday practices was strongly emphasized by one socially active, middle-class Presbyterian woman. She attended church most Sundays with her two daughters and was heavily involved in church and community social institutions, including teenage camps, the couples' club, the Parent-Teacher Association, and the Girl Scouts. She commented, "I don't think you can isolate the spiritual part of your life from your whole existence. More than an ethical code, it's all integrated, all tied in. This is much more difficult than a lot of people realize. The way people live in their actions and relationships to one another is relevant to what they believe. It's something I feel very strongly about, but [it's] difficult to express. If a person states, 'I am a Christian,' and doesn't carry through in all phases of activities and relationships, can he call himself a Christian?"

The invocation of a Golden Rule morality by many of our study participants and their parents underscores the code's long presence in American society. Our participants, especially the Protestants, readily accessed the Golden Rule with much the same ease shown by their progeny, the baby boomers, and they did so irrespective of their level of religious commitment.[14] Because the Golden Rule is universal, determining whether individuals invoke it because of its religious or its secular underpinnings, or because of both, is difficult. Most of our participants had attended Sunday school as children or adolescents (see chapter 3), and therefore we cannot identify whether exposure to Sunday school may have uniquely prompted their Golden Rule ethic in adulthood.

It is noteworthy, however, that though tied to the Bible the nonsectarian emphasis on the command to be decent and honest in everyday life was the *doxa* institutionalized in both public and Sunday school education in the late nineteenth century (e.g., Beyerlein 2003; Boylan 1988; McGreevy 2003). The public school curriculum, Boylan argues, "represented a kind of lowest-common-denominator Protestantism, acceptable . . . to both Unitarians and Baptists" (1988: 20). And even Sunday school curricula were largely nonsectarian in content, reflecting efforts to increase interdenominational cooperation.[15] Given the denominational character of many Catholics' schooling in America in the nineteenth century and throughout much of the twentieth century (see, e.g., Greeley 1977), Catholics were not exposed to the nonsectarian (lowest-common-denominator Protestant) Golden Rule ethos enshrined in public education to the same degree their Protestant peers were. These different denominational histories were reflected in our study by the greater tendency of Protestants than Catholics to invoke the Golden Rule.[16]

In sum, notwithstanding its Protestant emphasis, the historically nonsectarian content of American socialization, penetrating even the religious education curriculum, underscores the cultural imprimatur given to the uncoupling of a Golden Rule morality from theology or church creeds long before this ethic came to be associated with current cohorts. Thus while it is understandable that observers today lament the paucity of theological content in the moral views expressed by contemporary Americans (e.g., Smith and Denton 2005: 118–71), a longer historical perspective gives pause to the assumption that this is solely a post-1960s phenomenon. The muted expectations currently associated with the rhetoric of a Golden Rule morality may well be unintended, but their original nonsectarian spirit was the brainchild of serious moral leaders intent on fashioning the common good.

RELIGIOUS AUTONOMY

Not all Americans in the course of a lifetime will display the self-confident religious independence of Michael Perry's grandfather (see the quote at the outset of this chapter). Yet when we listened to ordinary individuals talk about religion, it became apparent that, in everyday life, religion is understood by many in highly autonomous and pragmatic ways. The data presented in this chapter illuminate how the American cultural emphasis on personal freedom translates into everyday religion. When interviewed at a time of heightened religious activity in America—in the late 1950s, when church attendance and confidence in religious institutions were at a peak—many of our study participants spoke about their religious habits and attitudes in ways suggesting that the yoke of religious institutions was not overly constraining. They spontaneously accessed a vocabulary of individual choice in regard to church, uncoupled faith and belief from church attendance, and invoked the Golden Rule rather than a more theologically specific moral code. These findings demonstrate that the cultural ethic of religious autonomy was imprinted on our study participants well before 1960s culture promoted individual freedom and choice.

Whether versed in the freedom of religious choice, the independence of faith-belief from church, or the independence of morality from a sectarian creed, our study participants in the 1950s spoke a distinctively American religious language. This vocabulary takes as its premise the assumption that individuals should not be shackled by religious traditions, institutions, and theologies in defining and interpreting their relation to God and church. A paradox of American religion is that, while Americans are active participants in religious traditions and are respectful of religious beliefs and institutions, their pragmatic individualism makes them opt for the sovereignty of the self as the arbiter of everyday religious belief and practice. This autonomy allows Americans to embrace the ethos of individual choice in deciding about church, to believe in God without going to church, and to aspire to live decent, moral lives independent of sectarian theologies. Thus the religion narratives of our study participants in the 1950s bridge the ideas of their revolutionary ancestors—for whom a rhetoric of liberty was a given—and those of their children, the baby boom generation, who came of age in the freedom culture of the 1960s and 1970s.

A discourse of religious autonomy, however—no matter how easily accessed—does not change the fact that religious and spiritual engagement matters in the conduct of everyday life. Religious commitment, even when its cloak of obligation is worn lightly, is a significant source of variation, differentiating the personal characteristics and social activities of religious and spiritual individuals from those who eschew the sacred (see chapters 8, 9, and 10).

5

The Ebb and Flow of Religiousness across the Life Course

D oes religious involvement change over the life course? This is a simple question, but it eludes simple answers because it requires access to long-term longitudinal data spanning many decades of the life course. Longitudinal studies require researchers to have not only the foresight to predict at the inception of a study what questions will be relevant to future scientists but also the patience to plant a seed whose fruit will be harvested only by later generations of researchers. It is not surprising, therefore, that only a few studies in the world include data necessary to trace changes in religiousness from adolescence to old age. The IHD study is one of them.[1]

THE GENERAL PATTERN OF CHANGE

Of the three phases of adulthood (early, middle, and late adulthood), a lot is known about how religiousness changes during the transition from middle to late adulthood. Much cross-sectional data indicates that church attendance increases in old age unless illness or some disability prevents this (see, e.g., McFadden 1999). Studies using national representative cross-sectional survey data (e.g., Hout and Greeley 1987; Rossi 2001) suggest that the steepest rate of increase in religiousness occurs some time between late-middle (age fifties) and late adulthood (late sixties, and seventies). These findings agree with the widely held view that Americans turn to religion increasingly as they age in order to deal with the challenges associated with old age: health problems, spousal bereavement, death anxiety, and the lack of purposefulness that may characterize the postretirement period.

Our findings clearly indicate that religiousness increased from late-middle to late adulthood. (We discuss the coding and ratings of religiousness in the methodological appendix.) As shown in the extreme-right portions of figures 1 and 2, the study participants increased in religiousness from their fifties to their seventies and did so irrespective of whether they were men or women, or whether they came from a mainline Protestant, nonmainline Protestant, or Catholic family background. The gradient of increase in religiousness among our aging participants was not very steep, however. In fact, their increase in religiousness would be hardly noticeable if we were able to meet them personally in their fifties and then again in their seventies. Nonetheless, it was statistically significant.[2] Therefore, if we had had longitudinal data confined to the fifteen-year age period between late-middle and late adulthood, our findings would have offered strong support for the assumption that religiousness peaks in old age and that this peak reflects a maturational imperative that transcends sociodemographic characteristics.

However, because we have data spanning the entire life course, we know that the increase in religiousness in the second half of adulthood is far from being the whole story. When we look at the pattern for the life course as a whole, it is apparent that late adulthood does not constitute the high point in religiousness (see figures 1 and 2). In late adulthood, in fact, our participants reverted back to the level of religious involvement that characterized them in early adulthood, and these gains still fell short of their levels of religiousness in adolescence.[3]

It is evident, overall, that the pattern of change is best described as a shallow U-curve, with high levels of religiousness in adolescence and in early and late adulthood and a dip in religiousness in the middle years. As shown in figure 1, the mean level of religiousness among the study participants as a whole decreased from adolescence to early adulthood (age thirties) and from early to middle adulthood (age forties). It then reached a plateau between middle and late-middle adulthood (age midfifties and early sixties), before increasing from late-middle to late adulthood (age late sixties and seventies).[4] In other words, there was a noticeable increase in the number of individuals who withdrew

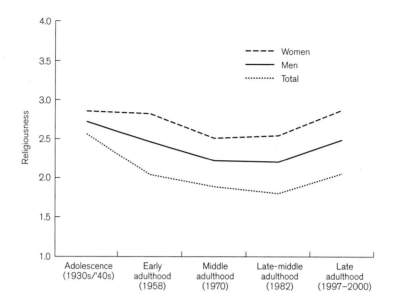

Figure 1. Mean change in religiousness over time by total sample and gender.

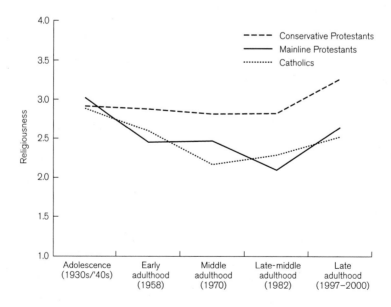

Figure 2. Mean change in religiousness over time by denomination.

from church between adolescence and early adulthood and an even more noticeable increase between adolescence and middle adulthood. Whereas over half the participants (57 percent) were moderately or highly religious as adolescents, this figure decreased to 48 percent in early adulthood, and just over a third (37 percent) were moderately or highly religious in middle adulthood. Although late adulthood brought with it an upswing in religiousness, the percentage of moderately to highly religious participants increased to only 43 percent, a figure close to that of early adulthood.

The high level of religious involvement among our participants in early adulthood is not surprising. A large body of research on religion in early adulthood indicates that, following a drop in religiousness during the college years (a period for which we do not have data), young adults who settle down in their twenties and thirties, and marry and have children, tend to generally resume church involvement. In short, having school-age children increases the likelihood of parental church attendance, though the age and gender of the parents, and whether parents are separated or divorced, affect this relation.[5] The strong connection between parenting and church participation is embedded in the cultural importance that Americans—even those not highly religious themselves (see chapter 2)—see in having children exposed to formalized religious socialization. It is also motivated by parents' appreciation for the social opportunities and supportive relationships that church can provide for both children and parents (see chapter 3; and Edgell 2006). The family-formation logic underlying parental religiousness was captured by one of our study participants: at age thirty, she and her husband attended church only at Christmas and Easter, but she commented at the time, "I expect we would go more often if we had children to be concerned about."

Because very few of the study participants did not have children, we could not directly test the effect of children's presence on parental religiousness. Nonetheless, the timing of women's drop in religiousness (see figure 1) fits with the findings from other studies underscoring the critical role that the religious socialization of children plays in increasing the religious involvement of parents, especially mothers. Responsibility for religious socialization belonged particularly to the women in our study, who, reflecting the more traditional gender social roles of the time, were by and large not in the labor force in the 1950s and 1960s, when their children were young. It is thus noteworthy that men's drop in religiousness occurred earlier than that of women, with the significant decline occurring between adolescence and early adulthood (age thirties). Although 48 percent of men were moderately or highly religious as adolescents, this number dropped to 32 percent by early adulthood. Women's religiousness, by contrast, did not dip until middle adulthood (age forties), and the decline was not as precipitous as men's.[6] Thus, a similar proportion of women (61 percent) were moderately to highly religious in early adulthood as in adolescence (64 percent), with the number declining to 51 percent by middle adulthood. Because the study participants tended to marry early and have children at a young age (as noted in chapter 4), the midlife decline in women's religiousness largely coincided with children leaving home and the attendant absence of child socialization pressures. The general fact that religiousness occupies a more prominent place in the lives of women than in the lives of men was reflected in women's significantly higher rates of religiousness during adolescence (see also chapter 3) and from early adulthood onward (see figure 1).

Whereas the comparatively high levels of religiousness in early and late adulthood are well grounded in existing research, comparatively little is known about religiousness in middle adulthood. An innovative contribution of our research is that it offers a bird's-eye view of the entire adult life course and thereby allows one to connect the two literatures on changes in religiousness in early and late adulthood by including data from middle adulthood. Once again, our findings are very clear: the interval from middle to late-middle adulthood was the nadir of religious involvement for the IHD participants irrespective of gender and whether they came from a mainline Protestant or Catholic background (see figures 1 and 2). This dip (and the general pattern of change as a whole) was also characteristic of both the younger and the older cohorts. The religiousness of the small group of participants who had been socialized in nonmainline Protestant families did not dip in midlife. That this group's religiousness was more immune to the tides of family and social change indicates, perhaps, the greater sacrifices and strictness associated with sectarian religious traditions (Finke and Stark 1992). Moreover, they had higher levels of religiousness across adulthood as well as a much more consistently stable pattern of religiousness than their mainline and Catholic peers.

But what explains the middle-adulthood decline in religiousness experienced by many of our study participants? The drop in religiousness certainly reflected parents' diminished child socialization pressures, as intimated by several of the participants themselves. But it was also related to the fact that many of the parents at midlife were busily engaged with additional career responsibilities—the new responsibilities that come with seniority at work (for the men) or that are encountered by women who enter or return to the workforce after their children leave home—and with increased involvement in community and leisure activities. Apparently, as a result of the confluence of children leaving home and newly emerging pressures exerted by work and other activities, our middle-aged participants assigned a lower priority to church involvement. The perceived need for church may also have dimmed because midlife is a time in the life course when individuals tend to see their mortality as still far off, belonging, as noted by Philip Roth, to the remote future (2006: 32). In any event, our longitudinal findings revealing a midlife dip in religiousness fit with the retrospective accounts provided by elderly individuals (Ingersoll-Dayton, Krause, and Morgan 2002) and fit with findings from the baby boom generation (Roof 1999), which point to a similar decline in midlife parental religiousness.

Ian Logan's life course pattern of religious engagement helps to illustrate how family role transitions and social and cultural changes can affect the religious attitudes and habits of even some of the most religious among us. From childhood, Ian was heavily immersed in the Methodist Church, attending weekly services and staying active in the church's young people's group. He also helped his father, a Sunday school superintendent, count and roll pennies and sort Sunday school papers. After graduating from high school in 1947, Ian, then nineteen, accompanied his family to the Philippines, where they lived for a year while his engineer father completed some contract work. Ian enjoyed his time living on the outskirts of Manila, and he too worked for several months in his father's firm. Upon his return to the United States, Ian enrolled in a Methodist junior college in California, became very active in its church group, and was elected state president of the Methodist Youth Organization. He spent a considerable amount of his time fulfilling the duties of this office, both before and after he went to the University of California, where he majored in engineering.

Soon after graduation, Ian married a woman he had known since childhood; both had attended the same Methodist Church and were members of its youth group. Ian joined the air force and served with noncombat forces, first in Sacramento, and later in England for about two years during the war in Korea. The first of his children was born before Ian and his wife left England, and they later had a second child.

Upon Ian's discharge from the air force, he bought a house and worked at his father's engineering firm in the San Francisco Bay Area.

Described as "guarded and unexpressive," Ian spent most of his leisure time during his thirties counseling a Methodist young people's group, which he found enjoyable. More religiously involved than his wife, Ian said that his church commitments restricted his family's activities, and his wife, a traditional woman who left college after two years to marry Ian, was, he said, "unhappy that I spend so much time at it."

Twelve years later, in 1970, Ian continued to be "self-contained and detached." His musically talented daughter was in high school, and his wife, taking advantage of the increased opportunities available to women in the 1970s, was going to school part-time to get a teacher's credential. Ian was very satisfied with his engineering career; he was now in a managerial position at a different company and enjoyed a lot of autonomy and independence. Financially the couple were "making do," but he felt that they could use more money; Ian had a pilot's license, for example, but no plane.

Now at age forty-two, Ian was less active in church than he had been at any time since adolescence. Although he still believed in "God in general"—in the "Judeo-Christian concepts of God with God as a Father, a personal-type God"—Ian expressed concern about the slackening of his own religious involvement and its larger meaning. He was somewhat "remiss" in regard to his adolescent children's religious training, largely because of the family's busy daily routines—"the hectic pace at which we operate"—which made "involvement in church activities not as much as it should be." It was also evident, however, that Ian's reduced commitment reflected a turmoil he was experiencing in response to the many religious, social, and political changes occurring in the late 1960s and the beginning of the 1970s. He noted the "change in approach of churches and in Christian education in general," and pithily remarked that "everything is changing rapidly, and I am not changing rapidly enough myself."

Illustrating the emerging therapeutic ethos penetrating traditional religion, Ian recounted that he had recently gone to Grace Cathedral in San Francisco one weekend "for what was purported to be an organ concert" and had been surprised to see so many people "bring their troubles forward like Lazarus and lay them on the altar." He continued: "Of course these were Episcopalians—but the Methodists are also changing to the point where I'm not even certain that I want to continue being a Methodist. So that's something I have to figure out for myself." Although Ian would never leave the Methodist Church, unlike his younger sister, who "had gone quite fundamentalist," his grappling with the problem of what constituted the "right" religious education was intense. He commented dryly, "In terms of getting my kids the kind of religious training that I got, and which by definition must be right—they're not getting that. And so, either I've got to find some way for them to get it, or I've got to change my concept of what is right, I guess."

Ian's struggle to know what was right extended beyond religion. His reassessment of his religious philosophy, like those of others in our study, was not isolated from broader cultural issues and political events. His views on the Vietnam War, for example, had also changed. Following the escalation of military offenses in Vietnam, Ian had become more opposed to the war than he had been a few years earlier. He commented, "My personal view was that we ought to back the president's policy and give him support. . . . I tended to feel that he and his advisers had more information on this basic kind of policy than I could know about, and I tended to put my faith in him. Lately I've begun to wonder about that, and whereas I still feel that the gradual withdrawing is the only way to go about it[,] . . . I feel it ought to be a little faster than what is going on now."

The sense of personal anomie that Ian conveyed at midlife was even more pronounced in late-middle adulthood. In 1982, the overarching theme of Ian's interview was that he was in a period of transition, searching for a new self-direction and plan. With his children no longer at home, he was "making a greater effort" to engage more in social activities with his wife, who was now teaching full-time, but it was clear that he preferred to do things alone. Ian had gradually resumed a busy schedule of church involvement: he was once again regularly attending Methodist Church services and was singing in the choir, and he was serving on the church's Commission of Education and as chairman of its administrative board. When asked by the interviewer what aspect of his life had most influenced his sense of self, Ian responded, "Probably my church activities."

In 1997, Ian was still attending the Methodist Church "almost every Sunday, probably some forty to forty-five weeks out of the year," and was heavily involved in organizing and teaching in its children's religious program. His wife continued to feel that he was spending too much time on church activities, though they both now sang in the church choir and in a local choral society. Retired since 1994, Ian was learning to play the oboe and had taken up golf. He identified church activities, family, and career as the things in his life of which he was proudest. Despite the earlier lull in his religious involvement, he had remained a committed Methodist and spoke warmly of the various group activities that he had been involved in, and of the relationships that he had formed through his participation in the Methodist Church, relationships that he "shared with people of similar thinking."

Clearly, being a religious dweller and staying connected to the Methodist Church and to people of similar thinking were part and parcel of how Ian thought about himself and organized his time. And when his church involvement dipped, this reflected an identity crisis. The crisis was not necessarily a midlife crisis per se, though it happened in his forties, but was one that emerged during a time of family, religious, and political change. The firsthand experience of these multiple changes prompted Ian to question the status quo, including the established views of church and religious teaching that had been central to his life since childhood.

THE EFFECT OF CHURCH CRISIS

The ebb and flow of religiousness during adulthood is also driven by the specific sociohistorical context that shapes a given generation's life experiences and the unfolding of their religiousness over the life course. In fact, the historical and institutional context informing our study participants' lives significantly influenced the overall midlife dip in religiousness that we found. The only important difference in the pattern of change between Catholics and mainline Protestants occurred in the twelve-year interval between 1970 and 1982 (from middle to late-middle adulthood). During this time, the mainline Protestants showed little change in religiousness, but Catholics declined significantly (see figure 2).[7] The decline among Catholics was largely concentrated among those who were relatively less religious rather than moderately or more highly involved: from middle to late-middle adulthood, the percentage of Catholics who were not religious doubled (from 21 percent to 42 percent). In comparison, the proportion of Catholics with moderate to high religious involvement showed little change during this time (38 percent in 1970 compared to 33 percent in 1982). This finding supports the "religious capital" thesis, which states that the more invested individuals are in a particular religious tradition, the less likely they are to decrease their investment (see, e.g., Iannaccone 1990), even when prompted to do so by events that challenge the terms of their religious commitment and identity (see, e.g., Dillon 1999).

The significant midlife decline in religiousness evident among our Catholics captured a larger Catholic institutional dynamic. It coincided with the decline in church attendance among American Catholics as a whole; their church attendance subsequently stabilized at a lower level. The dip came from their disaffection with the Vatican's ban on contraception issued in 1968 *(Humanae Vitae)* and its unwillingness to continue reforms initiated by the Second Vatican Council (see Greeley 1985; Hout and Greeley 1987; Seidler and Meyer 1989). Similarly, in our study, Catholics (and Protestants) increased in religiousness by late adulthood. And for the Catholics, this was sufficient to bring their involvement largely back on a par with their early adulthood commitment. Our data thus track the immediate rupture that *Humanae Vitae* produced among American Catholics as well as its long-term accommodation.

Ellen Quinn was described at age sixteen as "a Catholic without conflict," and as "accepting of and integrating authority." She went to church every Sunday without protest. During her adolescent interview, she commented that she "would not think of not going." Ellen was also friendly, outgoing, and popular. And at seventeen, when asked what characteristics she would like to instill in a child, she said, "To be obedient, to be a good Catholic, to watch out for himself and his own interests, . . . to be self-reliant." Ellen's father was an insurance bookkeeper, and her mother worked part-time as a telephone operator; Ellen did not go to college but worked in an office and subsequently built a successful sales career.

At nineteen Ellen got married in church to a nonpracticing Episcopalian who took the formal Catholic instructions required of non-Catholics who wanted to marry Catholics. Although her Irish-born mother was, according to Ellen, a devout Catholic who went to church every morning, she did not object to Ellen's marriage to a non-Catholic. In fact, she was relieved that, after a few years of being interested in "wild" boys, Ellen had found someone who was sensible and who had a stable job as a sales representative. His parents, however, were concerned that their twenty-year-old son was marrying a Catholic, but this was not a source of tension with Ellen's in-laws after the marriage. Subsequently Ellen and her husband had three children, and they had an emotionally and economically secure family life. In the 1950s, putting into practice the aspirations she expressed as a teenager, Ellen took her children to church with her every Sunday, sent them to Catholic schools, and was active in the Parent-Teacher Association and the Brownies.

But in 1969, one year after the Vatican had affirmed its ban on artificial birth control, Ellen stopped going to church; she said that, like her kids, she could no longer be bothered to attend, "just sitting there bored." Ellen was using birth control pills, and when interviewed in 1970, she emphasized that she was "absolutely in favor of birth control" and also favored the legalization of abortion. Her views on these issues caused conflict between her and her mother, who thought "it's God's wish how many kids people have." By contrast, Ellen felt "there was nothing more immoral than bringing children into the world who couldn't be taken care of." Despite her lapsed attendance and her disagreements with Catholic teaching, Ellen still regarded herself as a Catholic, just like many dissenting Catholics today (D'Antonio et al. 2001), and she continued to believe in God, though she was unsure about an afterlife. Her increased disregard for church authority was, she said, part of her new awareness that "Catholicism is not the last, absolute word," an awareness further fueled by the various "shifts in doctrine" that she associated with the post–Vatican II church and which differed from what she was taught while growing up.

The change in Ellen's attitude toward authority was not confined to religion. Like Ian Logan, she had also changed her political views. Talking about the Vietnam War, she too said that, although she had initially thought the war in Vietnam was necessary, she subsequently had "learn[ed] not to believe everything [the] government and authorities say" and now believed that the United States should "get out as quick as we possibly can." She came to this opinion, she said, partly in response to the views and experiences of some military pilot friends who had served there.

Almost thirty years later, when she was interviewed in 1998, Ellen was a widowed grandmother. She was in good health and enjoying her life, especially travels with her friends. She was working two days a week at a gift shop for which she had been a successful buyer-manger since the early 1960s, and she spent some of her free time delivering meals to AIDS patients. Ellen had resumed her weekly attendance at the Catholic Church, and spontaneous prayer was an important part of her daily life. She was quick to point out, however, that, while she believed in God, "I can't say I believe in everything that they [the church] teach you." Ellen did not point to any one reason as the motivation for her return to church; it seemed to come from a mix of factors. With her husband's death in 1990 after a short illness, and her own reduced work schedule, she clearly had more time on her hands. And while there is some research indicating that adult children can influence the religious involvement of parents (Sherkat 2003), this was not true in Ellen's case. Her son went to church only occasionally, and her two daughters and their families were not at all religiously active. This lack of church involvement did not bother Ellen; she was glad her children had some religious background and, reflecting the cultural hold of the Golden Rule, she added that honesty and moral living were more important than church attendance: "Your conscience more than anything else guides your behavior."

Although Ellen was not as strong a Catholic as Ian was a Methodist, both exemplify how church involvement is variously shaped by social context. Clearly, as illustrated in both lives, early socialization into a religious tradition exerts an enduring influence on people's long-term religious involvement. But over time the extent of that commitment can be altered by various life course, social, and historical changes. The absence of child socialization pressures in midlife, or the increased availability of free time as a result of changes in spousal, family, and work roles in the postretirement period, shifts the context informing people's religious involvement. Similarly, large-scale political and cultural events and religious institutional changes and controversies can cause people to rethink their taken-for-granted values and habits. Both Ellen Quinn and Ian Logan lapsed somewhat in their religious commitment for several years in midlife. But, highlighting the ebb and flow rather than the irreversibility of religious behavior, for them and for many others in our study, this was a temporary change rather than a once-and-for-all rupture, since they subsequently and without fanfare eased back into their weekly church routines.

LIFETIME VARIATION IN RELIGIOUS HABITS

Although the religiousness of the study participants ebbed and flowed over time, as illuminated by the decline in religiousness in middle adulthood (see figure 1), a more fine-grained analysis that divided the participants into discrete groups based on common trajectories of change indicated that stability was the norm for many others. Some interviewees maintained a stable adulthood pattern of high religiousness, and still others maintained a stable pattern of little or no interest in religion (see figure 3). It is particularly noteworthy that a substantial proportion of our study participants kept a good distance between themselves and organized religion throughout their adult lives. Even in 1958, at the peak of American religious practice, a quarter (26 percent) of the study participants were not religious at all; clearly, many did not just talk of religious autonomy (see chapter 4) but felt free to keep away from church. In fact, the group with low religiousness included more than half the study's participants, who, throughout adulthood, either were not religious at all or displayed sporadic religious involvement. Compared to their peers who were consistently high in religiousness, the group with consistently low religiousness included—not surprisingly—more men than women, and individuals who as adolescents were less conscientious and less religious.[8]

"The Holy Grail!" Jack Adams quickly asserted when at age sixteen he was asked by the interviewer to identify Leonardo da Vinci's painting of the Last Supper. Typical of his defiance, Jack was the only one in the study to refer to the picture by ignoring the central figure of Jesus (though, of course, as the interviewer noted, he was right in that the Last Supper is when the Grail was last seen). Jack was a self-described staunch atheist all his life; he died in 2001, at age seventy-nine, from a stroke. He grew up in an economically comfortable but emotionally repressive family. His father, a college baseball star in his youth, was physically and verbally abusive and instilled a strong masculine bravado in Jack, though it was tempered by what observers saw as Jack's "good-natured" and easygoing ways.

Jack's father was an atheist, and he objected to his wife's Catholicism, which he consequently suppressed. Although Jack's mother had him baptized while his father was out of town, he was among the small minority in our study (13 percent) who did not receive any religious training, attending neither church services nor Sunday school. After he graduated from high school, Jack worked in his father's small retail business. Following the bombing of Pearl Harbor, he immediately, as a newly married man, joined the marines and served in the Pacific. While he was modest and generally positive about his war participation, seeing it as a character-building experience that made him appreciate his abilities, Jack had problems in adapting to civilian life upon his return. He bought out his father's business but encountered financial troubles in running it, and suffered a series of business failures during the 1950s. Jack coped with his acute sense of failure, and what he saw as the challenge it posed to his manliness, by resorting to heavy drinking and spending long evenings away from home, from his wife and two young

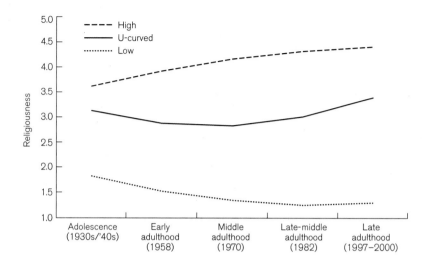

Figure 3. Lifetime trajectories of religiousness.

daughters. He eventually opted for a career selling life insurance and did quite well financially.

In 1958, Jack boasted that he had "no religion. I mean I'm an atheist, I don't believe in God." He conceded that some of his fellow-soldiers had found comfort in their religious faith during dangerous military situations, but not he. And just as Jack's father had squelched his mother's Catholicism, Jack said he had "squelched" his own wife's Catholicism before they got married by refusing to be married in a church. For Jack, the "most important thing in life [was] health and happiness," and, underscoring the cultural potency of the Golden Rule even among the nonreligious, he gave an inverted definition of its ethos as his moral philosophy. His rule for living, he said, "would be the Golden Rule, or not doing anything you would change if people knew, or which you would not want to see in the papers." When the interviewer made the leading remark that apparently his living by the Golden Rule was not connected with religion, Jack replied with a resounding "Right!"

By 1970, Jack's two daughters were married, and he reported that they too were atheists. This was so despite the fact that he had sent them to Sunday school—because his atheistic father had advised him that "girls should have religious training." In any event, he said, "they didn't believe in all the fish stories and so forth, and so that ended it."

After he retired in 1980, at age fifty-eight, Jack spent most of his time welding metal statues and working on a new house that he had recently bought. He started learning French and taking piano lessons, and had an electric piano inserted in the thirty-five-foot trailer that he and his wife took on trips within the United States and to Canada. Jack remained vigorously antireligious and, during the 1982 interview, criticized what he saw as the trouble religion causes across the world:

> I figure that most religions are the cause of more death and suffering among people than anything else. Starting back as far as you can name in history, there's always been somebody killing somebody else because they don't believe in their way of religion. . . . They're fighting over in Ireland over religion; the fighting in the Middle East is over religion; a lot of the fighting in Africa is over religion; and it just goes on and on. I don't want any part of that. The words are fine, but when it comes to deeds . . .

When he was interviewed fifteen years later, Jack was suffering from emphysema and heart trouble. Despite his illnesses, he was still finding enjoyment in his metal statues and working in his garden, from which, reflecting his good nature, he generously gave seasonal fruit to his neighbors, a gesture, he suggested, that helps "to cement friendships." Jack was still an atheist, and he reiterated his negative view of religion, saying he was "irreligious and antireligion . . . because religion has caused so much grief and death and bloodshed. . . . The Catholics and the Protestants, the Sunni Muslims and the Shiite Muslims, the Jews and the Muslims. It seems like everybody's killing each other instead of turning the other cheek."

Although religion can provide people with comfort and meaning during times of adversity, and the onset of illness or some other unexpected personal trouble can prompt a nonreligious person to turn to the church, the stability in the lifetime nonreligiousness of Jack and of several others in our study highlights the fact that, even in the face of danger, illness, and death, some do not waver in their aversion to the church. Jack's defiant atheism was not ruffled by the many tough challenges he faced over the years. He remained impervious to, and decidedly uninterested in, any personal comfort or meaning that religion might have brought him when he was a young paratrooper or when he subsequently faced long nights of alcoholic despair, or in his late life, when he endured painful illnesses. Quite the contrary. And Jack found substantial reinforcement for the reasonableness of his own lack of religiousness in, as he cited, the multiple ways in which religion inflames ongoing political conflicts around the world.

Our analysis of life course trajectories is also important in demonstrating that many of our study participants remained highly committed to religion from adolescence through late adulthood, across sixty years of major life course and social and cultural changes. The stability of individual religiousness could not be better illustrated than by Jay Campbell, a lifelong Presbyterian. Unlike Barbara Shaw, with whom we opened this book, and whose consistent church involvement belied her internal struggle with the Baptists' everyday strictures, Jay saw his churchgoing as a direct expression of his beliefs, and he seamlessly merged his religious outlook into his busy life. Born in 1922, Jay was brought up in a fairly conventional, though interdenominational, family; his mother was a Presbyterian and his father a nonpracticing Episcopalian. Jay and his brother accompanied their mother to church every week, and both boys also went to Sunday school. Although Jay was sociable, he was also seen by institute researchers as being "under stress of religious and moralistic demands to conform." After graduating from the University of California, Jay served in the navy for thirty months during World War II and subsequently remained active in the naval reserve. He regarded his time in the service as one of the lowest points in his life; he was especially homesick for his family and for his fiancée, whom he married without delay upon returning from the war. Coming from a middle-class background, Jay used the GI Bill to pay for graduate studies and to put a down payment on his first house, thus securing his status in the quickly expanding suburban middle class.

Work, family, and church have been the pillars of Jay's adult life, leaving little time for socializing with friends or getting involved in community activities. By 1958, at age thirty-six, Jay and his wife had six children, and he was immensely fulfilled in his work as a history professor at a California university. A nonsmoker and nondrinker, Jay attended church with his wife and children "at least fifty Sundays a year," and while in Europe for a year on sabbatical, he went to the Anglican Church. Conscious of the boundaries between different religions, Jay explained that his brand of Presbyterianism was "strictly evangelical Trinitarian Protestant."

Jay spent most of his free time playing basketball with his kids; he did very little socializing with friends, and, unlike many religiously active Americans, he considered himself a nonjoiner, outside of his church, the naval reserve, and professional organizations. Politically, he described himself in 1958 as "a liberal conservative"—liberal on social issues and conservative on economic issues. When asked what he considered to be the most important thing in life, Jay responded, "The most important is the moral, spiritual values in life. . . . Unless one solves this aspect of life, there is little lasting basis of satisfaction." He also expressed a forward-thinking view of diversity and multiculturalism and was critical of the increasingly visible consumerism, stating, "I feel that material gain and comfort are not the most important aspects of life. There are many other satisfactions that are more worthwhile than having a new automobile or a fur-lined bathtub or whatever is the most conspicuous aspect of luxury. Of course, I feel that most Americans are too preoccupied with conspicuous consumption, having something that looks flashy and costs [a lot] of dollars."

For Jay at midlife, his academic career continued to be a major source of personal satisfaction. Still attending the Presbyterian Church every Sunday, Jay commented that he felt "an obligation" to regularly attend church: "It continually reaffirms or reassures a person that religion is part of life or part of that individual's continual kind of revitalization on the spiritual side of life." Jay's view that religious belief should be accompanied by church attendance was part of his larger belief that individuals should publicly witness their avowed commitments: "I also think regular participation is an example to the children and an example, not in a goody-goody type example, but an example to your friends and associates. . . . A person can hardly claim that they're a church member if they go once or twice a year to church. . . . I think that it also tends to make contacts for yourself and your family with people who have similar sets of goals and beliefs."

In 1982, Jay was still heavily involved in his successful career and traveling often to Europe on extended research trips. With the children grown, his wife had gone back to college and was completing a nursing degree that she had started before they got married. Jay was still attending the Presbyterian Church, and though he acknowledged that he'd "always been involved in the church in a way," he was quick to say that he wasn't deeply religious: "I wouldn't say that I am deeply religious. I don't think it's superficial either. . . . I don't have to understand it, totally, to believe it. . . . I accept it more or less on blind faith, because it's not worth it for me to spend that much time [worrying about it]."

Reiterating the views he expressed in 1958, Jay still emphasized the importance of example and practice as a way of showing respect for religion. Modulating the individual-choice view of church expressed by many others in our study (see chapter 4), he stated that religion was largely "inherited by example." Hence, he argued, children need at least to be exposed to a particular church even if they reject it later. Commenting that he, his wife, and the children remaining at home went to church every Sunday, Jay said,

> I can't force them to do anything more than that, but I do think they need that sort of element. They don't have to go to the church we go to, as long as they're attending church. This is for as long as they live at home. I feel that, under these circumstances, I've done what a parent should do. From then on, it's up to them. . . . But at least they can't say they weren't exposed. . . . Some people say, "Well, I'm gonna let my kids decide on their own." That's already a decision against [religion], if they say that, because it basically makes [the children] not religious, makes them not believe. But if it's offered, they take it if they want it, or they reject it if they want to, but at least it's been presented.

When interviewed in 1998, Jay, at seventy-six years of age, was officially retired, though he still maintained an active research program and continued playing basketball with his kids and grandkids. He was still going to church every Sunday, "except when there's something that makes it impossible to do so." Although mostly satisfied with his life, Jay was disappointed that three of his children had divorced. He was also disappointed, unlike Ellen Quinn, that some of his children had little interest in church; he was particularly worried about his grandchildren's moral well-being, because, he felt, they "don't have an opportunity for any sort of exposure to nonmaterial things[,] . . . to Christianity, theology, or whatever you want to call it."

Not surprisingly, in elaborating on the beliefs and values that guide his life, Jay emphasized his Christian ethos:

> Christianity is the fundamental value that has guided my life. I know that Christianity can have lots of different manifestations, but I would say that fairly conservative Christianity is closer to what is guiding me. . . . Having a Christian orientation gives one a certain idea of what his responsibility is—to look out for yourself, look out for other people, be as generous as you can to causes that are worthwhile. . . . I think that the example of any person, but particularly people who profess to be Christians, the example that they set for other people ought to be very important in guiding what they do. It's not entirely for their own benefit that they are good; it's for the example they set for other people. . . . Setting a good example is a fundamental requirement for a person who believes, who expresses the Christian faith.

Clearly, work, family, and church formed the consistent centerpiece of Jay's adult life. Committed to living by good example, Jay had a keen sense of obligation that meant he was unwavering in his commitments in each of these domains. For Jay to have absented himself from church, even as a temporary lapse during his overseas research trips, would have been a personal betrayal of his strong belief that deeds must give constant expression to values. Life course and family transitions, a highly successful career, and the many large-scale social and cultural changes he lived through did not alter the stability of his strong religious commitment. Though he traveled widely for his work, he was clearly a dweller when it came to religion; he willingly accepted his religious inheritance and did not seek any religious answers or experiences outside his own denomination.

DYNAMIC CONTINUITY

After a general fall-off in church activity between adolescence and early adulthood, the proportion of individuals who were involved to various degrees in church at any given time in adulthood was relatively stable, and at each time point, women had significantly higher levels of religiousness than men. We saw, however, that the study participants as a whole decreased in religiousness between early and middle adulthood and, subsequently, increased in religiousness between late-middle and late adulthood. This shallow U-curve pattern held for men and women, for both cohorts, and for mainline Protestants and Catholics. Underscoring the fact that religiousness is not abstracted from the everyday world but is shaped by individuals' immediate social context, as well as by specific institutional and historical forces, there were some notable differences in the timing of our study participants' dip in religiousness: women decreased their religious commitment later than men, and Catholics had a sharper decline than mainline Protestants.

Although statistically significant, the average change in religiousness over the life course was relatively small. The largest change in religiousness—the decrease from adolescence to middle adulthood—would have been only marginally observable in everyday behavior. Excluding adolescence, the decrease from early to middle adulthood and the increase from late-middle to late adulthood, though statistically significant, were relatively small. Overall, our data indicate a rather gentle ebb and flow in religiousness over the adult years, rather than more abrupt shifts in religious commitment. In this regard, our findings support Robert Atchley's emphasis on the adaptive continuities that characterize the aging process (1999). He argues that adults develop robust and relatively enduring patterns of thought and behavior that allow them to accommodate a considerable amount of ongoing change without experiencing a crisis or the necessity for radical transformation. This general pattern of stability does not, of course, preclude a small number of individuals from experiencing marked increases or decreases in religiousness (see chapter 6).

The findings in this chapter demonstrate the importance of considering the entire life course in interpreting changes in religiousness that occur within any one of its phases. Taken in isolation, the finding that religiousness increased significantly from middle to late adulthood could be interpreted as strong support for the thesis that older adults become more religious in response to the social and existential challenges associated with late adulthood. However, when changes that occurred at other phases of the life course are brought into view, it is remarkable that, for our study participants, late-adulthood religiousness was not more pronounced than early-adulthood religiousness.

In support of the life course paradigm (e.g., Elder 1998), our data demonstrate the importance of analyzing change over time in terms of trajectories, the timing of role transitions, and the surrounding socio-historical context. While it makes sense to ask whether religiousness changes over the life course, our findings show that this question has no one answer. Among the study participants, there were three distinct adulthood trajectories: stable high, stable low, and a curved pattern. The two stable trajectories appeared to have been uninfluenced by either social role or life transitions (e.g., becoming a parent, career mobility, illness, and retirement), or by the larger historical context. By contrast, the curved trajectory illustrated the way in which life course religiousness is potentially shaped by both role transitions and social change. The mix of trajectories that emerged in our data confirms the life course theoretical expectation that trajectories and transitions interact with each other; in short, tracing lifetime religiousness among the IHD participants revealed that some trajectories are more contingent than others on life course and socio-cultural change. And, additionally, trajectories of adult religious involvement are also influenced by such factors as adolescent personality and religious socialization.

6

Individual Transformation in Religious Commitment and Meaning

We know from the findings presented in the previous chapter that the study participants as a group showed relatively little change in their level of religiousness across adulthood, despite the dip in their religiousness around midlife evident in the 1970 interviews. But this information does not tell us whether individual members of our study who were more religious than others in early adulthood tended to remain comparatively so in middle or late adulthood. And conversely, it does not tell us whether individuals who were not religious in their thirties or forties tended to remain so in old age. After all, a sample that is highly stable as a group can show a lot of individual variability as long as increases in religiousness among some of the members are offset by declines in religiousness among other members. By the same token, a high level of individual stability in religiousness or any characteristic from one time period to another does not preclude group-level decline or increase in the same characteristic. This is demonstrated, for example, by the fact that fifth graders as a group do better in math than they did as third graders (showing a group-level increase), even though the same boys and girls who were best at math in third grade may remain so in fifth grade (showing individual rank order stability).[1] Assessing change in individual levels of religiousness—discovering who increased or decreased in religiousness during their adult years—is a focus of this chapter.

In general, much more is known about group-level change in religiousness over the life course than about individual (rank order) stability in religiousness. This is the case for two reasons. Group-level changes typically occur as a result of general social and maturational forces impinging on individuals. A shift in social roles, for example, may result in young parents, as a whole, showing a higher level of church attendance than college-age students. Group-level change can also occur as a result of specific sociohistorical occurrences, as illustrated by the response of Catholics to the Vatican's ban on contraception in the late 1960s (see chapter 5). From a more psychological perspective, group-level change is exemplified by maturational effects, such as the improvement in cognitive functioning that results in better math performance in our earlier example of fifth graders. As a result, group-level changes interest both the sociologists who study how social and life course changes affect individuals, and the psychologists who study the maturational effects of aging as a developmental process. In contrast, rank order stability, with its emphasis squarely on the individual, piques the attention of psychologists more than other social scientists. This is because instances where a given characteristic changes in some individuals and not in others typically lead to explanations invoking individual differences in such characteristics as personality, intelligence, or some other emotional or cognitive attribute construed as independent of social and cultural change.

The other reason why relatively little is known about stability of religiousness among individuals, in contrast to group-level stability, is that coefficients of stability can be computed only by using longitudinal data. To continue with our math example, the only way to determine whether the same youngsters who scored highest on math in third grade continued to score highest in fifth grade is to test a group of children when they are in third grade, wait two years, and retest the same children in fifth grade. In contrast, changes on a group level can be investigated cross-sectionally by comparing results for a group of third and a group of fifth graders tested on the same day. The need for longitudinal data to establish stability at an individual level means that it takes at least fifty years, as in the case of our study, to gather data needed to find out whether adolescents who score higher or lower than their peers on religiousness continue to do so in late adulthood. There is only a handful of such studies in the world, and most of them focus on psychological development over time rather than on changes in individual religious and other social behavior.

How stable, then, was individual religiousness in our study? The data indicated two distinct patterns of individual (rank order) stability over time (see table 2). First, the average correlation between religiousness in adolescence and religiousness at any of our study's four time points in adulthood was only moderate (average $r = .49$). This means that, although a high proportion of the study participants who were highly religious in adolescence continued to be religious throughout adulthood, they were not universally so. Rather, a large number of individuals who were highly religious in adolescence became less religious in adulthood and, conversely, a substantial number of nonreligious adolescents became religious later in life. In short, adolescent religiousness is a robust, but not an overwhelmingly strong, predictor of religiousness.

There are several explanations for this finding. Adolescent religiousness is more immediately constrained by parents' expectations than adulthood religiousness is; the latter is more freely determined by the individual. This means that adolescents who attended church primarily because of parental expectations are likely to cease doing so once they leave home and gain independence. Ray Tatum typified a postadolescence religious decline. In adolescence he attended weekly Quaker services with his strict stepmother but was going only "once in a very great while" when interviewed in his thirties. Like many young people of all generations, especially men, he had fallen away from church as soon as he left his parents' house. And although Ray felt that a person should go to church, he acknowledged that he had "procrastinated" through the years and had not gone. His lack of attendance was, in part, related to years of personal turmoil. Socially withdrawn since childhood, when he was deserted by his real mother, he himself had a very unhappy marriage and, not long before the 1958 interview, had been deserted by his wife. He struggled to care for their two children and establish a plumbing business. He subsequently remarried, and although he continued to believe in God and an afterlife, Ray's procrastination in regard to church attendance continued through late adulthood.

Other adolescents and young adults may develop an interest in religion for the first time in college, in the military, or through other work and social contacts. Marriage, in particular, through spousal influence, is one of the most important predictors of religious affiliation and involvement (see, e.g., Hout and Fischer 2002; Sherkat 2003). The vast majority of our participants got married between the ages of eighteen

TABLE 2. INTERCORRELATIONS OF
RELIGIOUSNESS FROM ADOLESCENCE
TO LATE ADULTHOOD

Age Periods	Age Periods			
	2	3	4	5
1. Adolescence	.54	.48	.47	.42
2. Early adulthood	—	.74	.69	.67
3. Middle adulthood		—	.84	.80
4. Late-middle adulthood			—	.89
5. Late adulthood				—

NOTE: $N = 142$. All p values $< .001$.

and thirty (i.e., by the time of the first interview in adulthood), and some had spouses whose religious affiliations and degree of church involvement differed from theirs. It is likely, therefore, that the spouses' religious affiliation and level of religiousness had a bearing on the participants' own religiousness, thus contributing to individual fluctuations in church attendance between adolescence and early adulthood.[2] In sum, given the freedom and new social experiences that individuals typically encounter during the interval between late adolescence and early adulthood, it is not surprising that, as other studies indicate (e.g., Stark and Finke 2000), this is the time of greatest individual variability in religious beliefs and practices.

The data collected in adulthood, by contrast, indicated a very high correlation between religiousness in early adulthood and religiousness in late adulthood (average $r = .77$), thus showing the strong tendency of individuals to preserve their individual rank in religiousness relative to others. In other words, individuals who scored comparatively higher in religiousness in their thirties also scored higher in their late sixties and their seventies.[3] Our findings of high individual stability in adulthood corroborate results from a handful of other longitudinal studies (e.g., McCullough et al. 2005; Shand 1990) suggesting that individual religiousness remains highly stable across different phases of adulthood.

Our data on individual stability have several implications for understanding religiousness in adulthood. First, the finding that individuals' religiousness tends to stabilize by their thirties is analogous to findings reported for general personality characteristics such as extroversion, neuroticism, and conscientiousness (see, e.g., Roberts and DelVecchio 2000). Because individual stability is independent of group-level change, the fact that individuals tend to preserve their respective levels of religiousness across adulthood does not preclude religiousness changing at a group level. It simply means that, when religiousness increased from late-middle to late adulthood for our study participants as a whole (see chapter 5), this increase applied almost uniformly among them. Thus, the individuals who were the most religious in their fifties continued to be the most religious in their seventies, though they were then more religious than they had been in their fifties.

Second, our results showing a lower correlation between adolescent religiousness and adulthood religiousness than was evident for scores on religiousness across adulthood support the research indicating that rates of apostasy (the abandonment of one's religion) and conversion peak between adolescence and early adulthood.[4] A high rate of individual stability (indicated by a high rank order coefficient) means that relatively few people experience radical religious transformations in adulthood (such as conversion or apostasy). Conversely, low individual stability (indicated by a low rank order coefficient) implies that such transformations are more widespread. Conversion, in short, means that an individual who scored low on religiousness at one point in time would score high at a subsequent point in time. If there are enough of such changes in individual religiousness, this inevitably lowers the coefficient of individual stability. (As we discuss later in this chapter, a small number of our study participants did undergo dramatic changes in religiousness during adulthood; nonetheless, such shifts were so rare that they did not depress the high rate of individual stability found in the study as a whole.)

Following this same logic, our finding of high stability in religiousness across adulthood challenges the view that individuals tend to increase in religiousness in response to stress or adversity. Some scholars argue that the increased rates of bereavement and health problems characteristic of old age, lead to greater religiousness among older adults compared to when they were middle-aged (e.g., Ferraro and Kelley-Moore 2000). Bereavement and poor health, however, tend to affect some adults in their seventies but not others. If these individuals were to respond to adversity by becoming more religious, then this should have lowered the index of individual stability indicated by the correlation between religiousness in late-middle and late adulthood.

Yet this did not happen. This finding does not, of course, preclude the possibility that a small number of nonreligious individuals responded to adversity by turning to religion (as we discuss in a later section); our data suggest rather that this was not a normative pattern that applied to the majority of our interviewees.

Finally, the high correlation between scores on religiousness throughout adulthood means there is a high probability that the social and psychological characteristics associated with religiousness at one point in adulthood can be predicted from religiousness at an earlier time. The predictive power of religiousness in early adulthood extends consistently to a number of behavioral and attitudinal outcomes in late adulthood, across an interval of more than forty years (see chapters 8, 9, and 10). Such findings are a direct corollary of the high stability of individual religiousness over time.

Moreover, notwithstanding the comparatively lower stability of individual religiousness in adolescence, adolescent religiousness was still a stronger predictor of religiousness in late adulthood than were sociodemographic and personality characteristics (see chapter 8). The long-term predictive power of adolescent religiousness is not a complete surprise, however, because there is a large body of research showing that Americans who grow up in religious families are more likely to be religiously involved during early adulthood (e.g., Myers 1996), and our study participants' adolescent religiousness was highly correlated with their parents' religiousness (see chapter 3). But the fact that the influence of adolescent religiousness can extend so far as to predict religiousness at the end of the life course is a major finding underscoring the long-term significance of youth participation in church and church-related activities. Our finding gains additional importance because religiousness makes a significant contribution to successful aging (see chapters 8, 9, and 10). This means that religiousness joins a small number of characteristics found among adolescents, such as personal competence (Clausen 1993) and altruism (Wink and Dillon 2007), that enhance positive functioning in late adulthood.

RELIGIOUS TRANSFORMATION

As we indicated at the beginning of this chapter, the fact that individual religiousness is highly stable across adulthood does not mean there are no individuals who experience dramatic change. In our study, a small number of the participants—3 percent—showed a marked increase in religiousness, and another 3 percent decreased in religiousness, after midlife. Thus approximately 6 percent of the sample exhibited the type of radical change in religiousness that lowers the rate of individual stability among the sample as a whole. And indeed, it was largely personal adversity that prompted nonreligious individuals to become religious.

Whereas Ian Logan and Ellen Quinn (in chapter 5) took a midlife break from religion in the 1970s and 1980s, other study participants during these same years were prompted by various personal circumstances to discover church. Susan Moore was one of the few people in our study who, though not very religious in early adulthood, became significantly more religious after midlife. Born in 1928, Susan had a wonderful childhood in an affluent family. Strikingly attractive, vivacious, popular, and engaged in a busy social life, Susan deftly managed her schoolwork and after-school pursuits, including taking many lead roles in school plays. Her family was described by IHD researchers as a "high-living, pleasure-loving family" in which "all members were treated as equals." Susan's parents too had a very busy social life, with bridge, dancing, and cocktail parties, which left little space for formal religious practices. The kitchen radio, however, was often tuned to religious programs that played in the background. Susan's mother believed in "a practical religion, not the churchgoing kind," and in adolescence, Susan described herself as "not interested in Sunday school"; indeed, she was one who preferred to sleep late rather than go to church.

After high school, Susan studied economics, and got married in 1950 to a handsome air force officer; they both found much enjoyment and emotional support in the well-organized social life available to military couples. In the mid-1950s, her husband left the air force and they moved to a small town in Montana, where he made a financially rewarding career in the oil sector. They had four children, and Susan was kept busy helping out with their school and after-school activities, as well as with her husband's social commitments. Religion continued to have little place in her early adult life; she and her husband went to a Protestant church only at Easter and Christmas.

Later, in middle age, during her 1970 interview, Susan said, "I believe so much in God I don't even go to church. I don't believe in church particularly. . . . I've wondered about God, and I've said, 'It can't be'—that sort of thing, but in my heart I believe in God. I've been so dang close to him and so lucky and everything. I know when I'm on good terms with him, and I know when I'm not on excellent terms with him, and I know when I'm not—within myself—doing right."

Nevertheless, Susan's feelings of closeness to God did not prompt her to go to church or to pray with any regularity. At this point in her life, with her children approaching adolescence, Susan was primarily worried about the soon-to-be-empty nest and her "capacity to survive" without her children.

Twelve years later, in 1982, Susan was definitely not debilitated by an empty nest, and she remained highly involved in the community's social and philanthropic activities. But a big transformation had occurred: both she and her husband had become active born-again Christians in the early 1970s, and subsequently each of their children had too. Prayer had become the center of Susan's life; she was now, she said, "dropping back more" and letting prayer direct her; she was giving her "problems to the Lord. . . . And seeing the Lord as my personal savior, where before I just believed in God. Now I have a very personal relationship with the Lord, as my husband does. That's been a very big part of our lives in the last eight or nine years, enormously big." Susan and her husband were attending a Baptist church every Sunday and were also involved with an interdenominational group of Christians from different churches in the area; the group made themselves available "to help people if they have marriage problems, are new to town, or just want somebody to pray with and to encourage them."

Susan's turn toward born-again Christianity was precipitated by opposing cultural influences. One of their adolescent daughters had gotten involved in the 1970s drug scene. Not knowing how to deal with the turmoil it caused in the family, Susan benefited from the welcoming outreach of evangelical Christianity. She recounted that she

> went into sort of a self-pity trip for a couple of years, . . . and as I was pulling out of that, some rather interesting things began happening. I call it a setup. We lived half a block from a very large church. . . . We weren't into churchgoing at all, . . . but we lived a half a block from church, and across the street was the pastor and his wife, who were a neat couple. . . . Our two youngest children became very close with them, the whole family did, actually, but particularly the two youngest. They began to go to church, and we began to see some incredible things happening in them. So we began to visit now and then at church, and shortly afterward we went to a chaperoned camp for a bunch of junior and [senior] high schoolers who were going to a church camp that summer. And I think the guy who taught them three times a day was way over their heads, but suddenly we knew there was a world out there that we didn't know anything about. . . . So that was one thing, religion and church, . . . but this other thing, this letting go and asking him [Jesus] into your life, was a whole other thing, which we really didn't know anything about.

When last interviewed in 1999, Susan and her husband, now living in a small town in Colorado, were still enjoying busy lives. Every Sunday they attended a nondenominational Christian church and also participated with about ten other people in a Wednesday night "cell group" that discussed the week's scriptural passages and how they applied to their lives. Susan and her husband prayed together every morning, and they also prayed alone in order to "have private time with the Lord." Three of their children were involved in Christian outreach activities, and Susan and her husband did a lot of volunteer work for a Christian pastoral organization. They even built a retreat on their property for pastors, who came from all over the United States to spend a week enjoying the wilderness of the Rockies, its costs underwritten by Susan and her husband. Throughout the interview, Susan made frequent references to the Lord, not only in talking about her various church-related activities but also in relating how her own personality and way of being had been transformed by her Jesus-centered life. She said that every area of her life had been affected by her born-again Christianity and her ongoing process of working at "releasing it all to the Lord." When asked, for example, whether she had acquired any personal wisdom while growing older, Susan replied,

> My mother was very wise. And I have always had a personal wisdom. I didn't have to be too old to realize that I had it. . . . I think a lot of it was very helpful to people. . . . But personal wisdom has to go through one brain and out to another person who is very different. What I have had to concentrate the hardest on . . . since I've become a Christian [is to] realize that God was calling on me to let it all go. . . . I find when I can empty out, so to speak, and just say, "God, have your way," and then go and feel the Word, the Lord will give me a word, or he'll give me an instruction. Or even without [my] realizing he's doing anything, he'll bring out something that, when I speak it, is the first time I've ever heard it. And I know it was from him. That's been a freedom for me. Because people used to count on me a lot—that I would have answers for them. . . . I can see now they needed something that I couldn't give them. But now, when it happens, I wait. I don't go out to them. I wait for God to bring them to me.

Clearly, over the course of Susan's life, religion had moved from background radio noise to the center point of her daily consciousness.

Bob Mears, the nonreligious shoe salesman whom we quoted in chapter 4 for his definite view that people should be deliberate church shoppers, experienced a transformative religious conversion in the late 1970s. Bob developed chronic, debilitating back pain in his fifties and, despite visits to several medical experts, found no relief. Driving one day on a freeway in San Diego, Bob experienced a moment of epiphany when he saw a giant billboard depicting Jesus on the cross and advertising a local Pentecostal church. Soon after, Bob, who since early adulthood had been respectful of religion but a sporadic churchgoer, became a highly committed member of the Pentecostal Church.

In 1970, when he was forty-nine and had not yet experienced his conversion, Bob explained his lack of religious involvement:

> I could probably, if I really wanted to, attend a church; I could probably find a church. . . . However, inwardly and mentally I'm satisfied with the religious attitude that I have. I don't have . . . a great desire for a religious connection and for really working at it. I don't have this feeling. . . . [But] I cannot in my mind believe that there is not someone or something with control or guidance for us mortals that could put together a human body or a solar system. . . . It just didn't happen by accident. It's too complex to be something that just came by itself. . . . I [frequently] contemplate belief in a Supreme Being. Especially if you get away from the rat race, out wherever, by yourself in the country or on the beach, and just relax and think about things and look around you and marvel at what we call God's work.

Twelve years later, reflecting on his transformation, Bob explained his religious submission:

> I did not deny a Supreme Being; I was just not active in religion. And then when I injured my back, I went through many of the emotions related to it, and a very deep depression. Why did this happen to me? Frustration. Despair. I figured I couldn't go any lower. And finally one day driving on the freeway [on the way back from visiting the chiropractor]—I can remember the exact spot, passing a church—I finally told myself that I would do what I could do to control the situation, and leave the balance up to God. And I had a great weight taken off my shoulders with that.

The idea that he would "leave the balance up to God" pushed Bob to explore the possibility of attending church on a regular basis, and, perhaps predictably, he implemented the deliberative approach to choosing a church that he had for so long emphasized:

> My wife (who was always more religious than me) listens to a preacher on the radio. We started watching religious broadcasting, and we decided that we should be going to church. . . . So we have been going to different churches to find out what their doctrine is like, and where we feel we would fit in. My wife contacted the people at this radio station for some suggestions as to any churches they were aware of, and ministers and pastors that were followers of the Bible alone. So many of them, we find, are doing things that the scriptures say we're not to do. So we're still looking. . . . We seem to gravitate toward one particular church in Stockton that seems to meet all our criteria. . . . It's an interdenominational neighborhood church.

Bob summarized his religious transformation, saying: "Religion holds a great part of my life now."

When interviewed in 1997, Bob still suffered from back pain, and his wife also had some chronic health problems, but this did not alter his positive view of religion. He attended weekly services at an interdenominational Protestant church, and he and his wife read specific Bible passages every day. He was less active than he had been in the Masons, but he reiterated his view (first expressed in 1958; see chapter 4) of the importance of the Bible, the Ten Commandments, and the Golden Rule as guides for everyday living. In recalling the events that led to his conversion, Bob explained that he found out through scripture that "we can't do everything by ourselves. And that if we place our trust in Jesus Christ and let him handle our problems, then we are better off. I find that's true in my case."

In contrast to Bob Mears and Susan Moore, Joan Sweeney withdrew from religion after midlife. Joan was someone for whom church had had a very important place in her life from her twenties until well into her fifties. She grew up in an upwardly mobile family; her father worked in insurance sales and her housewife mother was heavily involved in the PTA and community activities. Socially reserved, Joan and her two older sisters went to Sunday school at a Protestant community church, even though her parents were not churchgoers and did not emphasize religion in the home. Joan majored in art at the University of California for two years but withdrew to get married. Her husband's work for a nonprofit organization meant that they traveled extensively in Europe, and did so with five children in tow. Although Joan's husband was raised Catholic, they were married in the Episcopal Church, and she was subsequently confirmed there. When interviewed in the late 1950s, while living in an East Coast city, both Joan and her husband were teaching Sunday school at the Episcopal Church and were active participants in the church's several discussion and social groups.

In 1969, when Joan was forty-eight, her much-loved husband died suddenly. Just one year after her bereavement, Joan was described as "very active, enthusiastic, and assertive" and as having "meaningful relationships with her children and friends." The interviewer predicted that Joan's "internal resources will . . . carry her through the entire grieving process and changing lifestyle with successful coping." Only two of her children were still living at home. Joan's extensive church activities bolstered her during the early years of widowhood. Her friends were mostly people whom she had known for many years from church and from her earlier PTA activities. She usually went to church services with a couple of her friends and stayed afterward to chat. She was a regular volunteer in the church's altar society, and she complemented her interest in church activities with a deep personal faith. She was also attending evening courses on house maintenance and appliance repair and art classes, and spending her time at home painting, sewing, and gardening.

In 1982, Joan was still active with church, family, and college classes and during the interview spoke extensively about her "enthusiasm for new ideas." In her art classes, she was focusing on photography and ceramics; she had also taken up aerobic exercise and swimming. At church she had become director of the altar society, which made her responsible for training new members. With two of her children and their families living close by, Joan enjoyed good relations with them and especially appreciated the time spent looking at maps with her grandchildren and teaching them geography. But fifteen years later (in 1997), Joan was significantly less involved in church, going mainly at Christmas and Easter but still helping on those occasions with altar decorating. Joan explained that she no longer needed the friendships and social activities that religion had provided while she was rearing children, and especially while dealing with the bereavement of her husband thirty years earlier, when, she said, it had helped to mend her heart. But now she felt she was "pretty much mended," and her art had become her life-enriching activity, continuing to provide her with fulfillment and excitement. For many decades Joan had enjoyed serving the church in various capacities, and the church in turn had provided her with a social network and an outlet for her generative interests—teaching Sunday school—as well as for her creative altar-decorating talents. In older age, however, she no longer felt the need for church-related social support: her grandchildren provided her with generative relationships, and she had found a broader canvas for her creativity.

In sum, our study included a small number of individuals whose lives showed a postmidlife religious transformation, either a major increase, like those of Susan and Bob, or decreased salience, like that of Joan. More typically, however, our longitudinal data following the same individuals over time revealed a high degree of stability in individual religiousness, especially across adulthood and moderately so between adolescence and adulthood.

CHANGES IN THE MEANING OF RELIGION OVER THE LIFE COURSE

Although most of the people in our study showed little age-related change in religiousness either individually or as a group, this does not rule out the possibility that the meaning of religion changed for them over the years. As we saw in the case of Barbara Shaw, although her pattern of church attendance did not change over time, the meaning of religiousness in her life did. Among American scholars of religion, James Fowler (1981), for example, argues that, as people age, their faith becomes less concretistic and more contemplative, and personal yet universalized in scope, and they become more inclined to accept the contradictions and paradoxes of everyday life. Fowler's view of age-related change reflects the ideas of cognitive-developmental psychologists who argue that, as a result of the need for varied life experiences, it is not until middle adulthood that adults acquire the ability to truly embrace the paradoxical nature of the universe and the relativism and uncertainty of human knowledge.[5]

The idea of age-related changes in apprehending the complexities of life is compelling, as is, by extension, the idea of age-related change in the personal meaning of religion. Fowler has been criticized, however, for not testing his model with longitudinal data and, especially, for not including data from older adults in the original study in which he outlined his thesis (McFadden 1999). Another source of concern is that Fowler's definition of faith is so expansive that it incorporates both religious and nonreligious attitudes in a way that makes it hard to empirically test his model.

Lars Tornstam (1994, 2005) argues that cumulative life experience pushes individuals toward a shift in how they view the world. This process, Tornstam maintains, makes one less concerned with materialism and rationality, and more interested in intergenerational spiritual connections, wisdom, and meditation, changes indicated by a decrease in material interests, self-centeredness, and superfluous social interaction, a shift that he calls "gero-transcendence." Among older Americans, retrospective self-reported accounts of changes in the content of their prayers suggest a shift toward less materialistic concerns (Eisenhandler 2003; Ingersoll-Dayton, Krause, and Morgan 2002).

Findings from the Ohio Longitudinal Study of Aging Americans (Atchley 1999), however, offer only partial support for the gero-transcendence thesis. Ohio respondents who attached importance to being religious were more likely to feel a greater connection with the universe and to take more enjoyment from their inner life—a response that suggests gero-transcendence. Contravening Tornstam's thesis, however, over three-quarters of the Ohio study participants reported that material things meant more (not less) to them in old age; they were likely to take themselves more (not less) seriously and to see less (not more) connection between themselves and past and future generations. In short, the research to date has not determined whether, and if so, how, worldviews change in old age.

We explored change in the subjective meaning of religion among our study participants by coding relevant themes from the extensive interview material on religion in early and late adulthood. We were interested in whether there were differences in how the participants spoke of religion when they were in their late sixties and their seventies compared to when they were in their thirties. We turned first to the frequency with which they invoked a Golden Rule morality (see chapter 4, note 5). We found that substantially more participants affirmed a Golden Rule philosophy during late adulthood (63 percent) than in early adulthood (29 percent). Those who invoked it ran the gamut of social differences in our sample: similar proportions of mainline (63 percent) and nonmainline (67 percent) Protestants, Catholics (65 percent), and individuals not religiously affiliated (63 percent) made reference to the Golden Rule in late adulthood. Nor did the use of it vary according to gender, social class, or level of religiousness. As in early adulthood, however, members of the older cohort (75 percent) were significantly more likely than the younger cohort (57 percent) to refer to Golden Rule values.[6]

We interpreted the increased reference to the Golden Rule in late adulthood as suggesting a developmental-maturational increase in the interviewees' appreciation of universal morality, because the Golden Rule assumes that you treat all others as equal irrespective of their differences (Erikson 1964). In addition, the use of the Golden Rule affords the possibility of being ethical without being religious, which in turn implies a complexity of thought that indicates higher stages of cognitive development. Because our study participants came of age at a time in American society when the language and ethos of the Golden Rule was already prevalent, it is unlikely that their increased tendency to invoke it in late adulthood was a function of an increase in its cultural accessibility to this particular generation. Nor is it likely that their greater use of the Golden Rule was wholly due to the specific questions asked at the different interview times. To the contrary, there is a partial overlap in the phrasing of questions used in both the early and the late-adulthood interviews.[7] The greater public acceptance of social and religious differences in America since the 1950s, however, likely had some influence on the interviewees as they aged. Our finding of an increase in the participants' invocation of a Golden Rule nonetheless lends support to scholars who argue that a more universalizing worldview is distinctive of late adulthood (e.g., Fowler 1981; Tornstam 1999).

Martha Wilson exemplifies not only a lifelong commitment to the universality of the Golden Rule but also how the meaning of this commitment broadens over time. Martha, a highly committed Presbyterian all her life, had taught Sunday school for many years, and in late adulthood she was active at a liberal Presbyterian church that accepted gays and accepted women priests. Martha attended weekly services with her husband, was a member of the board, and was involved in its outreach community work with seniors and homeless people. Martha also sang the Taize chant, what she described as "a beautiful prayer for peace," at the Catholic Church and prayed, she said, "all the time."

Martha was not one of the study participants who came to an appreciation of the Golden Rule only with age; when interviewed in her thirties, she had cogently summarized her moral philosophy by saying that it was "Love thy neighbor as thyself" (see chapter 4, page 75). Yet at that time she had also acknowledged that she was often prejudiced toward people who were different from her. In late adulthood, however, there was a discernible shift in her attitude. Her explanation of the practical challenges posed by the Golden Rule nicely captured the expansive worldview associated with gero-transcendence, as well as suggesting that she herself had come to a deep acceptance of the beliefs of others. When asked to describe her beliefs and values, Martha elaborated:

> I think it really is true that you do have to love your neighbor. I do believe that God really did create us all equal, although we haven't figured that out quite yet. I believe you really, really have to love one another. You don't have to like everybody, but you do—if we're ever going to live in this world in peace—you do have to love everybody. I think that people have got to quit worrying about sexual preference. God made us the way we are; and if you're gay or lesbian, that's the way you were made, unless you strayed off the track somewhere and you're a voyeur or whatever. I believe that you have to accept people, truly accept them. And as I said, I don't think you have to like everybody—I don't think that's possible. But I do think you have to love everyone. And this includes the criminals and everybody—no matter how hard that is. There are a lot of people who are not very lovable. (Age seventy-seven, 1998)

Martha's ethic of love extended to include a pluralistic and individuated view of religion notwithstanding her own strong commitment to Christianity:

I think you come to God in your own way. If I didn't believe that, I'd be very upset with my older child, who's so involved with Hinduism. I believe that she sees God, or feels God in her life, the way I feel the presence of God in mine. And no less. I believe you have to find the way that's right for you. It happens that our church—let me just say something: there are two big Presbyterian churches in [this city]. First Presbyterian, . . . and then Saint Andrew's, which is just up here. The First Presbyterian is very fundamental, very basic. Saint Andrew's is the one . . . that does not question people's sexual preferences. We are very much for ordaining women and ordaining gays and lesbians. I couldn't go to First Presbyterian even though it's the same church. I believe you have to find the way that is the best for you. I think that what's true is a personal thing.

We also explored whether the personal meaning of religion changes with age by reviewing other themes. We coded the study participants' religion narratives to see whether there was an age-related shift in emphasis away from the more social to the more faith-based functions of religiousness. In the early adulthood interviews, when responding to open-ended questions about their religious beliefs, attitudes, and habits, 55 percent of the study participants referred to religion's social dimensions. Considerably fewer—26 percent—commented on religion's personal meaning to them in terms of faith or as a theological resource in trying, as one woman said, to apprehend "unanswered questions." In late adulthood, by contrast, only 17 percent referred to religion's social aspects, and 36 percent invoked its faith elements.[8]

For example, a Presbyterian woman who drifted toward the Methodists and who occasionally went to church said in later adulthood, "I enjoy going to church to hear a sermon, but I don't want to be hit for joining committees to do this or do that, and have to sit and introduce myself to the people next to me, and all this holding hands. I like to go to church and sing or hear the music, but I don't like all this that they have added, say, in the last twenty years. I would rather go to a church service in a city where I am not known. That would be my choice." These are the words of Allison Foley, the same person who, in adolescence and early adulthood, was socially involved in church—she was one of our adolescents who, with her friends, took much pleasure in routinely visiting others' churches (see chapter 4, page 67).

In late adulthood, a widowed Presbyterian woman who varied her choice of church, depending on which of her religiously diverse friends she went with, responded without hesitation that her faith guided her life: "Oh yes, my faith. My religion, if you will. It's been a part of my life all through my seventy-five years. [It gives purpose to my life.] In the book I read, it says, 'There's a time to die, a time to be born, and a time to love and a time to hate.'" When she was interviewed in her thirties, this woman was attending church almost weekly and had taught Sunday school. And although then, too, she had said that she always had "faith in the sense of prayer," she had wondered whether church attracted her "as a matter of wanting to belong to a social group."

Similarly, a nondenominational Protestant woman in her late sixties said, "I want to live as the Lord wants me to live. I want to try to do what is right, what he would have me do. He knows. He has a plan for everyone's life. I want to do that. It says that 'he will show you the way.' That's what I want to try to do." By contrast, when this woman was interviewed in early adulthood (in 1958, at age thirty), she did not explicitly mention the importance of faith in her life, and she did not mention faith-related reasons for attending church. Then attending a Baptist church, she said she went mostly because her children liked it.

A Catholic woman whose church attendance was somewhat irregular because of her health problems commented in late adulthood,

> We're taught in the church that the purpose of life is to know, love, and serve God. . . . I think I've served this purpose by the life I've led. . . . I can't take pieces out of my religion, because it's all one piece—it is part of the whole, if you know what I mean. I can be out digging in the garden and saying my prayers if there is something bothering me—maybe by talking to God in my own words. I don't have to run to church and kneel down in front of the altar to say my prayers. It's a living religion, and if you live your religion, really live it, I think it automatically solves a lot of problems for you. I wouldn't say *automatically*, but it does solve problems for you.

When interviewed in early adulthood (in 1958), this woman described herself and her husband as "pretty dedicated" and explained that they attended Mass every week and sent their children to parochial schools, and that she was a member of the ladies guild and her husband of the building finance committee. Though faith may have underpinned and motivated this woman's dedication to the church back then, she made no mention of it.

Irrespective of the underlying reasons, faith-related references and experiences certainly seemed to come more easily into our study participants' conversations about religion in late rather than in early adulthood. The increased prominence of a vocabulary of faith in older adulthood—though not necessarily indicative of an increased religiousness—fits with Tornstam's idea that the aging process makes people more detached from concrete material and personal ambitions and more at ease with nonmaterial matters and their place in the larger universe. This perspective was captured by one highly successful professional man in the study who went to the Congregational Church twice a month. Among the characteristics of his late adulthood, he said, were a greater awareness of beauty, nature, and music, and a greater attentiveness to "religious feeling. . . . A feeling of humbleness and being properly insignificant as a person. Because when you're young, you're pretty much self-centered. You know everything is yours. And the whole world revolves around what you do. And as you get older, you realize that you're not very much. You're just another little speck in the universe." This contrasts with his attitude when interviewed in early adulthood. At that time, he was Presbyterian, and though he acknowledged his commitment to being a good citizen, he also spoke about how much he valued "the idea that each man has the opportunity to achieve as much for himself as possible, and to live his own life as an individual." In fact, it was this view and his dislike for doing things on Sundays that largely contributed to his sporadic church attendance back then.

Another man, a Presbyterian who was highly religious throughout his life—who attended weekly services, said grace before dinner at home every evening, and had a history of service on various church boards and of participation in couples' and other church social groups—consistently spoke at each interview time about the faith and social aspects of his extensive church involvement. He gave a hint nonetheless that in late adulthood his perspective on the self might have changed slightly. In his late thirties he had commented that "having a Christ-like life is desirable and a guidepost that one can use to measure one's self against." Sermons, he said, make a person see that "you think you are a lot more important than you are," and he felt that "religion stimulates self-analysis, which [is] good and important." Forty years later, using very similar language, he said that "a mature faith was something that can enhance your life and give you some guideposts to live by." But taking some of the energy away from his earlier focus on self-analysis, he said that while core Christian ethics guided his life, they were "amplified by Christ in love. I think that's it, things are done with love." In view of this, he might be judged, he said, as "a good and faithful servant."

Lillian Sinnott, for whom the social aspects of church were very important in adolescence and in early adulthood (see chapters 3 and 4), continued to value the sociability of church throughout adulthood. In her late sixties, Lillian was attending Unitarian Church services every week and singing in a choral society. She was also on the church's board and the children's religion education committee. But now, rather than talking of church primarily in terms of how it provided her with "an audience" (as in adolescence), or how it suited her particular social needs (she was the young woman who chose to get married in an Episcopalian church because it was the right size for the number of guests invited; see chapter 4), she spoke of it in terms of greater communal mutuality. "The church," Lillian said, "is my community, I think. That's why it's important to me more than anything religious. It's my community. It's a group of people that I like and enjoy being around because they're intelligent and we always have something to talk about."

Additionally, Lillian now expressed a more universal and reverential view of the sacred and related her values to a broad mix of sources, including the Golden Rule, religious teachings, self-worth, nature, and a universal spirituality. She believed, she said, in the

> worth and dignity of all human beings. And the web of life on earth we live in. The ecology. All that. . . . Do the best you can, and without hurting other people. But also do what's best for yourself. Don't shortchange yourself in order to be a martyr. No one really appreciates martyrs, I think. Not that I have to be appreciated. But I saw my mother be a martyr and slave to her children. . . . My main values, I guess, are the values of the greatest teachers and philosophers through time. The Golden Rule is a good one. And they all taught that. And I like the sevenfold path [toward] enlightenment. The Buddha. And I like the teachings of Jesus. I guess those are pretty much in my value system. . . . I'm a very spiritual person, and I get it in different ways. When I'm singing some magnificent works, I get tremendous spiritual uplift. And there are certain talks and certain things that uplift the spirit to do better things. To me, *spiritual* is being the highest you can be in life. I don't know how to describe it. It's personal. I guess everybody has their own feelings about these kinds of beliefs, and they can't be described to other people. I can't even describe them to myself. I just feel them. . . . When you're singing a great Mass or something—and I don't even know what the words mean, I'm just singing it—there's something about the music, the feeling that comes over you, where you just get goose pimples all over you, and you're shaking. You get so emotional you can hardly sing. . . . That, to me, is a religious experience. That's all I can say. I don't know what it is. But it just is. And how could anything be so magnificent? Nature to me is magnificent, how it keeps pushing through the cement, and it's going to bloom. It's going to come up, and the birds keep coming back despite all the spray and everything. I don't know. Whatever makes this happen—I don't know what it is, some creative spirit, though I don't know how spirit can make something happen. . . . But it's still magnificent.

7

Spiritual Seeking

Recent years have witnessed a significant increase in the proportion of Americans who are unchurched believers, who distance themselves from church and organized religion while still believing in God or a Higher Power (Hout and Fischer 2002; Roof 1999) and adhering to a personal religion that is uncoupled from conventional forms of religiousness (Smith 2002). Although the interest in seeking sacred meaning independent of church participation was accentuated by the cultural changes of the 1960s, spiritual seeking has long been present in American culture, and present even longer in Christianity. The early Gnostics challenged the religious authority of the church and sought revelation through a personal relationship with God (Pagels 1979). In America, the first "spiritual awakening" dates back to the 1830s and 1840s and is associated with the emergence of the transcendentalist movement and such renowned figures as Emerson and Thoreau. The transcendentalist movement was itself indebted to the writings of the eighteenth-century Swede Emanuel Swedenborg and his emphasis on the metaphysical and mystical nature of experience (Fuller 2001: 24–26).

For Emerson (Fuller 2001; Miller 1956/1964), the "Over-Soul," a depersonalized cosmic force, permeated or inhabited the world and was accessible to self-reliant individuals who, forsaking conventional beliefs and practices, opened themselves to experiencing the underlying spiritual reality.[1] Emerson's ideas were clearly influenced by German romanticism, with its emphasis on the primacy of the unconscious, the importance of undertaking a journey of self-discovery, disdain for conventionality, and pantheism (Fuller 2001; Miller 1956/1964). However, as argued by the distinguished cultural scholar Perry Miller, the yearning for an intimate connection with God, and the conviction that he could be found in the world around us, was far from alien to such paragons of Puritanism as Jonathan Edwards. What differentiated Emerson from Edwards, according to Miller, was not the basic impulse to seek union with the Divine but Emerson's rejection of the notion of original sin and the resultant belief in the possibility of actually finding the Universal Being in nature (1956/1964: 185).

More recently, Leigh Schmidt (2005) argues that, unlike the Puritans before him, Emerson's and the transcendentalists' conceptualization of spiritual seeking was not confined to Christianity but was inclusive of other, particularly Eastern, religious traditions. Emerson's notion of spirituality aligned itself with the liberalism of Adam Smith and Jeremy Bentham and thus was characterized by rejection of an uncritical submission to scripture as well as recognition of the validity of other faith traditions in ways that were unthinkable, Schmidt argues, to Jonathan Edwards, but which foreshadowed the cultural changes of the second half of the twentieth century and beyond.

Clearly, the major themes found in contemporary spirituality have been present in American and Western culture for a long time. What is new about American spiritual seeking in the post-1960s era is its pervasiveness (Marty 1993). Prior to the 1960s, only a small proportion of Americans attempted to fulfill their spiritual needs outside the domain of denominational religion. Since then, a vastly expanded spiritual marketplace—with its tantalizing mix of Eastern philosophies and practices, alternative ways of thinking about the sacred, and a variety of self-help therapeutic groups and manuals aimed at satisfying the inner needs of Americans (Glock and Bellah 1976; Roof 1993, 1999; Wuthnow 1998)—has produced a growing trend toward uncoupling religion and spirituality (see, e.g., Fuller 2001; Roof 1993; Zinnbauer et al. 1997).

THE RELATION BETWEEN SPIRITUAL SEEKING AND RELIGIOUSNESS

Not surprisingly, the increased prevalence of a spiritual vocabulary has resulted in a fair amount of ambiguity in how the word *spiritual* is used in both popular and scholarly conversation (Wulff 1997). The main source of this ambiguity is the fact that, whereas close to a fifth of Americans define themselves as spiritual but not religious, approximately three-quarters indicate that they are both spiritual and religious (Roof 1999; Zinnbauer et al. 1997).[2] More specifically, over two-thirds of Americans who have a religious affiliation describe themselves as both religious and spiritual; by contrast, among those who have no religious preference, 15 percent think of themselves as, at most, moderately religious, but 40 percent describe themselves as spiritual (Hout and Fischer 2002: 176). Clearly, these two groups invoke spirituality to convey different things. Individuals who identify themselves as both religious and spiritual are predominantly church members ("religious dwellers," in Wuthnow's distinction [1998]) who use the term *spirituality* to underscore the sincerity of their beliefs and their personal striving to relate to God within the boundaries of organized or church-focused religion (see Hout and Fischer 2002; Zinnbauer and Pargament 2005). This usage is in line with a long-standing tradition: after all, no one can question the profound spirituality of Saint Thomas Aquinas or Saint Theresa of Lisieux, and that of many ordinary churchgoers who use conventional prayer to forge a close relationship with God.

We use *spirituality* in a different way. Following Roof (1993, 1999) and Wuthnow (1998), we define *spirituality* in terms of spiritual seeking and contrast it with church-centered religiousness (paralleling Wuthnow's distinction between spiritual seeking and religious dwelling). Our decision is not premised on the belief that an Emersonian type of spiritual seeking is superior to the more traditional spiritual quest of many ordinary churchgoers.[3] Rather it reflects our judgment that this conceptualization of spiritual seeking is particularly apt for capturing the post-1960s cultural shift toward a more personal and negotiated understanding of religion and its interplay with the newly available, diverse spiritual resources of the post-1960s period. Our study is especially suited to identifying whether the changes in the American spiritual marketplace made a difference in individual lives. In the late 1960s and the 1970s, the study participants were negotiating midlife, a time in the life course known for its exploratory possibilities, at the same time that new spiritual resources were becoming accessible. One might expect, then, to see some evidence of a trend toward spiritual seeking among our study participants coinciding with this cultural change.

As we have discussed in previous chapters, Americans are remarkably autonomous in how they construe traditional or institutionalized religion. Many individuals and families slip in and out of church involvement over their life course; they choose churches based on pragmatic considerations of convenience and satisfaction; and they have a flexible view of the connections among church attendance, faith, and everyday morality. This autonomy, however, is an autonomy that tends nonetheless to be construed in relation to established or institutionalized ways of being religious or of thinking about faith. For example, many church-attending Catholics—like Ellen Quinn (see chapter 5)—reject the institutional authority of the Vatican to demarcate what is acceptable behavior in the domain of sexuality. Yet despite the autonomy inherent in their Catholicism, what strands they selectively accept and identify with, it is still contained within the Catholic tradition—they continue to be Catholic, to dwell within the Catholic tradition, even if their dwelling is very much self-defined (see, e.g., Dillon 1999).

By the same token, some born-again Christians are skeptical of churches and denominations, and many prioritize private prayer and Bible reading over corporate worship (see, e.g., Roof 1999). Nonetheless, because they anchor their faith and their prayers and religious reading squarely within Christianity—it is after all a Christocentric born-again narrative that they embrace—we see them as engaged in church-centered religiousness ("dwelling with Jesus") rather than as spiritual seekers. Ted McRae was one of our study participants who described himself as a born-again Christian in late adulthood, after having been relatively nonreligious throughout his life (he was the boy whose stepmother occasionally took him to the Catholic Church, though his Masonic father encouraged nonreligious activities on Sunday; see chapter 2). He explained what it meant to be born-again: "It is a faith; it is not a religion. . . . When you say *religious,* there are a lot of things that *religious* means. *Religious* means a lot of different things to different people. Christianity is not a religion. It's a faith . . . faith in the Christian faith, and if you go by the Bible, what Jesus said, there's only one way. And he is the way."[4]

The autonomy associated with spiritual seeking is different. It charts a path that may have relatively little truck with the ways established in traditional religious beliefs and practices. It is constituted by a personal autonomy that tends to be somewhat removed from, rather than in singular conversation with, church-based religion. In short, for spiritual seekers, institutionalized religion may be a resource but not an anchor. And when spiritual seekers draw on institutionalized religious beliefs or symbols, they tend to expand the meanings traditionally associated with such beliefs. Our five-point rating of spiritual seeking assessed the extent to which, in the context of American society, noninstitutionalized or non-church-centered religious beliefs and practices were important in the person's everyday life. (In the methodological appendix, we discuss the coding and rating procedures informing our assessment of spiritual seeking.)

The diversity of spiritual resources available to contemporary Americans who are active spiritual seekers was apparent in our study. Like Jane Bell, some of our spiritual seekers found sacred meaning primarily through Indian-inspired and other intense meditation practices; others participated in Native American drumming circles, in centering prayers, in nature-based ceremonial rites, and in other spiritually focused groups. Still others combined participation in Christian denominational traditions and church liturgies with Eastern meditation or participation in nonchurched spiritual reading and fellowship groups.

SPIRITUAL SEEKING ACROSS ADULTHOOD

In the absence of longitudinal studies tracking the development of spiritual seeking across adulthood, the understanding of spiritual development is based primarily on clinical case studies and a handful of cross-sectional studies (see, e.g., Bianchi 1987). Several adult development theorists (e.g., Jung 1953; Sinnott 1994) consider spirituality to be a postmidlife phenomenon that is the outcome of the maturational processes associated with aging. According to Jung, the first half of adulthood is devoted to establishing oneself in the adult world, particularly by developing a career and a family. In going through these processes, individuals tend to rely on their existing personal strengths and use resources that favor adaptation to conventional social roles, including adherence to traditional religious beliefs and practices. However, Jung argued, midlife brings with it a greater sense of personal stability that, in turn, decreases the pressure for conventional adaptation, and it brings an increased awareness of mortality that pushes the individual to confront the ultimate meaning of life and the individual's place in the world. These joint forces promote a turn away from the external world of career and family responsibilities and toward the inner self and engagement in the process of self-discovery (cf. Jung 1958).

Despite the intuitive appeal of the idea that spirituality emerges later rather than earlier in life, this thesis has not previously been explored with longitudinal life course data. Our ratings of the IHD study participants' spiritual interests and practices across adulthood indicate that fewer than one in ten were spiritual seekers in early and middle adulthood, and the proportion who were spiritual seekers in late adulthood increased to just under 20 percent. Spiritual seekers' average scores increased significantly from their forties (interviews conducted in 1970) to their fifties (1982) and especially from their fifties to their late sixties and their seventies (1997–2000; see figure 4). The late-life increase in spiritual seeking occurred across the board, among men and women, the younger and older cohort, those raised Protestant or Catholic, and those from higher and lower social classes.

However, just as in the case of religiousness (see chapter 5), behind this general pattern of change we found important sociodemographic differences. Women and men did not differ in their levels of spiritual seeking in early or middle adulthood. But women, because of a higher rate of spiritual growth, were far more spiritual than men in late-middle (age fifties) and in late (age late sixties, and seventies) adulthood. This gender difference in spiritual seeking underscores the gendered nature of religious engagement as a whole: women have a greater presence than men not only in traditional church-centered religion but also in newer forms of spiritual practice.

Both cohorts increased in spiritual seeking from their fifties on, and members of the younger cohort alone also increased in spiritual seeking from their forties to their fifties (i.e., between 1970 and 1982; data not shown). As a result of the different timing of change, by late adulthood the younger participants scored higher on spiritual seeking than the older participants.[5]

Moving from the long-term pattern of change to looking at who among our participants were spiritual seekers in late adulthood, we noticed that women from the younger cohort—those born in 1928–29, who entered midlife just as the cultural changes of the 1960s took hold—were significantly more likely than either men or older women (those born in 1920–21) to be spiritual seekers. Spiritual seekers were also more likely to have had mothers who were college graduates and to have been raised in mainline Protestant families than in nonmainline or Catholic families. It is particularly interesting that a mainline Protestant background provided the bridge to spiritual seeking. This finding is a reminder perhaps that, as Perry Miller (1956/1964) long ago noted, the original New England Protestants and their nonchurched transcendentalist peers were more united in their quest for the divine than is often appreciated. It is also interesting that, despite the clear disaffection

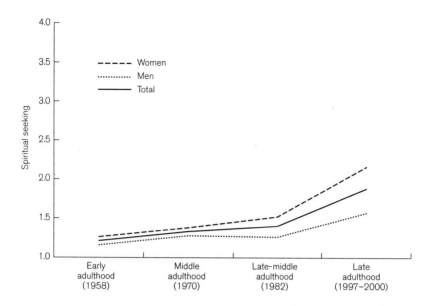

Figure 4. Mean change in spiritual seeking over time by total sample and gender.

among our study's Catholics (and among American Catholics in general) in the 1970s, this did not turn them toward the seeker spirituality fermenting at the time.[6]

Although the upward trend in spiritual seeking in the second half of adulthood was similar to the pattern we documented for religiousness, there were two notable differences. First, the size of the increase in spiritual seeking from late-middle to late adulthood was much greater than for religiousness, and it reached a level of change that could be observed in the context of everyday interaction.[7] Second, whereas average scores on religiousness across adulthood indicated that many of our study participants had been at least somewhat religious all their lives, average scores on spiritual seeking indicated that spiritual seeking was virtually invisible in the lives of the study participants before midlife. And while there was very little change throughout adulthood in individuals' relative levels of religiousness with respect to others (i.e., there was high individual or rank order stability; see chapter 6), there was considerable interindividual variability in who scored high and who scored low on spiritual seeking over time (see table 3). This means that knowing, for example, whether someone was ranked high or low in spiritual seeking in early adulthood did not tell us much about the

TABLE 3. INTERCORRELATIONS OF SPIRITUAL
SEEKING FROM EARLY TO LATE ADULTHOOD

Age Periods	Age Periods		
	2	*3*	*4*
1. Early adulthood	.39	.36	.34
2. Middle adulthood	—	.53	.54
3. Late-middle adulthood		—	.64
4. Late adulthood			—

NOTE: $N = 142$. All p values < .001.

person's ranking in late adulthood. In fact, our data suggest that spiritual seeking does not stabilize on an individual level until late-middle adulthood, when people are in their fifties.[8]

In sum, our longitudinal data support the expectation that spiritual seeking is largely a postmidlife phenomenon. This finding does not mean, however, that aging or maturational processes are the sole nurturers of spirituality. The postmidlife trajectory we document also has a social and cultural explanation. The study participants entered middle adulthood in the late 1960s, and consequently their negotiation of midlife identity during this time of cultural upheaval may have opened them to the new currents in America's vastly expanding spiritual marketplace (cf. Roof 1999). Clearly, these newly accessible spiritual resources could be utilized by someone with a preexisting disposition toward self-discovery. Or the public accessibility of these new resources may have generated a new spiritual awareness among individuals who, independent of any inner psychological process, were attracted to these innovative elements in the popular culture. Moreover, the fact that the vast majority of our study participants were living in California, the cauldron of new forms of spirituality, greatly enhanced their access to spiritual ferment and exploration. Thus the greater salience of spiritual seeking for our study participants from late-middle age onward most likely had as much to do with an expanded spiritual marketplace and geographical context as with chronological age or phase in the life course.

The cultural explanation for the postmidlife increase in spiritual seeking is strengthened by the fact that the younger cohort (those born in 1928–29) experienced an increase earlier in life (recorded in 1970, in their early forties) and showed a steeper increase subsequently. From a maturation perspective, in 1970 they were less likely to have had a settled adult identity (Levinson 1978), compared to the older participants who, born in 1920–21, were approaching age fifty. Additionally, the younger cohort were more likely to have teenagers living at home during this time, and this would have further exposed them to the influences of the cultural changes of the 1960s. Indeed, analyses of the study participants' personality data show that at midlife (as recorded in the 1970 interview), but not in early adulthood (as recorded in the 1958 interview), members of the younger cohort were more likely than the older cohort to show evidence of identity exploration.[9] Our emphasis on the significance of cultural context in aiding the postmidlife spiritual growth of individuals does not negate the maturational thesis that the postmidlife phase in the life course necessitates an adaptive shift in an individual's identity toward spiritual concerns. It simply affirms the fact that individual lives take shape and develop in particular sociohistorical and cultural contexts and thus are invariably influenced by the larger culture.

The complex entanglement of maturational and cultural influences in the development of spiritual seeking is illustrated by the life narrative of Peter Jones, a man who received a high score on spiritual seeking in late adulthood. Born in 1929, and thus a member of the younger, more spiritual cohort, Peter was highly intelligent, charming, healthy, and handsome. Yet he suffered chronically low self-esteem from childhood throughout most of his adult years. Both his parents were college graduates, and his father owned a successful grocery business that was badly hit by the Depression. Financial insecurity, exacerbated by Peter's status-conscious and emotionally unstable mother, characterized his life until 1943, when Peter was in junior high school and his family's economic situation improved considerably.

Religion did not figure much in Peter's family life, though his mother occasionally attended Congregational and Unitarian church services and was an active community volunteer. Peter went to a Christian Science Sunday school for a while and was a member of the Boy Scouts at the local Presbyterian church. But, socially awkward and curious, he was much more interested in magic and doing chemistry experiments. In adolescence he described himself as agnostic. Midway through college, Peter was drafted into the army. After basic training, which to his surprise he enjoyed, he returned to Berkeley, married a woman whom he did not know very well, and, after a week's honeymoon, went to Korea, where he was assigned to a logistics division. After returning from Korea, Peter went back to college, graduated as a business major in 1955, and went to work for his father in his wholesale deep-freeze business. Commenting on this decision when interviewed in 1958, Peter said that if he were "more mature and self-confident," he would quit working for his father, although he felt some loyalty to him and the business. Work was not the only source of frustration for Peter: his marriage was also strained. His wife had a troubled personal background and was suffering from depression. He was especially disappointed because, having built his wife and young son "a new home with all mod cons [modern conveniences]," he thought this would improve their relationship, but it hadn't.

When interviewed in 1970, Peter indicated that his life had spiraled downward. He was now divorced and had been depressed, out of work, and living in a boardinghouse for a few years prior to the interview. Nonetheless, he was trying to take hold of his life and give it some direction. Like Jane Bell, he found new resources and opportunities for self-growth in the newly expanding therapeutic culture. Peter was involved in a transactional analysis (TA) therapy group that met once a week, and he was also exploring yoga and meditation. It was clear that Peter was quite taken with TA, and its therapeutic language dominated much of the interview. Peter felt strongly that this system of psychotherapy had given him a greater understanding of his behavior and how he perceived himself:

> One of the concepts they have [in TA] is that of the good guy. . . . The good guy is somebody who's too worried about his image and functions in terms of how he thinks other people want him to function. . . . Rather than doing what he feels is the right thing to do, he says, "I wonder what so-and-so would think if I did this; would they like it?" . . . I think I have a tendency to be a good guy. . . . One of my contracts [tasks] in TA is to get over being a good guy, because I don't particularly like it. Over the years, I have found it very destructive.

It was through some friends at the Unitarian Church which Peter had attended on and off for several years that he first heard about TA—an acknowledgment of the fact that the religious and the therapeutic intertwine. Highlighting the diffuse creed of the Unitarians, what Peter liked about Unitarianism, he said, was that he "didn't have to have all kinds of [particular] religious beliefs to fit in."

Twelve years later, Peter's life seemed to have taken a positive turn. After selling a service station that he had owned for a few years, Peter had gone back to college and received a master's degree in ecosystem management and technology. Among the new opportunities in the post-1970s environment-friendly marketplace, Peter had at last found a vocational niche. He had a small woodstove business and was also engaged in other alternative energy projects and organic farming. Peter was now in his third marriage, after a second short and stormy one in which he had had another son. His second wife had been active in the Baha'i religion, and she in turn had gotten him involved. It was through Baha'i activities that he met his current wife. Both had subsequently left the Baha'i religion because of what they felt was its hypocrisy, especially about women's equality. As Peter explained, in the personally authoritative and self-oriented language associated with the therapeutic culture (Bellah et al. 1985), "We replaced the faith with our beliefs regarding energy and self-sufficiency, and how we want to handle our own lives and where we are going" (1982, age fifty-three). His wife, a nurse, was younger than him but "mature and levelheaded"; they had a son together and enjoyed a cohesive family life.

When interviewed in late adulthood (1998), Peter was still happily married and had a very close relationship with his youngest son, though he was not close to his older children. Describing his marriage as "very good," Peter did not invoke the therapeutic language one might have anticipated based on his past interviews. He now used a more old-fashioned or prosaic vocabulary, much like middle-class Americans tend to do (see, e.g., Swidler 2001: 114–16). He stated, "Finally I recognize that what it takes for a marriage to work is commitment, almost more than anything else." Commitment was also apparent in Peter's spiritual life. He identified himself as "a neo-pagan" who regularly engaged in nature spirituality practices, and he also attended the Unitarian Church most weeks, served on its board, and was active in its worship committee. Indicative of his commitment to paganism, Peter and his wife built a "worship circle" on their property. He elaborated:

> I would consider myself a neo-pagan. I have friends that I consider close friends who are part of our group. My wife and I have . . . a circle at which we hold celebrations. It's on the property here. . . . [We] have developed a very successful kind of—it's almost more nature worship or nature spirituality or earth-centered spirituality than it is—it's not witchcraft or what's called Wicca. It's . . . worshipping or celebrating the seasons and nature and the earth. . . . We are to some extent part of a larger organization, in that we are a chapter of what's called CUUPs, the Covenant of Unitarian Universalist Pagans, a nationwide organization. Our main reason for having connected with the CUUPs organization is that being tied in with a church—a regular denomination (it's an old denomination)—being affiliated, gave it

more legitimacy, we felt. Also we get information; we use it as a resource for pamphlets and information about that type of thing.

In addition to his pagan and Unitarian activities, Peter was the organizer of a local organic farmers' market, ran a wholesale food-buying club for twelve families, and was on the boards of the community hall and the local conservation district. He described his values thus: "My values tie right in with this earth's spirituality. . . . I think my values are very, very environmental, and I'm very concerned that we as human beings are destroying our home, our earth. I'm concerned that it's going to affect my son's life and my grandchildren's lives. Not mine necessarily. . . . So my values are very much those of attempting to live lightly on the earth" (1998, age sixty-nine).

For someone who in adolescence and early adulthood had felt deeply inadequate and incompetent, it is clear that from middle adulthood onward, and after many-work related troubles and personal calamities brought on by his lack of maturity, Peter had carved out a stable and committed life. His dabbling in various religious (Congregationalism, Unitarianism, Baha'i) and nonreligious traditions (paganism) illustrates the fact that multiple options are available to Americans with religious or spiritual interests. Though it took a while, Peter managed eventually to commit to Unitarianism and to an earth-centered spirituality, the obligations of which, in turn, tied him into a whole web of personal and community relationships.

We cannot, of course, rule out the possibility that Peter's integration of spiritual practices into his life in late adulthood resulted from the maturational or aging process itself. We are struck, however, that changes in the post-1960s cultural environment provided resources that allowed Peter to journey toward purposeful engagement by means of practices that gave him spiritual meaning. Similarly, while his family history may have independently motivated Peter to seek psychotherapy at some point, the cultural accessibility of transactional analysis in the 1970s and its apparent suitability to Peter's specific needs may have enhanced his growth and maturation. By the same token, the expanded range of religious options in post-1960s America—including, for example, the Baha'i religion, which, along with unconventional forms of spirituality such as paganism, became more visible during this time—also played a critical role in creating new resources and social opportunities for Peter. Further, the culture's new environmental consciousness provided a legitimate outlet for Peter's late-blooming vocational interests.

TURNING ADVERSITY INTO SPIRITUAL GROWTH

Peter Jones was one of few in our study whose spiritual interests and habits were nature centered. Some of our spiritual seekers, like Jane Bell, engaged primarily in Eastern meditation practices, and still others, such as Kate Ward, whom we are about to introduce, found spiritual discipline and growth across a mix of church-centered and newer spiritual activities. But though their specific practices varied, spiritual seekers in late adulthood were as a group unified by a trajectory of postmidlife spiritual growth, early religious involvement, and introspection. Of further interest, spiritual seekers tended, like Jane and Peter, to have experienced significant emotional turmoil, especially in their thirties and forties.[10] Spiritual seekers' personal crises developed in association with their experiences of negative life events, such as bereavement, family illness, and divorce, and from conflicted family and other personal relationships. Religiousness in late adulthood, by contrast, was not related to antecedent negative life events. These findings further underscore the point that spiritual—and religious—engagement does not occur in a vacuum. In addition to the maturational, life course, and cultural forces that shape an individual's spiritual and religious commitments, the person's particular sociobiographical context also matters. It is noteworthy, moreover, that, in the case of our spiritual seekers, their having had a religious background meant they were able to incorporate its resources into their process of spiritual growth in response to personal crisis. This further highlights the bridge between traditional and newer forms of spiritual engagement, and it underscores the importance of early religious socialization as a resource for subsequent spiritual exploration (see also Wuthnow 1999).

The fact that spiritual growth, and personal transformation in general (Stokes 1990: 176), may be prompted by personal turmoil suggests a parallel between spiritual seeking and wisdom whose development, too, has been linked to the experience of stressful life events (see, e.g., Wink and Helson 1997). In any case it was certainly true in our study that spiritual growth was boosted by emotional pain and the ability to positively learn from and integrate that pain. Our data thus give flesh to an insight by Schopenhauer (1788–1860): "For man to acquire noble sentiments[,] . . . for the *better consciousness* to be active within him, pain, suffering and failure are as necessary to him as weighty ballast is to a ship, which attains no draught without it" (emphasis in original as quoted in Safranski 1990: 198). Or in the more prosaic wisdom of a

Chinese proverb, "A smooth sea never made a skillful mariner." We are not implying that religious dwellers are incapable of noble sentiment. Rather, our findings suggest that different paths lead to different types of religious engagement in old age. In the case of spiritual seekers, this process involves active confrontation of one's inner demons and an integration of them that results in positive change. In contrast, for religious dwellers, a sustained religious commitment relies less on open struggle with personal adversity.

Kate Ward's life story illuminates how the active confrontation of emotional pain can lead to spiritual growth. She also exemplifies the compatibility between church-based religiousness and engagement in spiritual seeking beyond church. Kate was one of the few women in our study who never married and who had no children. Born in 1929, the youngest of three siblings, she grew up in a high-status family in which intellectual and community activities were emphasized. She was a popular girl, vibrant and smart, yet easygoing, who had a good sense of humor; she was actively involved in sports and was a leader in classroom and school activities. Although her parents were not churchgoers, they sent Kate to the Episcopal Sunday school. During her interview in early adolescence (in 1943, at age fourteen), Kate said she liked the way the pastor "boils down the sermon so you can understand it," and like many of her peers, she also enjoyed the church's social activities. But at sixteen, Kate had stopped attending church. She explained, "I've been pondering over what I believe this year, and can't quite take the Bible and the sermons. I'm not an atheist, but I'm not a believer. I can't decide if I am religious. I believe in the spirit of religion, but I can't believe in the details."

Kate certainly had the introspection that characterized the spiritual seekers in our study. Talking about herself at age sixteen, she stated that, although she was a "good sport" and adaptable and nonrebellious in social situations, "in an argument, I'm apt to take a stand on the opposite side, but I always know what I think. No one makes up my mind for me. I'm honest with myself." Similarly, the psychologist who interviewed Kate at this time (in 1945) described her as "honest [and] full of surprising insights about herself and others."

After high school, Kate went to a prestigious college in the Northeast, majored in social science, and began a career in public administration. But in early adulthood, in 1958, she said she felt that her life was at a "depressed impasse," that she was not living up to her potential. She was grieving over the sudden death of the one man with whom she had had a meaningful relationship, and she spoke of her longing to be married to a man who "is strong, competent, and intellectually interesting, who would not only permit but who would expect me to be a person in my own right." Kate went into psychotherapy in her early thirties for three years, mostly "as an existential thing" but also because she felt helpless and had suicidal thoughts. Psychotherapy, by her own account in 1970, did not make her lose her hang-ups, but it "completely changed [her] whole life direction"; it made her more aware of her strengths and weaknesses and helped her "find a way to grow and develop."

Kate was working at an interdenominational, church-based teenage social action program in Philadelphia, and she chose to live in the integrated inner-city neighborhood in which she worked, though there was "constant theft." Kate's interest in social problems extended beyond the inner city to include a broader critique of how society in general was organized. Explicitly articulating the anti-institutionalism that national opinion polls were beginning to document in the late 1960s (cf. Roof 1999: 50), she was especially critical of institutions—"universities, churches, hospitals"—stating, "I think they're all bad, all need to be changed." But despite her constant readiness to engage in institutional critique, Kate was passionately involved in the everyday work of institutions. She continued, for example, to be an active member of the Episcopal Church—highlighting our study's general finding that religiousness in early adulthood (age thirties, 1958) was positively related to late adulthood spiritual seeking.

Kate was uncertain, however, whether she believed in God, though at the same time she expressed awareness and appreciation of a divine presence:

> I don't know what to say. I think *God* is a wretched term—and I just don't know. I believe, perhaps, in something, some kind of power or force. I don't know whether it really exists, or whether I can rationalize it and say, "Well, man just needs to have this, so that's why we have it." But in times of stress and trouble, it kind of makes sense. And it's helpful. . . . It's very comforting to think that there's something else. I think religion—it doesn't matter what religion it is—gives depth . . . and meaning to life that life in and of itself simply does not have.

At midlife (age forty-one, 1970), Kate held out the possibility that she might still marry and have children, but she primarily talked about the future in terms of her commitment to self-growth: "I would almost do anything to allow myself options to grow and to develop and to do different kinds of work and not to be into one thing. . . . I don't ever want to get locked into one thing. . . . I just really want to be able to have the opportunity to keep options open."

Twelve years later (1982), Kate was co-owner and manager of group houses for troubled teenagers. Her spare time was taken up with her spiritual development: "Spiritual discovery and development and growth has been very influential in determining my sense of self," she said, and she talked at length about the many domains of her life in which she experienced both personal growth and coming to terms with who she was.

Although Kate had shown signs of spiritual seeking already in adolescence and during her early adulthood existential crisis, she, like others in our study, experienced the most spiritual growth from her early forties onward. On returning to California in the mid-1970s—during the blossoming of the new religious consciousness (Glock and Bellah 1976)—Kate "felt the spiritual nudging again." She first got involved with a group of Catholic charismatics, until she found a progressive Episcopal church: "So now that is where I am, and that's my sort-of home," a spiritual home that also provided her with much social and emotional support. At that time she was also a member of a "house church" composed of twelve adults who met weekly for spiritual sharing and discussion.

In referring to the flowering of her long-term spiritual quest, Kate used language most usually associated with evangelical transformation, a vocabulary becoming increasingly accessible as a result of the evangelical resurgence in American society in the late 1970s and early 1980s. She explained, "What happened was that, in quotes, I was 'born again.' I can't think of any better way to put it than that." The catalyst for Kate's "born again" experience was an episode of physical and emotional exhaustion brought on by intense work-related pressures. During this time Kate gradually realized that she needed to surrender to God rather than control everything herself. She explained,

> I've never been a true believer [in anything]. Let's put it that way. I've
> had a lot of interests and a lot of enthusiasm in everything I've done. . . .
> Unfortunately, now I'm a true believer [laughs]. I never made a commit-
> ment to anything in my life before, ever. Not 100 percent. . . . It's a constant
> struggle. Constantly you're giving up. You have to—every day you have to
> give up. It's a real struggle. If you're going to do this Christian number, it's
> a constant struggle. It's a constant giving up of yourself. . . . You cannot get
> away with being sloppy and self-centered. And I mean it's really demand-
> ing. . . . I never believed in the divinity of Jesus Christ, . . . so for me to

actually believe in all this is really remarkable. . . . It was an act of total surrender. . . . [When she was near total collapse and finding her work very demanding,] I said, "Lord, if you want me to continue with doing what I am doing, which is obviously good work, then you're gonna have to help me with this. You're gonna have to do it. I've just had it. I just can't do it anymore. I can't give anymore." . . . Mine was sort of an act of surrender. I lived with that for a month or two. . . . So then I thought, well, what do I do now? All that I know is that I didn't go back to being the same person or living the same way; something had changed. . . . This whole issue I've had about the divinity of Jesus Christ seemed to go out the window. It was totally unimportant. I just accepted that. I thought, I'll never figure it out. It's an intellectual mystery—no one will ever prove either that it is true or it isn't. I'm choosing to say that it is. I could not make any intellectual justification today at all for that.

Upon her retirement, spiritual seeking continued to be a dominant force in Kate's life. She was involved in a couple of different non-church-based women's spiritual groups and, as she said, feeding her soul through a lot of varied activity: attending the Episcopal Church almost weekly and enthusiastically involved in the United Church of Christ—going to weekly services, participating in a morning "science and spirituality" discussion group, and being on the church's retreat-planning committee. When asked about what kept her going in times of trouble, Kate said that a practical attitude—the thought that "it can't stay this bad all the time"—and her strong faith had supported her. She explained, "I have a belief, a faith—I'm not quite sure what the correct word would be—in a universal spirit that's connected to human spirit. If you are plugged into that, you get renewed. You receive guidance, and you keep going. That's where I am now. And I've gone through it all, absolutely a great variety of religious experiences—I can't say *beliefs*, but religious experiences. That's kind of where I am." One of the ways Kate's belief in a universal spirit renewed her was through her extensive reading and meditating on the complex connections between nature, science, and spirituality and the search for a meaningful cosmic order.

Despite the centrality of religion in Kate's life, she was hesitant to describe herself as religious, preferring to say she was spiritual. Echoing remarks she had made forty years earlier, she explained,

The word *religion* is a really, really wretched term. I look upon it negatively now. It's a system of beliefs, and even though I'm a churchgoer, I'm totally unorthodox in any Christian beliefs. I take the good things. I don't believe in original sin or in any particular theology, but there are many good things to be exemplified and utilized in Christianity. . . . And I feel the same way about Buddhism. I find many tenets of Buddhism to be excellent dictums by which to live. And their whole concept of meaningfulness is great. I think that that's a good way to be and to live and [a good thing] to strive for. But religions per se have given us as much trouble as they have given us good. Our morals and our way of trying to control human beings have all come out of religions, sometimes for ill as well as for good. In the long run, I guess you have to say it's good that we had something like that, that man created religion. But not when you have people killing one another over it; it's ridiculous. . . . I would say that I'm a spiritual person, or I strive to be a spiritual person, not necessarily a religious person. I make the distinction there. I am very much a spiritual person—that's something growing in me.

Thus while Kate was critical of religion's association with violence and coercion, unlike Jack Adams, our defiant atheist who was similarly critical of organized religion (see chapter 5), she spent much of her adult life nurturing a spirituality that derived from both church and nonchurch activities. And unlike Bob Mears and Susan Moore, who, like Kate, also surrendered to Jesus, Kate's surrender was partial—it was not intellectually justifiable to her—and it was not exclusively to Jesus. She continued to maintain her "unorthodox" Christian beliefs and her *doxa* that non-Christian tenets also offered pathways to transcendence and the divine. Thus, through her diverse religious and spiritual activities, Kate's life conveys how individuals can be highly active spiritual seekers while being highly committed, though selectively so, to institutionalized religion. The compatibility between religiousness and spiritual seeking shown in Kate's life thus illuminates Ann Patrick's evocative simile of religiousness and spirituality as two rivers with shared tributaries that can unite and flow together (1999).

8

The Activities, Personality, and Social Attitudes of Religious and Spiritual Individuals in Late Adulthood

The aging of the populous baby boom generation has increased public interest in identifying the nature of positive functioning in older adulthood.[1] According to a traditional assumption, late adulthood is a time in the life course when individuals experience a decline in personal meaning and purpose as a result of their diminished social roles and physical and cognitive impairment, but a spate of more recent studies suggest otherwise (see, e.g., James and Wink 2007; Rowe and Kahn 1998; Vaillant 2002). Nonetheless, surprisingly little is known about the everyday functioning of the "young-old," those in the postretirement interval extending from around age sixty-five to age eighty. For the majority of Americans, this is a stage in life when they have the freedom of the postretirement period without the concomitant care-dependency needs that increase sharply among the "old-old" (those over eighty years of age). Yet there is little research documenting their experiences and indicating whether, in particular, religion makes a difference to everyday functioning in the postretirement period.[2]

SOCIODEMOGRAPHIC CHARACTERISTICS AND LIVING CIRCUMSTANCES IN LATE ADULTHOOD

At the time of our interviews in late adulthood, the older participants were approximately seventy-seven years old on average, and the younger participants were sixty-nine.[3] Most of them still resided in California or in a western or southwestern state. The study participants' living circumstances in late adulthood were impressively good and conducive to positive everyday functioning. Almost half (47 percent) were college graduates, and in social status over half (59 percent) the participants or their spouses were upper-middle-class professionals or executives, a fifth (19 percent) were lower-middle class, and another fifth (22 percent) were working class. Most of the participants were economically well-off. More than two-thirds (69 percent) had an annual household income of more than forty thousand dollars, a figure substantially higher than that of similar-age married households nationwide, and 17 percent reported an income exceeding one hundred thousand dollars. Nonetheless, though all participants were past the traditional retirement age of sixty-five, a quarter of them (26 percent), irrespective of cohort, were still working for pay, mostly part-time, and this was also true of a similar proportion of spouses (22 percent). Despite income variation among the study participants in late adulthood, a remarkable 90 percent said they were not financially prevented from doing any of the activities they wanted to do.[4] Neither religiousness nor spiritual seeking was related to education, social class, or income.

Most of the participants were still married (70 percent), some were divorced (9 percent), and quite a few were widowed (17 percent). Seventy-one percent (85 percent of men and 55 percent of women) were living with their spouse or a partner, figures that parallel the census data for same-age Americans.[5] Among those who were married, a majority (55 percent) said they were exceptionally happy and that their marriage fulfilled most of their expectations, and a further third (33 percent) described their marriage as good. Men, irrespective of cohort, reported being more satisfied with their marriage than women. The modal number of children per participant was three, and the modal number of grandchildren was five. Most of the study participants reported feeling close to their children, and it was apparent that they enjoyed their grandchildren's company and took pride in their activities and accomplishments.

Although marital satisfaction was high among our study participants as a whole, it is noteworthy that high scorers on religiousness were more likely than others to report being highly satisfied with their marriage. Paralleling gender differences in marital satisfaction, the positive relation between religiousness and martial satisfaction was significant for men but not women.[6] In addition, highly religious individuals had a greater number of children and grandchildren.[7] In contrast to religiousness, spiritual seeking was unrelated to marital satisfaction and to the number of children or grandchildren. Spiritual seekers in general and spiritual-seeking women in particular were, however, more likely to have been divorced, which indicates the prominence of emotional and personal conflict in their lives.[8]

PURPOSEFULNESS IN LATE ADULTHOOD

Not surprisingly, given the positive economic and social circumstances of our study participants' lives in late adulthood, most of them were leading an active older adulthood. Large majorities of men and women frequently read newspapers and magazines (92 percent) and books (66 percent). Many frequently engaged in some form of physical exercise such as walking, tennis, swimming, or golf (55 percent), traveled (44 percent), informally visited with relatives (55 percent) or friends and neighbors (44 percent), participated in community service (25 percent), and engaged in a range of personal hobbies (36 percent), including gardening, arts and crafts, and woodwork projects. A good few enrolled in adult education classes (21 percent), went to concerts, plays, museums, or lectures (21 percent), played a musical instrument (6 percent), sang in a chorus (8 percent), or played competitive card and board games such as bridge and chess (17 percent) or played solitary games or did puzzles (19 percent).[9]

Frequent involvement in these purposive activities was particularly characteristic of the study participants who scored high on either religiousness or spiritual seeking. This was reflected in the positive association among religiousness, spiritual seeking, and involvement across a wide array of everyday activities (see table 4). Given the well-documented finding that churchgoers tend in general to be "joiners"—to be involved in church activities and a range of social groups and organizations (see, e.g., Putnam 2000)—we were interested in whether the daily activities of individuals who scored high on church-based religiousness differed from those who scored high on spiritual seeking. We sought an in-depth understanding of the relation among religiousness, spiritual seeking, and everyday purposefulness by categorizing our study participants' activities according to whether they revolved around socially engaging pursuits such as socializing with friends and family or doing community service, or around more self-expansive, creative, and knowledge-building activities.[10]

TABLE 4. RELATIONS AMONG RELIGIOUSNESS, SPIRITUAL SEEKING, AND EVERYDAY ACTIVITIES IN LATE ADULTHOOD

Everyday Activities	Religiousness		Spiritual Seeking	
	r	*Partial* r	r	*Partial* r
Social	.27**	.23**	.17*	.10
Community service	.34**	.31**	.18*	.08
Creative	.24**	.13	.41**	.30**
Knowledge-building	.00	−.02	.27**	.26**
Total[a]	.28**	.22**	.24**	.17*

NOTE: $N = 157$. Everyday activities were assessed using Harlow and Cantor's Life Task Participation Scale (1996) as described in chapter 8, n. 10. In the case of religiousness, the partial r controls for spiritual seeking, and in the case of spiritual seeking, the partial r controls for religiousness.
[a] Total = sum of involvement across twenty-six different activities.
* $p < .05$; ** $p < .01$.

This categorization highlighted some interesting differences among our participants. Reflecting the overall positive relation between religion and involvement in everyday activities, both religiousness and spiritual seeking correlated positively with engagement in social activities like visiting family and friends, with participation in community aid projects, and with involvement in creative activities such as writing or painting. The only exception was the lack of an association between religiousness and an involvement in knowledge-building activities like auditing college courses and attending evening classes and lectures (see table 4). However, once we controlled statistically for the overlap between religiousness and spiritual seeking, it was evident that only religiousness was positively associated with engagement in social activities like visiting family and friends and with participation in community service. In contrast, with the effect of religiousness statistically removed, only spiritual seeking was positively associated with involvement in activities that had a self-investment dimension, such as painting, sculpting, writing, and other creative and intellectual efforts. This finding adds to the growing body of research on the links between spirituality and artistic pursuits (e.g., Wuthnow 2003). In sum, our results indicate that the more a person emphasizes religious dwelling devoid of seeking, the more he or she is likely to engage in social- or other-oriented activities at the expense of self-oriented pursuits. Conversely, spiritual seekers who do not incorporate elements of institutionalized religiousness in their lives are likely to be more self-focused in their everyday activities compared to others.

The contrast between spiritual seekers and highly religious individuals was further apparent in that high scorers on spiritual seeking (and not on religiousness) were more likely to say that they derived their sense of well-being from personal growth activities—as exemplified by Jane Bell (chapter 1)—whereas high scorers on religiousness (and not on spiritual seeking), like Barbara Shaw (chapter 1), largely derived their sense of well-being from warm and positive interpersonal relations.[11] Similarly, high scorers on religiousness but not on spiritual seeking tended to describe themselves as able to easily become emotionally close to others, as comfortable to depend on others and have others depend on them, and as not concerned about interpersonal rejection.[12]

But what about the everyday purposefulness of individuals who were neither religious nor spiritual? To find out whether the everyday involvement of our nonreligious study participants differed from that of religious and spiritual individuals, we divided the sample into two groups. One group consisted of individuals who scored moderately or high on religiousness, spiritual seeking, or both. The second group was composed of individuals who scored low on both religiousness and spiritual seeking. Our analysis showed that religious or spiritual individuals had a significantly higher level of involvement in social, community-service, creative, and knowledge-building activities than those who were not religious or spiritual. In other words, individuals actively engaged in religion, irrespective of whether it was church centered or seeker oriented, also tended to participate in more daily activities, and more frequently, than those for whom religion or spirituality were of little or no relevance. These findings were statistically significant.[13] However, the relatively low magnitude of the difference between the religious and nonreligious groups means that many nonreligious and nonspiritual older individuals were living purposeful lives. Nonetheless, being religiously or spiritually engaged, as opposed to having no religious or spiritual interests, was more conducive to involvement in everyday activities.

Of course, the fact that religiousness and spiritual seeking were associated with purposeful engagement in late adulthood does not mean this can be attributed directly to religious or spiritual beliefs and practices. It is possible, for example, that engagement in everyday activities is a function of good physical and psychological health, and, should highly religious and spiritual individuals be healthier and less depressed than others, this could account for our findings. In support of this conjecture, we did find that overall involvement in everyday activities among our study participants was related positively to good physical health and negatively to depression. Nevertheless, controlling for health and depression did not diminish the positive relations among involvement in daily activities, religiousness, and spiritual seeking. This suggests, therefore, that the purposefulness of highly religious and spiritual older adults cannot be easily explained by nonreligious factors such as their physical and psychological health.[14]

RELIGION AS A PREDICTOR OF EVERYDAY PURPOSEFULNESS OVER TIME

In our longitudinal analyses, we found that the pattern of activities associated with religiousness in late adulthood could be predicted using individuals' religiousness based on their high school interviews (1930s or 1940s), recorded close to sixty years earlier. In other words, the study participants' adolescent religiousness was as significant a predictor of their late-adulthood involvement in socializing and community service activities as their scores on religiousness obtained in late adulthood or, in fact, in early adulthood.

The predictive power of early-adulthood religiousness (age thirties) derives from the fact that there was a high level of stability in patterns of individual religiousness throughout adulthood (see chapter 6). One consequence of this personal stability is that individuals who scored high on religiousness at age thirty were likely to be engaged in socializing and community activities in late adulthood largely because they tended to continue being more religious than others throughout adulthood, and being religious reflected and reinforced their tendencies to be socially and communally engaged.

The same logic of stability, however, cannot wholly explain the long-term relation between adolescent religiousness and everyday activities in late adulthood, because the correlation between religiousness in adolescence and religiousness in late adulthood was only moderate (see chapter 6, table 2). There were, in short, many adolescents active in church and church-related activities who subsequently had little or no involvement in religion. Our finding, then, of a long-term relation between adolescent religiousness and social and community involvement in late adulthood may be a function of the fact that church involvement in adolescence provides a foundation for social engagement more generally, a foundation that can persist for the individual over time even if his or her religiousness subsequently declines after adolescence. This may be especially true of mainline Protestants, the majority of our sample, coming as they do from a tradition whose religious socialization gives special emphasis to social and civic engagement (cf. Coble 2002). It may also reflect the positive association between church involvement and sociability (extroversion) that we found to be particularly characteristic of highly religious adolescents ($r = .18$, $p < .05$), an association also evident in adolescents' remarks about the importance of the social aspects of church to them (see chapter 3).

In contrast to the long-term link between adolescent religiousness and late-adulthood daily activities, the everyday activities associated with being a spiritual seeker in late adulthood could be gauged only from a much shorter interval. The late-adulthood activities of spiritual seekers could be predicted from their level of spirituality in late-middle adulthood—an interval of fifteen years—but not from earlier interview times. Though the predictive duration is much shorter, this finding is a function of the personal stability apparent in spiritual seeking. As noted in chapter 7, this stability was comparatively lower than for religiousness. It was really only from late-middle adulthood, from the study participants' fifties onward, that their spiritual seeking developed. The daily activities of spiritual seekers in late adulthood could be predicted from their level of spirituality in late-middle adulthood because the routines they were likely to develop at that time continued into late adulthood.

We noted in the preceding chapter that adolescent and early-adulthood religiousness was a bridge to spiritual seeking in late adulthood. Looking at the long-term connections between late-adulthood activities and religiousness at earlier phases in adulthood revealed an interesting glimpse of the currents beneath this bridge. We found that early-adulthood religiousness (but not late-adulthood religiousness) was a significant predictor of late-adulthood involvement in creative activities and of well-being from personal growth. These connections held even after controlling for the overlap between religiousness and spiritual seeking. Remember, however, that spiritual seeking in early adulthood was not a significant predictor of engagement in either creative or personal growth activities in late adulthood. We interpret this set of longitudinal findings as suggesting that individuals who scored high on religiousness in their thirties and who had an interest in self-growth and creative activities were likely over the course of adulthood to decrease their involvement in church-based religion and instead gravitate toward spiritual seeking later on in life.

RELIGION AND PERSONALITY

The patterns evident among religiousness, spiritual seeking, and engagement in everyday activities raised the possibility that the study participants' different forms of religious engagement express broader personality differences. And indeed, our analyses of the personality traits associated with religiousness and spiritual seeking revealed some remarkable connections and long-term trends.[15] In late adulthood, religiousness was positively related to agreeableness and conscientiousness. Thus those individuals who scored high on religiousness were described as warm, giving, protective of others, sympathetic, and likeable, and as people whom others turn to for advice—all characteristics associated with agreeableness. They were also described as dependable, productive, ethically consistent, perfectionist, and prone to overcontrol their personal needs and impulses—all characteristics associated with conscientiousness. Spiritual seeking, in contrast was not related, either positively or negatively, to agreeableness or conscientiousness (see table 5). This means that, while spiritual seekers were not seen as being, for example, sympathetic toward others or as particularly likeable and dependable, neither were they seen as unsympathetic or unlikeable and undependable. It was simply that agreeableness and conscientiousness did not emerge as the most characteristic traits of spiritual seekers.

Both religiousness and spiritual seeking correlated positively with the personality characteristic of openness to experience. The positive association between religiousness and openness did not hold, however, when we controlled for the overlap between religiousness and spiritual seeking. Hence, personality traits such as intellectual independence, introspection, being interested in cognitive and creative activities, and having wide interests (all characteristics of openness to experience) are particularly indicative of spiritual seekers. Neither religiousness nor spiritual seeking were related (either positively or negatively) to such personality characteristics as outgoingness, assertiveness, anxiety, personal vulnerability, and hostility (the extroversion and neuroticism dimensions of the Big Five; see note 15).[16]

Although individuals' immediate family and social context, as well as larger cultural and historical forces, clearly shape their patterns of religious engagement over time (see chapters 5, 6, and 7), it is also true that personality has a determining influence (as noted in chapter 5). In fact, adolescent personality emerged as a long-term significant

TABLE 5. RELATIONS AMONG RELIGIOUSNESS,
SPIRITUAL SEEKING, AND PERSONALITY
IN LATE ADULTHOOD

Personality	Religiousness		Spiritual Seeking	
	r	*Partial* r	r	*Partial* r
Extroversion	−.02	.00	−.07	−.06
Agreeableness	.27**	.26**	.09	−.01
Conscientiousness	.14[a]	.17*	−.03	−.09
Neuroticism	−.07	−.05	−.06	−.04
Openness	.17*	−.02	.52**	.49**

NOTE: $N = 181$. In the case of religiousness, the partial r controls for overlap with spiritual seeking, and in the case of spiritual seeking, the partial r controls for overlap with religiousness.

[a] $p < .10$; * $p < .05$; ** $p < .01$.

predictor of late-adulthood religiousness. The study participants who were assessed in adolescence as being conscientious—that is, those who were dependable, responsible, and self-controlled as adolescents—were significantly more likely than others to be religious in late adulthood, almost sixty years later. This relation remained even after we controlled for adolescent religiousness and for the long-term stability of both religiousness and conscientiousness (see figure 5). Our results indicated, therefore, that adolescent conscientiousness was a significant independent predictor of religiousness in late adulthood above and beyond the influence of early religious socialization and independent of the fact that, in late adulthood, conscientious individuals tended to be highly religious.[17]

The long-term stability of the relation between religiousness and conscientiousness is crystallized in Ian Logan, who was active in the Methodist Church from his childhood days, when he helped his father sort Sunday school papers, through late adulthood, when he continued to be involved in the church's religious programs (see chapter 5). In ninth grade, Ian was described by one of his teachers as responsive, realistic, and conscientious and meticulous about his work; another teacher commented on his perfectionism, which she attributed to the "family's exacting punctiliousness." And when interviewed at age seventeen, Ian himself described all the members of his family as "being a bit on the serious side." He also indicated that the type of girl he would

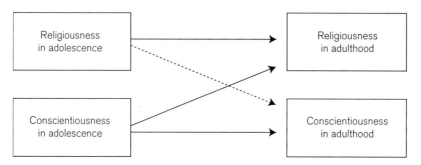

Figure 5. Lifetime relationship between conscientiousness and religiousness. Note: Solid arrows indicate a significant path, and dotted arrow indicates a nonsignificant path from a cross-lagged model (Wink, Ciciolla, Dillon, and Tracy in press).

like to marry would share his interests in church and music, and he emphasized dependability as a characteristic that he would want to instill in a child. As elaborated in chapter 5, Ian's entire adulthood continued to be characterized by dependability and scrupulousness, exemplified in his high level of religious involvement across the life course, notwithstanding a small dip in middle adulthood.

While Ian Logan illustrates lifetime stability in the positive relation between conscientiousness and religiousness, Patrick Doyle highlights how personality is independent of, and trumps, religious socialization. Patrick grew up in a large, close-knit, lower-class Catholic family. His childhood was overshadowed by a domineering, emotionally unpredictable, and indulgent mother; large family gatherings; and an absent father, a merchant sailor rumored to be a philanderer. At age fifteen, Patrick was described by one of the interviewers as friendly and easygoing but "loath to give up the role of baby in the family"; the interviewer also noted that Patrick was "finding it easy to accept without giving." Patrick attended church weekly, went on to win a scholarship to a Catholic high school, and contemplated becoming a priest, an aspiration not served, however, by his poor academic record and his general lack of responsibility. As he moved from one unrewarding job to another, Patrick's impulsive and sensation-seeking characteristics (indicative of low conscientiousness) led him, despite a strong religious background, to drug use and promiscuity and left little place for religion in his adult life.

It is not accidental that we have selected men to illustrate the long-term relation between conscientiousness and religiousness. Although the association between the two was evident for the participants as a whole, nonetheless, it was stronger for men. We did, however, find a long-term positive relation between adolescent agreeableness and religiousness in late adulthood that was present only among women.[18] Thus, sympathetic, likeable adolescent girls grew up to be more religious than their peers. Furthermore, girls who were religious in adolescence were in turn seen as more sympathetic and likeable as older women. This finding suggests the presence of a reciprocal relation whereby adolescent personality influences religiousness in late adulthood, and adolescent religiousness shapes personality in later life.

The intricate interplay between agreeableness and religiousness in the course of an individual's life is exemplified by Elizabeth Brown. Elizabeth grew up in a highly religious middle-class family burdened by medical debts. In adolescence, she was described by her teachers as friendly, pliable, cooperative, and "always very nice." Elizabeth loved music, and as a teenager she began earning money by playing the church organ and giving music lessons. Although always a churchgoer, by the time she was in high school Elizabeth appeared to attend church primarily for the music. At eighteen, she earned enough money from her music not only to support herself but also to buy clothes for her parents. Elizabeth married a very warm, likeable, generous, and highly religious human rights activist, and they both devoted their working lives to a faith-based organization focused on easing the plight of low-income immigrant families. When interviewed at age seventy, Elizabeth continued to impress others with her personal warmth, generosity, and likeability, and it was also clear that religious faith and church attendance now occupied a central place in her daily life.

Ian Logan, Patrick Doyle, and Elizabeth Brown illustrate the long-term relation between adolescent personality and religiousness in late life, but they also highlight how personality characteristics interact with family and social context. Elizabeth married a man whose warm, generous personality matched her own, and their joint faith-based work surely reinforced her generosity and agreeableness and fostered her religious commitment. In stark contrast, Patrick Doyle's impulsiveness led to a lifestyle not conducive to religious involvement, despite the fact that Patrick's religious socialization was as strong as Elizabeth's. Ian Logan, on the other hand, had a family background that fostered both the personality characteristics and the religious socialization that together ensure religiousness and conscientiousness in late adulthood.

Not surprisingly, adolescents who showed openness to experience were more likely than others to become spiritual seekers in late adulthood (see, e.g., Jane Bell and Kate Ward). Moreover, this long-term association remained after controlling for adolescent religiousness, which was itself positively related to spiritual seeking in late adulthood (see chapter 7). The association between adolescent openness and spiritual seeking in late adulthood was also independent of the father's social class but was related positively to the mother's educational background. This finding offers some support, therefore, for the idea that a long-term positive association exists between family cultural capital (Bourdieu 1984) and the intellectual openness and creative pursuits that characterized our spiritual seekers in late adulthood.[19]

Our findings on the personality characteristics associated with religiousness and spiritual seeking fit with those of a growing body of research that links conventional forms of religiousness with agreeableness and conscientiousness, and more unconventional forms—such as non-church-based spiritual seeking—with openness to experience (Saroglou 2002). As far as we know, however, our study is the first to extend research on the relation between adolescent personality and religiousness beyond early adulthood (see, e.g., McCullough, Tsang, and Brion 2003) and to highlight the long-term interplay across the life course between adolescent personality and religious and spiritual engagement in late adulthood. The robust effect of different personality characteristics on religiousness and spiritual seeking suggests that we might expect to see it extend into individuals' social attitudes in late adulthood, a question we next address.

SOCIAL ATTITUDES IN LATE ADULTHOOD

In the current political landscape characterized by cultural polarization (see, e.g., Hunter 1991), it is typically assumed that highly religious individuals embrace a socially conservative agenda that includes a strong stance on law and order; support for the death penalty; and opposition to gay rights, abortion, and gender-role equality in traditional male institutions such as the church and the military. Empirical support for this perception is provided by the large body of research indicating that church involvement predicts an authoritarian attitude constellation characterized by deference to law and order, adherence to conventional rules, and intolerance of groups seen as deviating from conventional morality (Altemeyer 1996).[20]

Given that the majority of our study participants were mainline Protestants affiliated with religious traditions that have a long history of preaching social tolerance (see, e.g., Thuesen 2002), we were surprised to find a strong and *positive* correlation between religiousness and authoritarianism. And we were doubly surprised by the fact that authoritarianism emerged as the only area of everyday life where religiousness and spiritual seeking showed a diametrically opposed pattern of relations, with spiritual seeking showing a significant *negative* association with authoritarianism. This divergent pattern emerged even though our study participants' political preferences—whether they described themselves as generally favoring the Democrats or the Republicans—did not align in accord with whether they were highly religious or spiritual seeking individuals.[21]

As we have shown in this chapter, highly religious and highly spiritual individuals differ in some everyday activities and personality characteristics. In these areas of functioning, however, a positive relation with one type of religious orientation was typically accompanied by the absence of, rather than a negative relation with, the other religious orientation. Thus, for example, whereas spiritual seeking was related to engagement in creative activities, religiousness was neither positively nor negatively associated with such activities. Yet, on authoritarianism, we see a clear gulf: here the tendency of highly religious individuals to submit to political and cultural authority, to adhere to traditional views of law and order, and to obey established social convention is diametrically opposite the stance taken by spiritual seekers.[22] What accounts for these unexpected findings?

In support of previous research showing that conservative Protestants are less libertarian than other Christians (see, e.g., Reimer and Park 2001), the small number of nonmainline Protestants in our study scored significantly higher on authoritarianism than mainline Protestants, Catholics, and those not religiously affiliated.[23] The average score for nonmainline Protestants indicated that they tended to agree (slightly to moderately) with most of the statements used to assess authoritarianism. Thus they tended to actively favor more law and order rather than the extension of civil rights, to endorse the punishment of individuals and social groups who are "troublemakers" or who deviate from the "normal way" things are supposed to be done, and to think that the United States would be better off with a strong leadership that aggressively imposes traditional cultural values. The average scores for Catholics and mainline Protestants indicated that they tended to take a neutral stance on these issues—that is, they neither agreed nor disagreed with statements asserting that individuals must submit to authority or with the advisability of taking an aggressive stance against culturally deviant groups. The average score for individuals not religiously affiliated indicated that they were in slight disagreement with these authoritarian themes.

Although nonmainline Protestants scored higher than others on authoritarianism, the positive relation between religiousness and authoritarianism remained significant, nevertheless, and virtually unchanged when we excluded the nonmainline participants from our statistical analyses. The link between religiousness and authoritarianism persisted even after we eliminated from our assessment of authoritarianism all the attitudinal statements whose content specifically related to religion. Thus, excluding statements such as "People should pay less attention to the Bible and the other old traditional forms of religious guidance, and instead develop their own personal standards of what is moral and immoral" did not make any difference to the strength of the relation between religiousness and authoritarianism.

We next focused on isolating the factors not associated with religion that might account for the positive relation between religiousness and authoritarianism and the negative relation between spiritual seeking and authoritarianism. First, we investigated whether the strength of these relations would decrease when major sociodemographic characteristics such as gender, age cohort, and education were controlled. Our results indicated that authoritarianism in late adulthood did not vary by gender, but it was significantly related to cohort, with the older participants more authoritarian than their younger peers. It was also negatively related to education, meaning that individuals who had fewer years of education were significantly more likely than others to endorse authoritarian attitudes. But despite these patterns, and despite the fact that women were more religious than men, controlling for all these variables (cohort, gender, and education) did not significantly alter the positive association between authoritarianism and religiousness and the negative relation between authoritarianism and spiritual seeking (see table 6, model 1).

Some individuals might argue nonetheless that the relation between religiousness and authoritarianism in our study is spurious. After all, we defined religiousness in terms of commitment to traditional or conventional (church-centered) religious beliefs and practices, and, because conventionality is a key component of authoritarianism, the relation between these two characteristics may reflect an underlying personality marked by conventionality and inflexibility. Conversely, it could be argued that the negative relation between spiritual seeking

TABLE 6. MULTIPLE REGRESSION ANALYSES
PREDICTING AUTHORITARIANISM FROM
RELIGIOUSNESS, SPIRITUAL SEEKING, AND
BACKGROUND VARIABLES IN LATE ADULTHOOD

Predictors	Model 1 (betas)	Model 2 (betas)
Gender	–.14	–.08
Cohort	.13*	.13
Education	–.29**	–.27**
Late adulthood		
Religiousness	.50**	.42**
Spiritual seeking	–.31**	–.22**
Flexibility	—	–.20*
R squared	.40**	.45**
Degrees of freedom	(5,149)	(6,115)

* $p < .05$; ** $p < .01$.

and authoritarianism reflects a presumption of flexibility present in our conceptualization of spiritual seeking. To investigate these possibilities, therefore, we recomputed the relations among religiousness, spiritual seeking, and authoritarianism while controlling for personality characteristics.[24] Once again, we found that the relations among religiousness, spiritual seeking, and authoritarianism did not change: even though, as expected, flexibility was a significant predictor of authoritarianism, it was negatively related to religiousness, and it was positively related to spiritual seeking (see table 6, model 2). In sum, the patterns evident regarding authoritarianism, religiousness, and spiritual seeking could not be explained by differences among our participants related to gender, cohort, education, and personality.

We next focused on whether our study participants' authoritarian attitudes in late adulthood bore any relation to their levels of religiousness and spiritual seeking in early adulthood. Once again, our results here further underscored the relative stability of religious engagement over the long term. Both the positive relation between religiousness and authoritarianism and the negative relation between spiritual seeking and authoritarianism in late adulthood remained intact in a new set of analyses using the participants' respective scores on religiousness and spiritual seeking from early adulthood. In this analysis, we similarly controlled for gender, cohort, educational status, and personal flexibility in early adulthood (as we did in late adulthood). In the case of spiritual seeking, its salience from early adulthood rather than solely from late-middle adulthood (as was evident in regard to the participants' everyday activities) points to the long-term stability of the social attitudes of spiritual seekers.

One final point: There is some discussion in the literature (Altemeyer 1996) that early religious socialization, because it establishes strict in-group/out-group boundaries at an early age, is directly associated with authoritarianism in adulthood. We did not find evidence of this in our study. When we investigated whether our participants' religiousness in adolescence was related to their authoritarianism in late adulthood, there was no association.

While authoritarianism captures an attitudinal disposition that is essentially submissive to authority and intolerant of minorities, its generalized focus does not allow for differentiation among minority groups. Yet the current political debates concerning the status of gays, women, and reproductive rights, on the one hand, and illegal immigrants, on the other hand, indicate the need to take a differentiated approach in trying to understand the relation between religion and social intolerance. Whereas the American Episcopal Church is currently divided over the doctrinal legitimacy of the ordination of gay bishops, and in Massachusetts the Catholic bishops are in the forefront of efforts to revoke the state's affirmation of the right of gay couples to marry, many faith-based organizations, including the Catholic Church, prominently advocate granting citizenship to illegal immigrants. Clearly, the fact that these churches do not articulate a uniform policy across the spectrum of social issues means that it is important to disentangle whether their adherents, too, tend to differentiate among the issues.[25]

We investigated the relation between religion and social tolerance by exploring our study participants' views of whether certain groups, for example, homosexuals and immigrants, had too much power or influence in American society.[26] Although the perception that a given social group has too much power cannot be equated with prejudice, using such a question has the advantage of minimizing social-desirability concerns. Whereas it is unlikely that many individuals (especially given the generally high level of education that characterized our sample) would openly endorse the view that they are prejudiced against racial minorities or immigrants, for example, it is much more likely that they would agree to endorse statements asking about societal power.

We placed the participants' responses to the questions regarding feminists and homosexuals into a single scale, based on the assumption that negative views toward gays and women's equality find some legitimacy in church teaching (see, e.g., Dillon 1999; Moon 2004), and particularly because church sanctions against homosexuality and gender equality were more pronounced in the 1940s and 1950s, when our participants would have formed their social attitudes.[27] We placed the questions about whether too much power was exercised by racial minorities, immigrants, labor unions, and older people into a separate scale, because Christian doctrine and history, with the exception of controversies over slavery, does not generally support a negative view of these groups (see Batson, Schoenrade, and Ventis 1993).[28]

Our initial findings showed that, indeed, highly religious individuals were significantly more likely than others to agree that homosexuals and feminists had too much power. But, contrary to our expectations, religiousness was also positively related to negative views of groups who are not stigmatized in church teaching. Spiritual seeking, in contrast, was negatively related to both forms of social intolerance (see table 7; see model 1 for gays/feminists and other social groups).

Given the clarity of our results, we were intrigued to discover whether they could be explained by the positive relation between religiousness and authoritarianism and the negative relation between spiritual seeking and authoritarianism. In other words, because the authoritarianism scale included items suggesting a negative view of minority groups, we wondered whether it was this overlap that accounted for our findings. After controlling for authoritarianism, we found that religiousness continued to predict the perception that gays and feminists have too much power, but it was no longer associated with the perception that racial minorities, immigrants, labor unions, and older people have too much power. In the case of the spiritual seekers, a reverse pattern was evident. After controlling for authoritarianism, spiritual seeking ceased to be a negative predictor of perceptions of the power of gays and feminists (it was now simply unrelated to such views), but it continued to be negatively related to the perception that other groups had too much power (see table 7, model 2). In sum, our findings strongly support the widely held assumption that sexuality and gender polarize Americans along a religious fault line. And, moreover, the negative views that highly religious individuals have concerning the

TABLE 7. MULTIPLE REGRESSION ANALYSES PREDICTING
GROUP ATTITUDES FROM RELIGIOUSNESS, SPIRITUAL
SEEKING, AUTHORITARIANISM, AND BACKGROUND
VARIABLES IN LATE ADULTHOOD

Predictors	Gays and Feminists		Other Social Groups	
	Model 1 (betas)	Model 2 (betas)	Model 1 (betas)	Model 2 (betas)
Gender	−.17	−.12	−.25*	−.19*
Cohort	.12	.04	.16	.08
Education	−.02	−.16	−.03	−.15
Late adulthood				
Religiousness	.53**	.23**	.38**	.09
Spiritual seeking	−.33**	−.15	−.42**	−.25**
Authoritarianism	—	.56**	—	.54**
R squared	.31**	.50**	.33**	.50**
Degrees of freedom	(5,111)	(6,110)	(5,111)	(6,110)

* $p < .05$; ** $p < .01$.

power of gays and feminists exist above and beyond their tendency to
defer to authority and social convention.

Despite the strong statistical association between religiousness and
authoritarianism, the attitudes expressed by any given religious individual can be nuanced and varied. Lives are always more complex than
captured by statistics alone, a point illustrated by the experiences and
attitudes of Dorothy Marshall. Dorothy scored significantly higher than
others in our study (more than one standard deviation above the sample
mean) on both religiousness and authoritarianism. Yet on several occasions in her life, she stood up to established authority. Dorothy grew up
in a family where the Masonic lodge was more important than church,
but she was always curious about church and, of her own accord, at
age ten walked up the steps of the Methodist church in her neighborhood and eventually struck up a close relationship with its bemused
pastor. Dorothy continued to attend the Methodist Church throughout
her adult life and maintained a strong religious faith. It was faith that
helped Dorothy deal with many onerous burdens: the untimely death

of her husband, a World War II veteran who subsequently was killed in the Korean conflict; the ensuing necessity of bringing up two daughters on her own; a later struggle with breast cancer; and, in late adulthood, a series of cardiac-related surgeries.

Following her husband's death, Dorothy challenged army officials and won the right to include a reference to his service in Korea on his tombstone—the army initially denied her request because the U.S. military action was never officially declared a war. Subsequently, she had to confront bankers reluctant to lend her money to buy a house; in the 1950s very few women bought homes in their names because, as recounted by Dorothy, they were deemed incapable of undertaking the physical maintenance, such as mowing the lawn, necessary to the home's upkeep. Once again, Dorothy won the fight. Working as a bookkeeper and office manager, she eventually purchased a townhouse and used it as rental property, and she bought some land that almost tripled in value before being resold. Dorothy never remarried—as she said, "They threw away the mold"—but maintained lifelong satisfaction from her relationships with her daughters and with close friends.

At age seventy, Dorothy described her main personal strength as an ability to handle problems: "I taught my girls, face your dragon. If you don't face your dragon, he'll chase you and get bigger." The resource that enabled Dorothy, a weekly churchgoer, to confront her own dragons was her faith: "People scoff, and religion is a very hard thing to talk about. People get uneasy—even my daughters. But I have always had an abiding faith that there is someone bigger than I, that there is a Lord." But although deeply religious, Dorothy did not privilege Christianity over other faiths. She adhered, rather, to the pluralistic explanation offered by her church minister that the various religions can all be seen as united and equal.

It is striking, however, especially given Dorothy's own independence and her success in confronting gender discrimination, that she had misgivings about gender equality. She was particularly critical of the women's movement, feeling that it "has caused friction." She noted, "I was brought up with rules, and we followed those rules, men and women alike. Nowadays there aren't any rules. Well, I like my door opened. I just think it's a courtesy when the man walks on the outside of the sidewalk. . . .You'll never be equal with a man. . . . Sure, some women are policemen, policewomen and so forth, but it's still a man's world." Although supporting the concept of equal pay, Dorothy wished that women "would back off just a bit on things. They [don't] have to have

100 percent equality." Yet Dorothy's concerns about women's pushiness did not extend to her views on racial equality. She was, in fact, very positive about the civil rights movement, and having lived for two years in Georgia, where she had seen segregation firsthand, she admired Martin Luther King Jr. and Rosa Parks.

SOCIAL INTOLERANCE IN CONTEXT

In view of the strong emotions that characterize debates over gender and gay rights in contemporary American society, it is important to recognize that, while our data indicated clear-cut patterns among religiousness, authoritarianism, and intolerance, they also revealed important nuances. Significantly, the negative views of gays and feminists that highly religious individuals tend to hold do not encompass other social minorities (e.g., racial minorities and immigrants). And, of course, while individuals can express negative attitudes about gays, for example, this does not necessarily mean they are prejudicial toward the gay people they know or encounter in day-to-day life.

Another nuance derives from the fact that, although we found a fairly strong relation between religiousness and authoritarianism, religiousness still accounted for only a relatively small amount of the variability in authoritarian attitudes. This means that a large portion is accounted for by factors other than religiousness. It also means that there are many highly religious individuals who are not authoritarian. Furthermore, the Catholics and mainline Protestants in our study showed a fair amount of neutrality (neither agreeing nor disagreeing) in regard to the various authoritarian statements. Therefore, although they were more authoritarian than the nonreligious, religiousness—unless it is associated with a nonmainline tradition—does not necessarily promote authoritarianism. Our findings suggest, rather, that church-centered religiousness does not actively encourage tolerance but neither does it actively discourage it.

What remains strikingly evident, nonetheless, is that authoritarianism and group attitudes are aspects of everyday functioning where the polarization between religiousness and spiritual seeking is the greatest. A narrow focus on this domain, therefore, is likely to exaggerate the contrast between church-centered religious individuals, on the one hand, and spiritual seekers and nonreligious individuals, on the other. Yet, regrettably, from the stance of trying to encourage civil discussion in the political arena, it is precisely such differences in outlook that tend to receive extensive media coverage, thus prompting assumptions about a culture war. We certainly do not want to negate the critical salience of issues revolving around sexuality and gender in contemporary American society. But we do want to make the point that there are other areas of everyday life where traditional church-centered and other Americans (spiritual seekers and nonreligious or nonspiritual individuals) either have things in common or, at least, are not worlds apart.

9

Spiritual Seeking, Therapeutic Culture, and Concern for Others

Much has been written in recent years about the threat posed to the communal web of American society by the increasing displacement of church-based religion in favor of an individualized, personal religion. Most notably, "Sheilaism," the personal religion embodied by Sheila Larson in the sociology best-seller *Habits of the Heart*, crystallized for Robert Bellah and his coauthors (1985) how a diffuse and therapeutic spirituality is both narcissistic and detrimental to social and community commitment. Sheila Larson was a nurse who spent many years in therapy; she described her "faith" as "Sheilaism"—"I believe in God. I'm not a religious fanatic. I can't remember the last time I went to church. My faith has carried me a long way. It's Sheilaism. Just my own little voice. . . . It's just try to love yourself and be gentle with yourself" (Bellah et al. 1985: 221).

Sheilaism captures well what Bellah and his coauthors (1985) and other cultural critics (e.g., Lasch 1979; Brooks 2000) perceive to be wrong with today's spiritual seeking. They argue that a therapeutic, self-centered, and narcissistic individualism underlies spiritual seeking, and that these self-oriented interests are displacing the socially responsible individualism that has historically characterized American society. In this view, the "triumph of the therapeutic" (Rieff 1966) in post-1960s

America, and the growth of interest in both psychotherapy and spirituality, is portrayed as reflecting a desire for immediate gratification among individuals for whom feeling good has become the prime goal in life in an era when the self is threatened by diminishing cultural and personal expectations and a decline in traditional supportive relationships. In essence, the elevation of personal experience as the arbiter of moral authority, and its lack of grounding in the authority imposed by an institutionalized religious tradition, is seen as detrimental to the practices of spiritual and social commitment that church participation obliges (Bellah et al. 1985). In contrast to the discipline associated with church attendance, Bible reading, and the fasting associated with holy days of obligation (such as Ash Wednesday, Good Friday, Yom Kippur, Ramadan), spiritual seeking is thought of as being ad hoc, diffuse, and motivated by the "hunger not for personal salvation, but for the feeling, the momentary illusion, of personal well-being, health and psychic security" (Lasch 1979: 33).

Jane Bell's midlife preoccupation with personal growth, and her emphasis on teaching her children "to be in touch with themselves and their feelings" (see chapter 1), and Peter Jones's drifting in and out of marriages in search of an authentic, confident self (chapter 7), could raise concern that self-seeking distracts attention from the needs of others. Whereas churches play a critical role in creating a responsible community, spiritual seeking typically does not entail the same degree of exposure to the parables of service to others repeated in scriptural readings and sermons, the church-based friendship connections that encourage collaboration in volunteer activities, and the organized service opportunities that many churches provide their members (see. e.g., Wuthnow 2004).

In short, skepticism toward an individualized spiritual seeking fits well with the sociological view that social institutions are essential to the maintenance of community and society. This skepticism also finds legitimacy in the belief that human nature is ultimately tainted with selfishness, and that consequently social engagement and ritual are vital in order to redeem "original sin." It reflects well what Perry Miller has referred to as the Puritan fear of the excessive "reeling and staggering" that comes from being intoxicated by one's own autonomy and self-expression (1956/1964: 192, 203).[1]

The dim view of spiritual individualism articulated by sociologists such as Bellah and his colleagues (1985) contrasts sharply with the stance taken by humanistic psychologists (e.g., Fromm 1941/1965), who, because they give primacy to the individual's obligations to the self rather than to society, welcome the spiritual seeker's focus on the self as a positive personal and social development. From this perspective, it is the established social order, tradition, and conventional religion that alienate individuals from their fundamental purpose in life, that is, from personal growth and self-realization. It is only when individuals reclaim their personal freedom (Fromm 1941/1965) and self-actualize that an altruistic concern for others and a mature individuated spirituality can flourish (Maslow 1964; Rogers 1961).

The humanistic tradition shares with Carl Jung (1953) the assumption that humans are born with a propensity for self-actualization or individuation, and that this aim is best achieved through the process of self-exploration in the "here and now." Although inner directed, this process of self-growth is not seen as resulting in narcissistic self-absorption or in selfish hedonism, because a highly individualized person becomes aware of the needs of others, appreciates the sacred, and develops a sense of unity with the universe (see, e.g., Jacoby 1990). In this view, negative emotions such as anger, envy, and selfishness are seen as the product of a damaged or frail self. It is assumed, therefore, that "the restoration of the self"—Heinz Kohut's evocative phrase (1977)—will result in the release of positive emotions including love, gratitude, and altruism (see also Winnicott 1965).

In sum, the humanistic perspective is associated with a firm belief in human goodness and the individual's propensity to care for others, even though, as others have noted, its proponents say little about the practical steps necessary to transform self-interest into social concern (Wallach and Wallach 1983; Bellah et al. 1985: 81). As Perry Miller intimates, the Emersonian view of pantheism brings with it the danger of a lack of sensitivity to how social context shapes social injustice. This, in turn, dampens fidelity to building the common good as first envisaged by John Winthrop and the Pilgrim settlers. After all, if the sacred can be found in all of nature, and if all things in the world are interconnected and are an expression of a single universal force—if "God is, in short, both the slayer and the slain" (Miller 1956/1964: 189)—why should one bother to rectify any manifest imperfections?

SPIRITUAL SEEKING, SELF-ORIENTATION, AND PSYCHOTHERAPY

At issue in the debate between the cultural critics of spirituality and its humanist supporters is not whether spiritual seeking is an outgrowth of self-investment. To the contrary, the fact that spiritual seekers are focused on the self is accepted as a given. What is controversial is whether this self-investment reflects a pathological and self-indulgent desire for immediate self-gratification or marks a more positive preoccupation with personal growth.

Spiritual seeking and narcissism are typically juxtaposed by social critics to highlight the dark side of the recent cultural turn toward therapeutic individualism. After all, following the destructive fate that befell the mythological Narcissus, who was so in love with his own reflection that he died of despair, it is customary to think of narcissism in negative terms. Yet, in psychology, narcissism is used in a more varied way (see, e.g., Cooper 2000; Stone 2000). Typically psychologists distinguish between narcissism that represents a healthy form of self-investment reflective of an autonomous and strong self, and its pathological counterpart, characterized by an excessive sense of self-entitlement, grandeur, and resentment toward others as well as an exploitative overdependence on them. And although it is common in everyday life to think of narcissists as being grandiose show-offs, psychologists in fact further identify a covert type of pathological narcissism, one that is characterized by an outward hypersensitivity and vulnerability but that ultimately masks a deep-seated or hidden grandiosity.[2]

Based on our close reading of *Habits of the Heart,* it is this hypersensitive narcissism that seems to offer a fair characterization of the individuals discussed by Bellah and his colleagues (1985) who seek relationships that are primarily based on therapeutic self-interests and feelings. The despair, fragility, and search for deliverance from personal pain that are said to characterize spiritual seekers (Beit-Hallahmi 1992; Wuthnow 1998) equally characterize hypersensitive narcissists. Because hypersensitive narcissists, unlike their willful counterparts, experience emotional pain and are prone to self-reflection, they are also more likely to seek privatized solutions to personal problems typified by a reliance on psychotherapy or spiritual seeking. It is reasonable to assume that, because of their self-focus and desire for immediate gratification and transient relationships, hypersensitive narcissists would have little truck with organized religion and its ethos of social responsibility and commitment to others. Rather, these individuals should be attracted to the therapeutic and spiritual discourse, with its emphasis on self-exploration, self-fulfillment, and feeling good.

Healthy narcissists, on the other hand, have a self-investment that derives not from vulnerability but from openness to new experiences and an interest in personal growth (see, e.g., Wink 1991a, 1991b). For this type of person, therefore, interest in spiritual seeking would be an extension of their commitment to personal growth and exploration. It could be argued, of course, that healthy self-investment should not be called narcissistic in the first place because it does not have pathological connotations or negative implications for psychosocial functioning. For the purpose of our research, however, the ultimate resolution of this categorization question is not important. Rather, what is central to our investigation is that being self-oriented does not necessarily have to be pathological.

We investigated the links between different types of narcissism or self-investment and spiritual seeking among our study participants, using ratings of narcissism from early adulthood, psychotherapy in middle adulthood, and spiritual seeking in late adulthood.[3] Between the interviews in early adulthood (1958) and those in middle adulthood (1970 through 1982), 25 percent of the study participants had at least some involvement in psychotherapy, a figure comparable to the national rates for middle-aged Americans during the 1970s.[4]

Our analyses uncovered remarkable findings that underscore the need for a nuanced understanding of the links among narcissism, psychotherapy, and spiritual seeking. We found that individuals in our study who scored high on hypersensitive narcissism in early adulthood (age thirties; 1958) were likely to seek psychotherapy in middle age, and we also found that psychotherapy in middle adulthood was positively related to spiritual seeking in late adulthood. Our data also showed that hypersensitive narcissism was negatively related to religiousness and indeed to altruism in late adulthood. These findings support the claim (e.g., Bellah et al. 1985; Beit-Hallahmi 1992) that fragile and depleted self-oriented individuals seek out psychotherapy and avoid commitment to others. However, we found no evidence indicating a relation between hypersensitive narcissism in either early or late adulthood and spiritual seeking in late adulthood. In other words, although our data showed a link between hypersensitive narcissism and psychotherapy, and a link between psychotherapy and spiritual seeking, there was no association between hypersensitive narcissism and spiritual seeking.

For Emma Mallory, psychotherapy did not lead to spiritual growth; she was also among our study's highest scorers on hypersensitive narcissism. Emma's childhood and adolescence were dominated by a strong-willed yet conflicted father who, in a rags-to-riches story, made money in the meatpacking and distribution business. Although they lived in an affluent neighborhood and Emma went to an elite private school, she was forced by her father to wear secondhand clothes from a thrift shop so she would not forget her family's humble beginnings. Although fiercely loyal to him, and sharing his sense of superiority over people who couldn't pull *themselves* up by their bootstraps, Emma felt resentful about her clothes and she envied those of her peers. She also felt humiliated that her father had no formal education.

After graduating from college, Emma married a very pleasant and accommodating medical doctor, whom she appreciated for his kindness but resented for his lack of ambition. Emma's embroilment in her parents' nasty divorce when she was in her midthirties precipitated an episode of depression, and she sought treatment by going into psychotherapy. Therapy made her feel better and got her "back on track," as she said in her middle-adulthood interview (in 1970), but it did nothing to change her deep sensitivity to slight and her resentment of others. When asked about belief in God, she responded, "I truthfully don't believe in God. . . . I don't feel the necessity for this belief." She did comment, however, that she had "a strong belief in the oneness of things, . . . that maybe there is an ultimate reality underneath things. You take psychological problems or physical problems or chemical problems or anything, and there will be some kind of formula or something at the root of it." Emma, however, did not build on her sense of "the oneness of things," and twelve years later, her life was devoid of any sense of awe, whether religious, spiritual, or secular. The IHD staff member who interviewed Emma in middle age (at age fifty-four, 1982) commented, "It was my impression that somehow the world existed only in relation to herself, that she had little perception of a relationship to the world other than as it impinged upon herself."

When she was interviewed in late adulthood (1999), Emma was still married, but she had no friends and was not involved in any hobbies or social activities. When asked about the place of religion in her life, she responded dismissively, "I don't know what that is. . . . My father was an atheist." Nor did she think there was any ultimate meaning or purpose for her life: she felt people were "no more than ants." The aging Emma also took a dim view of the world's future and thought it was heading "to a not very good place."

But the story of our research on narcissism and spiritual seeking does not end with Emma Mallory. Having failed to find a relation between spiritual seeking and hypersensitive narcissism, we next explored the relations among spiritual seeking, psychotherapy, and autonomous narcissism, the healthy self-investment associated with a strong, self-actualizing self. In accord with the expectation that this type of person would be likely to engage in spiritual seeking, our data showed that this was in fact the case. We found a positive relation between autonomous narcissism in early adulthood and spiritual seeking in late adulthood. The analysis showed, however, that this relationship became insignificant when psychotherapy in middle adulthood was taken into account. But we found instead a significant path from autonomous narcissism in early adulthood to psychotherapy in middle adulthood and from therapy in middle adulthood to spiritual seeking in late adulthood (see the bold arrows in figure 6). Thus, psychotherapy acted as a mediator of the path from healthy narcissism in early adulthood to spiritual seeking in late adulthood. Moreover, the path between autonomous narcissism in early adulthood, psychotherapy in middle adulthood, and then spiritual seeking in late adulthood remained significant after we controlled for religiousness, spiritual seeking, and psychotherapy in early adulthood.[5]

Our results thus indicated that spiritual seeking in late adulthood was particularly characteristic of individuals who in early adulthood were highly autonomous—who were characterized by independence, high aspirations for the self, and wide-ranging interests—and who subsequently entered psychotherapy by midlife. In the 1970s (when our participants were in middle adulthood), psychotherapy was not as popular as it is today. It is likely, therefore, that those who went into therapy did so because of some personal crisis, as we saw with Jane Bell, Peter Jones, and Kate Ward—all of whom were spiritual seekers in late adulthood and had had personal crises and therapy in early or middle adulthood.

In sum, although both autonomous and hypersensitive narcissism in early adulthood were related to involvement in psychotherapy in middle adulthood, it was only the autonomous narcissists who were spiritual seekers in late adulthood. This suggests that spiritual seeking tends to develop as a result of personal strength (autonomy) rather than fragility (hypersensitivity). Psychologically depleted individuals who therapeutically use others to prop themselves up and who thus exploit rather than mutually engage with others are similarly unable to commit to the discipline of a spiritual path and are, perhaps, unwilling to inject a sense of mystery and awe into their lives. In short, then, narcissism and psychotherapy are connected to spiritual seeking, but this connection bears fruit only for those whose narcissism is grounded in healthy

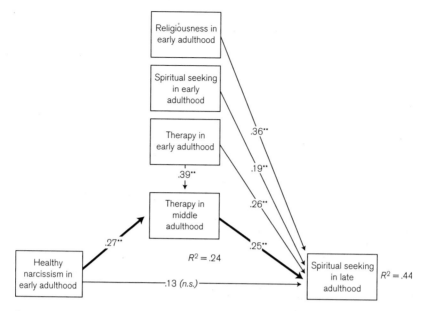

Figure 6. Path analytic model depicting relations among narcissism, therapy, and spiritual seeking. * $p < .05$; ** $p < .01$. Redrawn with permission from Paul Wink, Michele Dillon, and Kristen Fay, 2005, "Spiritual Seeking, Narcissism, and Psychotherapy: How Are They Related?" *Journal for the Scientific Study of Religion* 44: 153, figure 3. Copyright Blackwell Publishing.

self-investment and who use therapy as a means to change rather than as an end in itself. But do these findings of a more nuanced relationship among narcissism, psychotherapy, and spiritual seeking go far enough to assuage concern that spiritual seeking may still nonetheless be detrimental to social responsibility and concern for others?

RELIGIOUSNESS, SPIRITUAL SEEKING, AND CONCERN FOR OTHERS

Not surprisingly, given the large body of research showing a strong positive association between religiousness and concern for others (e.g., Putnam 2000; Rossi 2001; Wilson and Musick 1997), the study participants who received high scores on religiousness also received high scores on generativity, a term coined by Erikson (1964) to refer to the individual's concern for the welfare of future generations. This was the case whether we used an interview-based assessment of the person's generativity or relied on their own self-reported answers.[6] It was evident from their interviews in late adulthood that our highly religious participants were generous toward others; they were aware of and sympathetic to the needs of others, and they responded to the perceived needs of others in a responsible and dependable manner (see table 8, CAQ Generativity Scale). Moreover, highly religious individuals reported that they were altruistic and caring toward others (see table 8, Loyola Generativity Scale).

The spiritual seekers in our study, however, also scored high on generativity. They were especially likely to show awareness of the needs of other individuals and groups. And, they were just as likely as their church-centered religious peers to report that they were altruistic and concerned about others. But unlike highly religious individuals, they acknowledged a desire to have an effect on others, and stated that they had creative and other worthwhile skills and knowledge they would like to pass on to others. The generativity of spiritual seekers thus included a strong self-expansive focus on making creative or artistic contributions that would variously effect others and that would endure beyond their lifetime, whereas the generativity of our highly religious study participants appeared to be motivated primarily by a selfless altruism—the desire to simply help others, irrespective of any long-term impact that doing so might have on their own personal legacy (see table 8).[7] Clearly, when people help others, regardless of whether their motivation is more self-expansive or selfless, they find fulfillment for themselves; it truly is in giving that we receive, as affirmed by the prayer of Saint Francis and by many of the proverbs of everyday life. This truth emerged again and again in our late-adulthood interviews. Nonetheless, how people act on their generative concerns necessarily reflects their own personal style and everyday context. The differences characterizing the generative interests of our religious and spiritual study participants fitted with their different personality traits and ways of being. Importantly, however, notwithstanding these differences, both religiousness and spiritual seeking were positively associated with concern for others.

Once again, as with our participants' everyday activities and social attitudes (chapter 8), our data showed significant long-term patterns over the life course. Specifically, early adulthood religiousness and late-middle adulthood spiritual seeking were related to concern for others in late adulthood. It is also noteworthy that the ethos of social concern historically associated with mainline Protestants found clear expression in our data. Irrespective of whether the study participants were highly religious or spiritual seeking individuals, generative interests and behavior were particularly evident among the mainline Protestants, in contrast to our study's nonmainline Protestants and Catholics.[8]

TABLE 8. RELATIONS AMONG RELIGIOUSNESS, SPIRITUAL SEEKING, AND GENERATIVITY IN LATE ADULTHOOD

Generativity	Religiousness		Spiritual Seeking	
	r	*Partial* r	r	*Partial* r
CAQ Generativity Scale	.33**	.28**	.28**	.13*
Givingness	.25**	.24**	.06	−.01
Social perspective	.34**	.22**	.54**	.48**
Prosocial competence	.18*	.21*	−.06	−.12
Loyola Generativity Scale	.20*	.12	.30**	.25**
Altruism	.26**	.21*	.24**	.17*
Impact on others	.14	.08	.20*	.17*
Outliving the self	.14	.08	.20*	.17*
Creative activities	−.30	−.11	.24**	.26**

NOTE: $N = 153$ for the CAQ Generativity Scale, and $N = 156$ for the Loyola Generativity Scale. In the case of religiousness, the partial r controls for overlap with spiritual seeking, and in the case of spiritual seeking, the partial r controls for overlap with religiousness.
 * $p < .05$; ** $p < .01$.

Because the generativity associated with spiritual seeking has a more self-expansive component than that associated with religiousness, it may well raise doubts in some readers' minds as to whether it truly indicates a concern for others and for the social good. We further probed this by examining the extent to which religiousness and spiritual seeking were related to social activism, based on our study participants' engagement in a variety of political and community issues in late adulthood, from helping the homeless to civil rights issues. The types of involvement we asked about included signing a petition, contributing money, attending a meeting, attending a rally, contacting a public official, and being a member of an activist organization. Based on the sum of our participants' diverse types of involvement across a range of social issues, our analyses showed that individuals who scored high on either religiousness or spiritual seeking tended to be active in helping the homeless. Religiousness was also associated with activism to prevent neighborhood crime and with support for the pro-life movement. In contrast, spiritual seeking was associated with engagement in environmental causes, civil rights issues, AIDS activism, antiwar efforts, and the advocacy of women's rights

TABLE 9. RELATIONS AMONG RELIGIOUSNESS,
SPIRITUAL SEEKING, AND INVOLVEMENT IN
SOCIAL CAUSES IN LATE ADULTHOOD

	Religiousness		Spiritual Seeking	
Social Cause	r	*Partial* r	r	*Partial* r
Homelessness	.22*	.13	.32**	.28**
Crime/Neighborhood Watch	.23*	.23*	.04	−.04
Pro-life	.38**	.38**	.09	−.04
Women's rights	.05	−.04	.24**	.24**
AIDS	−.07	−.15	.21*	.24**
Environment	.07	−.08	.41**	.41**
Civil rights	.04	−.07	.39**	.30**
Antiwar/peace	−.08	−.23*	.36**	.41**

NOTE: $N = 117$. Involvement in a cause is an average of self-reported ratings on signing a petition, contributing money, attending a meeting, contacting a public official, membership in an activist organization, and attending a rally. In the case of religiousness, the partial r controls for overlap with spiritual seeking, and in the case of spiritual seeking, the partial r controls for overlap with religiousness.
  * $p < .05$; ** $p < .01$.

(see table 9). In sum, both religiousness and spiritual seeking were associated with individuals' engagement in various social causes, though the focus differed, except in the shared activism on behalf of the homeless.

Given that our data replicate the well-established positive link between church-based religiousness and social responsibility, it is all the more credible that these same data also demonstrate a link between non-church-centered spiritual seeking and concern for others. Our findings on the relationship between spiritual seeking and social responsibility, therefore, make an especially innovative and significant contribution. The increasing prevalence of Americans who dissociate from organized religion (Hout and Fischer 2002) accentuates the related concern that the role of churches in fostering social responsibility is diminishing. Importantly, our findings indicate that spiritual seeking is conducive to altruism and to achieving the social perspective that leads individuals to care for others and to actively contribute to the common good.

Our findings on spiritual seeking may not fully mitigate the concerns of cultural commentators who recognize the critical role that churches have played in fostering social responsibility, but these findings should offer assurance that concern for others can spring from many different streams. Further, our data also suggest that we should be willing to look for evidence of concern for others in places and activities not typically associated with church-based community caregiving. As Amanda Porterfield notes, Americans revitalize the spiritual culture of their communities through participation in diverse activities, many of which have no relation to church (2001: 20). While spiritual seekers and highly religious individuals share a commitment to altruism and social activism, some of their generative interests clearly differ in distinct ways. These differences matter. Nonetheless, although the practical implications of helping out in one's neighborhood are clearly different from leaving a legacy of artistic drawings, both acts touch others' lives in enriching ways. By extension, these activities can help others to cultivate trust in and appreciation for the web of social relations that all individuals are by definition necessarily involved in. Such appreciation, in turn, can foster a greater sense of social responsibility among all (cf. Bellah et al. 1991: 275). Most critically, self-investment and concern for others are not antithetical (see, e.g., Erikson 1964), an insight illustrated by the lives of two of our study participants, Laura Goodall and Melissa White.

EXEMPLARS OF GENERATIVITY

LAURA GOODALL

On Christmas Day 1975, Laura, at age forty-seven, was vacationing with her husband and children in their Sierra mountain cabin when her husband announced he wanted a divorce. He then promptly drove off, leaving Laura with the immediate logistical problem of packing herself and their five adolescent children into her sports coupe for the four-hour journey back to the Bay Area. This logistical hurdle was compounded for Laura by the chronic arthritis and bad psoriasis that she had been having for the previous six years. The divorce settlement left Laura in deep financial straits. Although a successful business executive, Jack, in the months prior to leaving Laura, had divested himself of virtually all his assets. Because Laura was a public school teacher with an independent income and pension plan, the divorce settlement gave Jack half her salary and retirement annuity. What Laura received was a court order to vacate the family home. The divorce was all the more painful for Laura because it revived memories of when her own father had deserted the family when she was in high school.

This narrative of family disruption and health problems might suggest that Laura would be more self-protective than socially generous. But this is far from true. In fact, Laura is one of the most selfless and generous participants in our study. She is also someone for whom religion is critically important.

Religion was not emphasized in Laura's family when she was growing up; both her parents were leaders in community organizations, and although her mother was a devout Christian, her father was an agnostic who believed that "the whole thing was hogwash," and that religion should not be forced on people. Nonetheless, in adolescence, Laura went to the Episcopalian Sunday school for a few years with one of her neighbors and also attended the youth group at the Congregational Church. Later in high school, she was confirmed an Episcopalian, something that her mother was "quite delighted" about but not her father.

In college, Laura met her husband, who had qualified as an engineer, and, in keeping with the baby boom demographic explosion following the end of the Second World War, they had five children in quick succession. Like so many young mothers in the 1950s, Laura was highly involved in the church: she attended weekly Episcopalian services and directed the church's youth group. Religion, she explained, "is very important in my life, and I feel it's terribly important for the children too. We never miss Sunday school or church if we can help it. And it helps. It's a wonderful crutch. It's something to lean on in a time of crisis." But religion also bolstered Laura's strong sense of social responsibility and her commitment to living her Christian beliefs. For Laura, being a "practicing" Christian demanded that she contribute her time to various church and community endeavors. She commented,

> I'm trying to be a good Christian. I don't know if I am one, but I really do try. I try to be a good mother. I do know that I'm always trying to do the best that I can. . . . I have an idealistic feeling about others. I do try to see the best in everyone, and think that others do too. I know some don't, and I do get so annoyed with hypocritical Christians. It bothers me. I like to look at things in a positive way and give people the benefit of the doubt. Often I've found that, when I haven't, I [then discover] that really they are very nice people.

Laura's positive view of human nature was aided by her belief that God gave each of her children, "and perhaps everyone in the world, something special." It was also evident that she admired generous people such as her mother, whom she described as someone who "sort of dedicates her life for others." Demonstrating moreover the mutuality characteristic of the ethic of care for others (Erikson 1964), Laura, at age forty-two, observed that getting a middle-ear infection and temporarily losing her hearing had been a positive experience for her, because she "came out with a totally, beautifully, new understanding of deaf people."

Religious faith was a constant resource for Laura throughout adulthood, and when in her late forties she was confronted out of the blue with her husband's request for a divorce, prayer helped her cope with its emotional trauma and everyday burdens. Indeed, Laura converted to Catholicism in 1976, "right during the divorce mess." As is usually the case with religious conversions, Laura's decision was neither impulsive nor based on any radical personal transformation, notwithstanding her divorce. She had long been interested in Catholicism and had spoken of this during her early-adulthood interview (1958), when she commented approvingly of its closeness to Episcopalianism. The catalyst for her decision was, ironically, a trip to Rome she had made with her husband and some of his business associates in the spring of 1975 as part of the church's Holy Year celebrations. Going to Rome, Laura said, "was a wonderful opportunity to see the Catholic Church firsthand—we had a thrilling trip. I loved it. I loved all the Masses and the beauty of it and the pomp and circumstance, and loved the darling people; it was just a thrill for me. It really was that stepping-stone I needed. I came back and started taking religious instruction, and . . . I had tremendous support and counseling from several priests."

Not surprisingly, Laura's impending divorce made her slightly hesitant about joining the Catholic Church, because she felt she might want to remarry and was concerned about the church's opposition to divorce. After much soul searching, Laura "finally decided it was important, and went ahead and joined the church. . . . It really made a difference in my life and future. It was a big step, a huge step. . . . It just turned out to be a very happy thing and super supportive. And it's just been marvelous, other than a few zaps—like my aunt, who will have very little to do with me, mainly because of Catholicism. But it's just been a beautiful part of my life and a beautiful healing."

In view of Erikson's reference to the prayer of Saint Francis as an exemplar of generativity (1964), it is noteworthy that Laura actually referred to it as one of the "beautiful" prayers she turned to for strength. Asked about her usual response to trouble, she said,

I have some good books, religious books. And I usually turn to those. . . . One, for instance, is *Instrument of Thy Peace*. It's all done from a prayer of Saint Francis's. And it's a beautiful, beautiful thing. Another one . . . is *What Do I Say to God?* There are prayers for all kinds of problems you might have in your life, particularly as a wife and mother. It was written by a woman, and she's done a beautiful job. It's interesting. I think there's a lot more of the Divine Being around us than we ever think about or give credit to. When I'm particularly troubled by something, I can open the book, and it always seems to be the kind of prayer I need. And I'll test it. I'll close the book and open it up again [laughs], and I'll find another one just as good, just as appropriate. It can't be coincidence. . . . I have another one, *Prayer Really Works*. That's my bible. It's the kind you can open up and get some really substantive point from at any time.

Although Laura experienced multiple health problems throughout adulthood, debilitating ailments that could have caused her to turn inward and become self-preoccupied, she continued instead to be remarkably energetic in caring for others. Quite impressively, after her older brother was killed in an airplane crash, Laura made a financial sacrifice so that she could take an active role in caring for his family. Up until midlife, Laura followed the typical "feminine" role pattern of marriage, mothering, and church involvement, and her caring for others was defined within these traditional contexts. Buoyed perhaps by the spirit of the women's movement, she expanded her social roles, completing a master's degree in special education in the early 1970s. "Physically and mentally exhausting," Laura's occupational decision to teach "superdependent" emotionally troubled children and adolescents for ten years was clearly generative.

Her subsequent work showed an even broader communal concern when, in 1980, she married her second husband (after she had received an annulment) and, catching the wave of public concern about the environment (see, e.g., Putnam 2000: 155–56), they started a nature store. They saw the store not as a moneymaking enterprise but as a service to a larger good. As Laura said, "It's a thrilling store, and we don't look to it as a means of making money. We feel very good about what we're doing. If it's just a message to the public, and we can scrape out a living from it, that's all we want" (1982, age fifty-four). Asked to comment on how she had changed now that she was in her fifties, Laura responded, "I think I use the church and the Lord more; I find a great deal of strength that way. I think there is often a reason, God-given, for things happening, and I think I'm learning to be more patient. In other words, if you want something and don't get it, he's saying something very loud and clear to you. So I've learned to be patient and know there is a reason things happen."

Fifteen years later, in 1997, Laura and her husband were still working full-time in their low-profit nature store despite her continuing health problems. They had good relationships with her five children and his two from an earlier marriage, and both enjoyed having their grandchildren stay with them during school vacations. Laura attended church weekly, and, saying that faith was the guiding principle of her life, she was still emphatic about her responsibility to live out her religion and to feel that she was "doing something really worthwhile. . . . It's always been important to me that I've done something I thought would contribute to society." Reflecting on her nature store, she commented,

> We have made a living for ourselves, but not much more than that. We're very happy with what we're doing. We believe in what we're doing. One of our major things is trying to make people aware, particularly children and the young generation, how fortunate we are to have this beautiful world, and [that we should] try and take better care of it. . . . We're contributing to help maintain this environment that is so beautiful, that the Lord created for us. . . . Probably my religion is more the here and now, and on earth. . . . I think I'm more concerned with the now. And maybe I shouldn't be. But I'd rather see us being better Christians here on earth at this point.

Laura's life epitomizes the tight connections we have long associated with church-centered religiousness and concern for others. Not all highly religious Americans display the same expansive commitment to others and to the common good as Laura did. Jay Campbell confined his generative concerns to caring for his large family and mentoring his students. Ian Logan's generativity was primarily seen in his long-standing commitment to working with his local church's youth group, while Joan Sweeney's altar-decorating activities were a generative outlet for her. Both Susan Moore and Barbara Shaw showed concern for others in their outreach to young married couples, and Barbara, of course, also hosted and organized social events for her local Baptist Church. Ellen Quinn's generativity went beyond church service: she cooked and delivered meals to AIDS patients in her town. Our data thus confirmed that religious individuals are likely to be engaged in activities that show concern for others, whether within church circles or further afield.

MELISSA WHITE

While the connection between religiousness and generativity is straightforward across adulthood, the slower development of spiritual seeking as a postmidlife phenomenon means that the association between spiritual seeking and generativity is more obvious in later life (as we saw with Peter; chapter 8). Melissa White illustrates the fact that, especially in late adulthood, spiritual seeking and commitment to the welfare of others can go hand in hand. Melissa also demonstrates the link between autonomous (healthy) narcissism and spiritual seeking. She grew up in a high-status (see chapter 3), but conflict-ridden, family that existed behind a facade of social conformity and politeness. Her father was moody and aggressive; her mother was controlling and critical and constantly negated Melissa's desire for privacy and independence. Melissa's younger brother dealt with family conflict by siding with his parents, leaving Melissa to be the family scapegoat. The family was not particularly religious, though Melissa attended a Presbyterian Sunday school regularly and in high school was a member of the young people's group at the Congregational Church, where she had a boyfriend.

During each of the four adulthood interviews, Melissa's memory of family life centered on a pivotal scene that occurred when she was in college: coming back home after a date, she was locked out of the house by her mother who saw and disapproved of Melissa kissing her boyfriend good night. For Melissa this was the final episode in a long series of family conflicts, and soon after the incident, she married her boyfriend, despite having serious misgivings about his emotional maturity. Not unexpectedly, the marriage turned out badly. When interviewed at age thirty, the "rock bottom" in her adult life, Melissa was depressed. She felt alienated from her husband and incapable of taking adequate care of her son and daughter. Following her realization that she was beginning to mistreat her daughter just as her mother had mistreated her, Melissa entered psychotherapy in the early 1950s and, at the time of her early adulthood interview (1958), was seeing a therapist every two weeks. After a long separation from her husband, Melissa divorced him. A potter, Melissa sold her work in local stores and galleries, qualified as an adult education teacher, and supplemented her income by teaching art classes to children and adults.

Melissa benefited considerably from psychotherapy. In particular, she developed insight into the feelings of passivity and lack of assertiveness that had contributed to her troubled interpersonal relations. The psychologist who interviewed Melissa in 1970 described her as someone who is "almost excruciatingly honest and direct" and who refuses to let herself "off the hook" over emotionally difficult issues (such as her relationship with her parents). During the interview, Melissa, at age forty-two, commented on her positive experience: "Psychotherapy literally changed everything I'd ever thought. I had to rework and undo everything I'd ever learned. . . . I felt it was so strenuous, that it was more than anyone could ever expect anyone to do. Like changing everything you've ever thought—it's just too much. . . . Like you have only so much adaptive energy and you use it up. I just felt like I was using up all my adaptive energy to change myself. And so it was really great for me."

Thus, unlike Emma Mallory, who used therapy simply to feel better, Melissa saw psychotherapy not as a formula but as an arduous task and a way of learning about herself and growing as a person. And, unlike Emma, she had the psychological resources and the desire to confront her inner demons, a process that in turn freed her to develop a sense of awe and grow spiritually. After entering psychotherapy, Melissa attended several different churches. She went for a while to the Unitarian Church but then stopped. She explained at the time, in 1958, "I have my own brand. . . . I really figure out what I myself think about religion. . . . I haven't thought about it hard enough to give it up, though. Theoretically I could just stop." She expressed a similar view in midlife, during the 1970 interview, stating, "I think everyone has their own brand of religion," and as a socially reserved person, she saw churches as having little relevance to her spiritual yearnings. "Churches seem irrelevant to it [spirituality]. Religion is such a social thing. I mean all these churches [I have visited]—I really didn't think they had anything to do with spirituality."

Asked whether she believed in God, Melissa said, "I think there might be some kind of a life force, but I wouldn't call it a god. I guess I don't like the word *god*. But I am certainly willing to believe. There is plenty that isn't known. I really object to organized religions being closed systems—like, they say they know everything." Melissa didn't believe in heaven or hell but entertained the possibility of reincarnation. She had a vision of the world as a total ecosystem, with all its living organisms equally sacred: "I think that everything is sort of sacred. . . . A person is part of everything that is alive, part of the total." Thus, for Melissa, cutting down trees was an act as "irreligious" as killing other living beings.

By age fifty-four, Melissa had found an outlet for her spiritual needs. She was a regular participant in two different meditation groups and an avid reader of Jungian psychology, and she had embarked on Shamanic journeys. From the early 1970s onward, Melissa had developed the habit of writing down her dreams and treating them like a "running commentary" on her life that tapped the (Jungian) archetypical forces within her psyche. These spiritual journeys led her to have out-of-body experiences, and she used these encounters as confirmations of some kind of life after death and of reincarnation. In addition to gaining spiritual growth, Melissa had also become more engaged in the outside world. She was active in a number of potters' groups, and supported several environmental organizations, including the Sierra Club, the Nature Conservancy, the Environmental Defense Fund, and Save the Bay.

When interviewed at age sixty-nine, Melissa was retired and spending contented days on a four-acre coastal property she had inherited from her parents, though she grieved for a close friend who had recently died and whose spiritual presence she felt when she undertook shamanic journeys, something she frequently did. Melissa had completed training that allowed her to be a senior peer counselor, a volunteer role to which she was highly committed. She liked "talking to people" and thus also enjoyed the peer-counseling-supervision discussion group she attended weekly, as well as a women's group. Melissa also maintained close relations with her adult children and continued to get a lot of satisfaction from her pottery and garden work, square-dancing with friends, and financially supporting environmental causes. For a time in her midsixties, Melissa had attended services at the Episcopal Church, where she liked the reform-minded and "dynamic" minister who had been kind to her around the time of her mother's funeral. But though she regarded it and other religious traditions as "fine," and described them as being "like different paths up the mountain," church liturgy and traditional prayers were too formalized for her; she preferred to get "into a real meditative state" when she prayed. She thus continued to practice intensive meditation and regularly participated in a drumming circle as well.

Talking about how she saw the place of spirituality in her life, Melissa said, "I think we are all connected, and there's not a lot of accident in who you meet, and what you are doing with them. It pays to live by the Golden Rule as often as you can." Notably, among our study participants Melissa scored well below the average on authoritarianism, and her antiauthoritarianism came through when she talked about her values. When asked to describe her beliefs and values, Melissa responded, "I'm not sure that I think in those terms usually. I guess I'm interested in finding out what's true versus illusion. I try not to be trapped in illusion. What comes to mind is what some author says . . . I'm not sure I can quote her right: 'Consider possibilities, believe nothing.'" Melissa interpreted this aphorism not as a sign of nihilism or of skepticism but as a reminder to keep an open mind and try to experience different points of view. She elaborated: "Open-mindedness is one [value]. I like to experience different points of view. I don't like for people to say, 'Well, that couldn't be true.'" Extending this ethos, she saw her own spirituality as something that "worked" for her, but quickly pointed out that she didn't know whether it was "ultimately true." And unlike Dorothy Marshall, she was unreserved in her support for the women's movement, seeing it as part of a larger struggle for social equality and part of the effort to "resist the dominator model."

In sum, Melissa illustrates how the generative interests and activities of spiritual individuals differ somewhat from those who are highly religious. Like other highly spiritual individuals in our study, Melissa enjoyed artistic activities, she had a strong interest in personal growth and self-realization, and, reminiscent of Kate Ward (chapter 7), she had a continuing interest in expanding her knowledge of the world. Despite her self-focus, however, she was not disinterested in others; she maintained good relations with her children, valued her friendships, and participated in social groups. In particular, Melissa's volunteer work as a peer counselor was clearly driven by altruism. Similarly, she cared about social equality and the health of the global ecosystem, and for many years she had acted on her environmental concerns through her financial contributions.

CARING FOR THE SELF AND OTHERS

Given the evidence of a shift in contemporary American society toward non-church-centered religion, it is clearly important for social scientists to empirically assess the social implications of newer forms of religious and spiritual engagement. Most of the research on religion and civic and social participation, however, compares churchgoers or the religiously affiliated with nonchurchgoers or uses measures of spirituality that rely on self-reported personal experiences and descriptors.[9] Such self-reported categorizations of spirituality do not require the same behavioral threshold that is customarily used in assessing traditional religious commitment indicated, for example, by weekly church attendance. Consequently, these studies do not fully discriminate between truly nonreligious and nonspiritual individuals and individuals who do not go to church but who are disciplined about their spiritual growth beyond simply describing themselves as spiritual. When these un-churched but spiritually disciplined people are pooled with religiously unaffiliated individuals in general, the resulting statistical findings may obscure the ways their social behavior differs from that of individuals who are neither religious nor spiritual (as well as how it differs from that of individuals engaged in church-centered religiousness).

The patterns in our findings provide strong evidence that spiritual seeking—assessed in accord with our high threshold definition requir-ing the individual to engage regularly in intentional spiritual practices, such as meditation, and not assessed simply on the basis of a self-re-ported personal descriptor—is positively related to altruism and dem-onstrating concern for others and society. Our results indicate that both church-centered religiousness and non-church-centered spiritual seek-ing are associated with concern for others. Clearly, the positive relation between spiritual seeking and generativity found in our study partici-pants may be a function of the sociohistorical context in which their lives unfolded—both cohorts are, after all, members of the long civic generation in America. It is evident, nonetheless, that disciplined spiri-tual seeking, similar to church-centered participation, is conducive to developing social awareness that focuses the individual's attention and behavior on the needs of other individuals and groups.

Although we found that spiritual seeking had a strong connection with the self-expansive aspects of generativity, our data also indicated that spiritual seeking was not driven by the narcissistic needs of a fragile self. Our spiritual seekers were self-invested, but this self-in-vestment sprung from their deep sense of personal autonomy and was not pathologically grounded. Indeed, narcissistically hypersensitive individuals were unable to use psychotherapy to turn their self-focus into spiritual growth. The patterns in our data on the links among narcissism, psychotherapy, and spiritual seeking underscored, in fact, the idea that the ability to take care of others necessitates a strong or autonomous sense of self.

Our findings indicating a positive relation between spiritual seeking and concern for others should help dispel concerns about the exces-sive self-absorption of spiritual seekers. Our study suggests that there is more than one pathway to the development of an ethic of care for others. Although involvement in a religious tradition provides individu-als with more systematic messages concerning the value of neighborly love, and structured ways of getting involved in caring for others, the individual journeying and self-growth associated with spiritual seeking are also conducive to developing a sense of connectedness and social commitment. The spiritual journeying of Melissa White, Peter Jones, and Jane Bell, and of Kate Ward (who complemented her spiritual journeying with a lifelong involvement in church and social concerns), was, in part, self-seeking and therapeutic, but its outcome resulted in an expanded social engagement rather than social withdrawal.

In this, the spiritual seekers in our study illustrate the power of American culture to orient action in a pragmatic and this-worldly way, rather than in a more mystical direction. Accordingly, just as American religion has historically emphasized socially responsible action in the everyday world (Parsons 1967: 419; see chapter 4), so too, perhaps, the American therapeutic culture, if harnessed to a disciplined spiritual seeking, can lead to engagement in socially responsible activities. Consequently, the social implications of both church-centered religion and a disciplined spiritual seeking may have more in common than is sometimes recognized.

10

The Buffering Role of Religion in Late Adulthood

When we interviewed David Allen at his sun-drenched home on the shore of Lake Tahoe in the summer of 1997, he was as articulate, insightful, optimistic, and energetic at age seventy-six as he had been during earlier interviews in his thirties, forties, and fifties. Retired from an economically successful career in which he combined high school teaching and a mountain resort business, David continued to work part-time restoring and managing rental property. He was highly involved in local community politics, and as a committed member of the League to Save Lake Tahoe, David was at the vanguard of a struggle to curb overdevelopment of the lakeshore. He was also active in the Sierra Club and a member of SIRS (Sons in Retirement), a retired men's group whose local chapter presented a monthly luncheon and speaker series. With no physical ailments or complaints, David continued to ski and hike, and he played in a weekly golf tournament with a group of mixed-age men with whom he also socialized. David and his wife had made several trips to Europe, and he took much pleasure in the good relations he had with his adult children, despite earlier tensions with them surrounding his divorce from their mother in the early 1960s. He was especially generous to his grandchildren and, on the day of the interview, had just purchased a new computer for his college-bound granddaughter. Two years earlier, David had invited four of his children and their children for an all-expense-paid skiing trip to Austria and Italy.

Although David was in excellent physical health and full of energy—he had played twenty-seven holes of golf in the sweltering Nevada heat the day before our interview—he fully accepted his age: "I look at [being older] as a part of the life process. . . . And I have no fear whatsoever of growing older and dying. I just hope that I don't deteriorate to a point where I'm a burden on myself or on anyone else." David's contentment and high life satisfaction in late adulthood derived in large part from his pride in having raised five fine children, although, at the time of the interview, he was still grieving over the death of his oldest son, Oliver. When Oliver's health had begun to deteriorate from AIDS, he had asked his father, who was licensed to perform weddings, to marry him and his partner. The ceremony took place at a family gathering in San Francisco. Sadly, less than two years later, David received a phone call from Oliver, who told him that he would not survive the night and had wanted to say a final good-bye. David also took considerable pride in the part he had played in shaping young lives as a history teacher. Several times during the interview, he mentioned unexpected encounters with his past students, and their various comments telling him, as one recently had, "You know, you were one of the most important teachers in my life." David clearly derived as much pleasure from the altruism of teaching as from the monetary rewards of a successful business career.

The vibrancy of David Allen's everyday life in his seventies is at odds with a view of late adulthood eloquently evoked in contemporary fictional literature (e.g., Roth 2006), a view that until recently was dominant among social scientists (e.g., Erikson 1951, 1982; Butler 1963). His aging is devoid of the personal despair thought to accompany the onset of the realization that one's mortality is no longer in the remote future but in the near future. As was true for the majority of our study participants, David's transition to late adulthood was characterized by continuity rather than change, and David lacked a tendency to dwell on past achievements, mistakes, and lost opportunities. When asked whether he now reflected more on his life, David stated, "I think occasionally I do, but it's kind of a rarity that I go back and try and dig [things] up. . . . I rarely reflect. I think I'm looking much more forward. . . . I just think you're a lot better off looking ahead and trying to plan for next year and plant a few fruit trees that twenty years from now will bear fruit."[1]

What is also striking about David's rich and purposeful life in late adulthood is that he was among the least religious of our study participants. David had been religiously involved as a youth, and for a while in his thirties he took the lead in organizing the building of a new Presbyterian church in the suburbs north of San Francisco. He had wryly commented at the time that, though he was active in building the church, he was not an active worshipper; he felt religion was more of a "wholesome social" than a spiritual experience. Church continued to be unimportant in David's life subsequently, though his religious background still informed his ethical views in late adulthood. He commented, "I'm certainly an agnostic and probably an atheist at this point. But the religious principles that [I learned at Sunday school] still have a good deal of influence. And I think also the Boy Scout oath and all of those moral principles are still quite strong [in me]." Nevertheless, David did not need church or the spiritual engagement that was so important to many of our study participants to anchor his life or enrich its meaning. He summarized his view of religion, saying,

> I don't think religiously, but I might sometimes think of the Lake God as being angry today when the waters are rough, or the Sun God as being particularly influential. But somehow I'm too much of an evolutionist to think of The God, whatever that is. And I think, is the Muslim God the same as the Christian God, the same as the Greek Gods? Now, I look at this a little bit, and I think, "We needed this [religion] in a primitive time," but I don't think organized religion is any longer a part of my thought processes.

Unsurprisingly, the view that late adulthood is a time of crisis promoted the idea that religion plays a central role in the process of successful aging. If indeed late adulthood is a time of increased social isolation and existential threat, then it may well be that religious engagement would provide an important source of personal meaning and social support for older individuals. But does religion in fact promote successful aging? Given the positive social and economic circumstances of our study participants in late adulthood, did religion have any role in enhancing their late-life experiences?

PHYSICAL HEALTH

When the study participants were interviewed in their late sixties and their seventies (between 1997 and 2000), a remarkable nine out of ten described their health as good or moderately good (89 percent) and their energy level as good (93 percent). Additionally, two-thirds (65 percent) felt their energy level was higher compared to that of others their age, while one in four (29 percent) said their energy was about average. This upbeat assessment of health and energy is typical of older Americans. It is not surprising, however, given our study participants' more socially advantaged backgrounds and living circumstances, that the proportion reporting good health was higher than among older Americans as a whole, approximately three-quarters of whom affirm that they are in good or excellent health (see, e.g., Ross and Mirowsky 2002). Reflecting the shift in medical and cultural attitudes toward smoking that occurred during our study participants' lifetime, only 10 percent reported smoking regularly in late adulthood, whereas a third of them had been frequent smokers in middle adulthood. But, as members of the generation that glamorized the evening cocktail, in late adulthood a large majority (77 percent) said they drank alcohol, and half of these reported having a daily cocktail or glass of wine.

During the late-adulthood interview, the study participants spoke extensively about their health. They talked in detail about their current ailments as well as their previous illnesses, the medications they were taking, and any personal health-related hospital and doctor visits they had had in the previous year. We used all this interview material to derive an objective assessment of the participants' general physical health. Based on their health narratives, it was evident that a solid 25 percent of our participants were, like David Allen, in excellent health with virtually no physical complaints. An additional 41 percent had relatively minor ailments. These included chronic problems, such as arthritis or high blood pressure, that were kept under control by regular medication. Notwithstanding the generally upbeat personal health evaluations made by the participants themselves, one-third (34 percent) had one or more serious chronic or life-threatening illness. The most common illnesses among our participants were diabetes, some form of cancer, and cardiovascular and related problems.[2]

As one would expect, members of the younger cohort—at age sixty-nine (on average) in 1998—were in better health overall compared to the older cohort, who were approximately seventy-seven years old by then. They were less likely to report having bodily pain or having physical problems that interfered with their daily activities. Similarly, in line with the literature on gender differences in physical health (e.g., Baltes, Freund, and Horgas 1999), men with health problems reported better physical functioning than women who had health problems. The men were less likely than the women to say that their health problems

interfered with routine personal and household care tasks or with ordinary activities such as walking outdoors, or to say that their health
problems prevented them from doing things they wanted to do, such as
traveling or visiting friends.

Religiousness and spiritual seeking were uncorrelated with the
study participants' health ratings in late adulthood. Thus individuals
who scored high either on religiousness or on spiritual seeking did not,
for example, experience fewer chronic physical illnesses and did not
report better physical health or less incapacity due to physical health
than their nonreligious and nonspiritual peers.[3] There was also no evidence of a long-term association between religion and physical health.
In other words, our various indicators of physical health in late adulthood were unrelated to religiousness and spiritual seeking in early or
middle adulthood and, in the case of religiousness, were unrelated to
adolescence. Further, we also found no long-term relation between either religiousness or spiritual seeking and mortality. Our findings on
religion, physical health, and mortality thus differ from the trends
documented by other researchers showing a positive relation between
various aspects of religion and physical health and mortality (e.g., Ellison and Levin 1998; Koenig, McCullough, and Larson 2001; Mc-
Cullough and Smith 2003).

What might explain the absence of a significant connection between
religion and health in our study? We believe that the answer largely lies
in the sociodemographic composition of our sample. Though illness often has a genetic basis, it is also the case that good health is associated
with social factors such as income and economic security, educational
background, marital quality, and good habits (see, e.g., Kahn and Pearlin
2006; Mirowsky and Ross 2003; Umberson et al. 2006). Our study
participants were socially advantaged, as indicated by their comparatively high levels of education, income, and marital satisfaction. They
were thus in a position to be protected from illness and, because of the
greater access to good health care associated with high social status,
to have a greater chance of recovery from any illness they might have
experienced. At the same time, our study participants' denominational
backgrounds were unlikely to directly enhance their health as a result
of particular lifestyle habits. Most were either mainline Protestant or
Catholic and thus were members of denominational traditions that, unlike sectlike traditions such as the Mormons, did not have strict lifestyle rules that might foster good health, such as would derive from, for
example, a ban on alcohol or caffeine (see, e.g., Koenig, McCullough,

and Larson 2001). Considered as separate factors, but especially when combined, our study participants' positive social and economic circumstances and their denominational background would dampen the expectation of an association in our study among religious engagement, health, and mortality.

Nonetheless, we did find some support in the data for the links between religion and health that other studies document. Specifically, there was evidence that religion does foster the good habits conducive to health. For example, we found a negative relation between religiousness and alcohol use. In late adulthood, highly religious men and women reported drinking less alcohol than the nonreligious study participants. And among those who were religious, it was the older participants (those born in 1920 or 1921), and Protestants rather than Catholics, who were least likely to drink alcohol. Further, using the data gathered in early, middle, and late-middle adulthood, we found that, at each of these earlier stages in the life course, men and women who were religious were less likely than nonreligious individuals to drink alcohol. We also found that religiousness was negatively related to divorce (as noted in chapter 8) and, as research shows, marriage stability, and an absence of marital strain, is linked to good health (Lorenz et al. 2006; Umberson et al. 2006). Religiousness, however, was not significantly related to any other health-related behavior such as smoking, physical exercise, or the frequency of medical checkups. In sum, therefore, while we found some strands of evidence that religiousness can make a salutary contribution to people's health, the study participants' social status and denominational affiliations were such that religiousness did not have a discernable influence on their physical health.

RELIGIOUSNESS AND PSYCHOLOGICAL HEALTH

Almost all our study participants (87 percent) were well satisfied with their lives in late adulthood. A third (34 percent) rated their life satisfaction level as very high and a further 53 percent as moderately high. Similarly, few individuals indicated any sign of depression: 14 percent of the participants were classified as being depressed, a proportion comparable to that found in other community-based studies (e.g., Braam et al. 1997; Braam, van den Eaden, and Prince 2001).[4] Given the study participants' high levels of energy and morale and their extensive involvement in hobbies and social activities (discussed in chapter 8), it is noteworthy that religiousness correlated positively with life satisfaction. In other words, despite the high level of functioning among our participants, high scorers on religiousness still displayed a greater level of personal contentment than those who were not religious or who were spiritual seekers. On the other hand, they were not less likely than their nonreligious peers to be depressed.[5] Thus, we found mixed support for the claim that, among older individuals, religiousness acts as a general buffer against feeling down.

A critically important way in which religiousness abetted the positive aging of our study participants, however, was its cushioning role during adversity. The assumption that religion props people up in times of trouble has long enjoyed much currency among pastors, scholars, and the general population. Our data provided much support for this assumption. We found a consistent pattern of evidence showing that the study participants who were in poor physical health—our proxy for personal adversity—and who were not religious were the most depressed or unhappy and the least satisfied with their lives (see figures 7 and 8). In contrast, the study participants who were in good physical health, irrespective of whether they were religious, were especially well satisfied with their lives and in good psychological health (i.e., they scored low on depression and high on life satisfaction). Clearly, these high-functioning, healthy people, like David Allen, did not need religion to prop them up.

The populist wisdom in the saying that "God helps his own," however, was also borne out in our findings. Remarkably, the study participants who were in poor physical health and who were religious were as well satisfied with their lives and as positive in outlook as their nonreligious peers who enjoyed good physical health. In short, among those who were physically ill, religiousness acted as a defense against feeling down and pessimistic about life. And religion's protective influence was such that these individuals were able to maintain the same optimistic outlook as those in the study who were not visited by illness. Our findings thus clearly affirm the positive effect that religion has in the lives of older individuals, which prevents them from submitting to the weariness that frequently accompanies a new illness or the debilitating presence of a chronic disease.

The protective effect of religiousness on psychological health was present after we took account of whether or not the study participants had relatives and friends with whom they were in close contact and who provided them with ongoing social and emotional support, and it was independent of gender. Therefore, although the religious individuals in

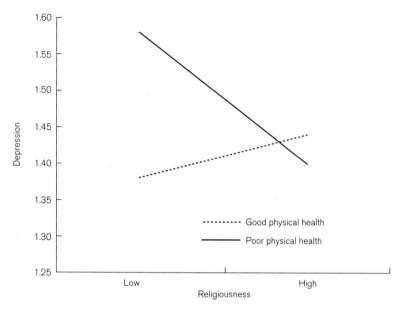

Figure 7. Depression as a function of physical health and religiousness in late adulthood. Redrawn with permission from Paul Wink, Michele Dillon, and Britta Larsen, 2005, "Religion as Moderator of the Depression-Health Connection," *Research on Aging* 27: 209, figure 1. Copyright Sage Publications, Inc.

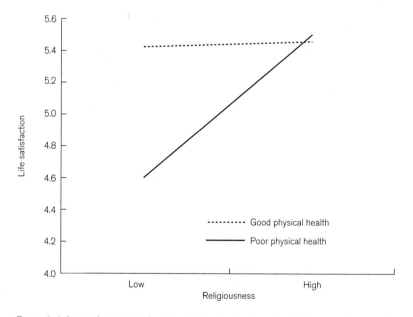

Figure 8. Life satisfaction as a function of physical health and religiousness in late adulthood.

our study tended to have closer emotional ties with family and friends than did the nonreligious, and although depression and life satisfaction were negatively related to social support, these interlinking connections in and of themselves did not explain why religious individuals were buffered against depression and a decline in life satisfaction. This suggests that something about being religious, independent of friends and social support, props people up during times of adversity. This finding fits with other research indicating that more than social support alone accounts for the positive way religion buffers people against depression (e.g., Ellison et al. 1997; Musick et al. 1998). Religiousness itself—independent of an individual's social support network—is a safeguard against feeling down.

We found, moreover, that the buffering effect of religiousness in late adulthood (age late sixties/seventies) could be predicted longitudinally from religiousness in middle adulthood (age forties; 1970). This held true even after we took account of variations in the physical health and psychological well-being of our study participants in middle adulthood.[6] Our results make it unlikely that the buffering effect of religiousness on psychological health in late adulthood is a function of the experience of adversity itself. Both the length of the buffering effect—close to thirty years—and its presence even after controlling for physical health and well-being in middle adulthood, make unlikely the possibility that the person either drifted toward religiousness in response to encountering adversity, or that religiousness was simply a proxy for good mental health. Our data thus argue against the notion that the protective effect of religiousness emerges because resilient older adults tend to gravitate toward religion in response to hardship. Our findings also make it highly unlikely that the protective effect of religiousness can be explained by the fact that severely depressed individuals do not have enough energy to go to church and, therefore, religiousness acts as a proxy for good mental health.[7] If this were the case, then, once again, we would not have expected a person's religiousness in his or her forties to have a cushioning effect against depression resulting from poor physical health some thirty years later.

The buffering effect of religiousness on psychological health was impressively long-term largely because our study participants maintained a remarkably stable pattern of religious engagement across adulthood. As we discussed (see chapter 6), very few of them made major shifts in the extent of their religious commitment. In this regard, our results indicating the stability of religious commitment across adulthood support the findings from short-term longitudinal studies showing that the stressors associated with aging, such as disability and poor physical health, do not have a significant detrimental effect on religious involvement (e.g., Idler and Kasl 1997; George, Ellison, and Larson 2002) (nor, as we noted in chapter 6, do they push nonreligious individuals toward church).

It is, of course, difficult to tease out what exactly about religiousness accounts for its positive effect. The remarks of our study participants such as Laura Goodall (see chapter 9), who had to deal with a midlife divorce and several serious illnesses from midlife onward, suggest, however, that she and others, such as Dorothy Marshall, used their religious faith to inject meaning into their adversity and, importantly, this provided them with the patience and will necessary to deal with pain. They were cushioned in times of trouble by their feelings of closeness to God and the sense that he was protecting them, and by the belief that illness or other adversity is part of God's plan for them. Prayer, whether at home or in church, solidifies these feelings and assurances and, in turn, buffers psychological health.

Sarah Jackson, whose father was confident about her spirituality in adolescence despite her penchant for playing tennis rather than going to church (see chapter 3), remained steadfast in her Christian faith throughout her life. She switched from the Congregational to the Episcopal Church in her forties because she "had a desire for the more formal partaking of the Holy Communion." Sarah led a fulfilled life: she was devoted to her husband and children, had a successful professional career, was a committed volunteer, and continued to play tennis well into her sixties. During each interview, in the context of talking about how she dealt with anxiety or personal trouble, Sarah commented on her confidence in the power of prayer. In 1970, at age forty-two, she stated, "I never know how I'm going to react to things, but I feel I have a great faith in how God will help me. I just know that by myself I can't handle the crises of life. . . . I need extra help, and I think I would get it. . . . I don't get terribly depressed, but when I feel depressed or worried I do pray. Prayer is part of my life—unloading. And while I know they won't come instantly, answers come eventually, and I've learned to accommodate."

Twelve years later she reiterated her belief: "I have a very strong faith and believe very strongly—I am a committed Christian. I believe very strongly in the power of prayer, and I would say that that's been my bulwark. . . . My faith in prayer has gotten better and stronger over the years." Again, in late adulthood, when we inquired about what held her up and renewed her hope during difficult times, Sarah unhesitatingly responded, "My faith. . . . I am a Christian. . . . My bookcases [are filled with] books of Christian faith and insight into life's journey, and that means a lot to me. I know there is a power out there that will help, and helps—not makes it all right but gives you courage and strength to face whatever comes. . . . My faith in Christ has been [the biggest influence on my life]. . . . It has given structure and meaning to everything. That is the inner soul. I consider this absolutely important, to have an inner soul and be in touch with your inner soul."

One of the people in our study who might have benefited from the cushioning effect of religiousness had she been religiously engaged was Ruth Manning. Ruth was born in 1928. Her Protestant parents were inactive except for celebrating the major holidays, and they sent Ruth to Sunday school for a few years. Ruth's family was quite well off, and her parents, both of whom worked full-time in their hardware store, made a good living in spite of suffering a 50 percent decrease in income during the Depression. Ruth was very attractive, poised, and highly intelligent, but art was the only subject she was interested in. She trained as a commercial writer and, after further study, as a designer. During the war, she worked for a time at a military installation, where she met her husband, a high-ranking officer. They had a son and a daughter.

In 1950, while pregnant with her second child, Ruth was struck with polio. She was severely incapacitated for several months, but after two years she was fully mobile and was able to walk without crutches, albeit a little awkwardly and with much pain. Swimming in the outdoor pool at her house had "saved" her and remained one of her lifelong recreational activities. When interviewed in early adulthood, in 1958, Ruth was satisfied with her life and showed no signs of self-pity or bitterness related to her polio. She had given up work soon after marriage, but art continued to be her main joy, and she displayed some of her paintings in her tastefully decorated home.

Twelve years later, when she was forty-two, Ruth looked healthy and attractive, but was "dissatisfied, depressed, and unhappy." Her primary source of concern was not her polio-related physical pain but her husband's alcoholism. Both Ruth and her husband liked to socialize, but her husband's alcohol dependence had significantly increased over the previous few years and was adversely affecting their marriage. She had gone to see a psychiatrist for six months but had not found it helpful, because, as she said, she was looking for a plan of action for dealing with her husband and was not interested in talking about herself and her emotional dependence on him, especially now that her children were away at college. She also had less energy and physical stamina for the voluntary work she enjoyed—raising money for Children's Hospital and helping out in Democratic political campaigns. Ruth continued to paint, however, and was active in an art group that met regularly. She was not religious but expressed a belief in God, saying she thought of God "as a Supreme Being, I guess. I would say that I probably don't always, but I usually come back to thinking that there is [a God]."

In late middle adulthood, Ruth was feeling even more distraught. Her husband's alcoholism had progressed; her daughter, whom she adored, had been diagnosed with a debilitating terminal illness; her own postpolio physical difficulties had worsened; and a love affair with a man with whom she had been friendly for many years had ended in a way that made her feel he didn't care for her at all. Ruth was doing very little painting, "a lonely pursuit," as she described it, and, because she felt that she "should get out with people more," was engaged in a lot of volunteer work. Nonetheless, Ruth described her feelings about life using strongly negative language: "I think I'm more depressed now, probably, than I've ever been. Because it seems like the whole world has just closed down. And there's no answer to any major problem. It's all just sort of a welter going round and round."

Ruth's physical and psychological health continued to deteriorate. Her postpolio disability had increased so much that, at the time of our interview in 1997, Ruth, then sixty-nine, was physically unable to do much for herself, though she continued to live in her nice home. Her husband had died in the early 1990s from a heart attack, and her daughter had died soon after that. Her son and his family had recently moved from the Bay Area to New Mexico. Ruth, therefore, was feeling down and bereft of any social and emotional support; she said her life satisfaction "would have to be near the bottom [of the scale]." In view of our research findings showing the buffering effect of religiousness on study participants with physical health problems, it is interesting that Ruth herself commented that if she had a religious anchor, it might be of some help to her. When asked what holds her up or gives her hope when life seems most discouraging and hopeless, Ruth replied,

> I imagine an awful lot of people would answer that with "religion." For me, unfortunately, I don't think I can say that. I do believe in a God, I think, and yet I still question this a lot because of all the terrible things that keep happening in the world, and [I wonder] why do they happen?

And I've never gotten over that. So I envy people who can say, "Well, this happened because God wanted it." I think that would be a wonderful way to be. I do envy it, and I wish I could say that that's the way I feel, but I don't. . . . I know I am not going to get better; and this postpolio syndrome, it just gets worse and worse and worse. . . . I can't hope that I'm going to get better, I can't hope that I am going to be able to walk better, and I can't hope that I'll have more family around. . . . So I guess I just hope that somebody will phone and say, "Would you like to do this, or would you like to do that?" or that something will happen during the day that can make me feel better about life. And if it doesn't, I have to accept the fact that it doesn't. . . . Hope is something I guess I don't have a lot of, because I can't see anything really changing except for the worse. . . . I don't know where, really, to say I look for hope. It's a hard one.

SPIRITUAL SEEKING AND PSYCHOLOGICAL HEALTH

Unlike religiousness, which was particularly effective in buffering physically ill individuals against the loss of life satisfaction and depression, spiritual seeking did not have such effects. We found no evidence among our study participants that spiritual seeking had any relation to psychological health in late adulthood. Thus, spiritual seekers did not report higher (or for that matter lower) levels of life satisfaction or lower levels of depression than their peers who were not spiritual seekers. Further, unlike for religiousness, there was no evidence to suggest that spiritual seeking had a buffering effect on either life satisfaction or depression in response to physical illness.

If high levels of life satisfaction and low levels of depression are considered core indicators of successful aging, then our findings suggest that spiritual seeking is not conducive to aging well. Alternatively, it could be argued that, because highly spiritual individuals have a personality profile that shows openness to experience (as documented in chapter 8), they are therefore likely to tolerate both positive and negative feelings in response to life events and experiences. In turn, this may mean that high life satisfaction or the absence of depression are not the most appropriate criteria in assessing how well spiritual seekers are coping with old age. For example, among our study participants, we found that spiritual seeking, but not religiousness, was positively associated with reflection and life review in late adulthood. Spiritual seekers were also characterized by high levels of "ego development," which meant they tended to evaluate themselves and others in nuanced and complex ways, and they also emphasized the importance of self-understanding.[8] This raises the possibility that spiritual seekers may respond to physical illness or other adversity by seeing it as an opportunity to take stock of their lives and to develop new insights about themselves. This process would typically elicit both positive and negative emotions as the person focuses on the good and the bad in a lifetime of feelings and behavior and tries to integrate both dimensions into a cohesive view of the self.

Taking stock of one's life may ultimately be conducive to a stronger and more integrated sense of self. But, in the short term, it necessarily uncovers negative feelings that may not be conducive to either high life satisfaction or low levels of depression. As argued by Carol Ryff (1989), a prominent scholar of adult development, happiness isn't everything. Of course, by making this statement, Ryff does not intend to negate the importance of happiness or life satisfaction as an important marker of successful aging. Rather she simply makes the point that happiness should not be used as the sole criterion of positive functioning, because this would skew our view of successful aging. An emphasis on individual contentment, moreover, can also shift attention away from the fact that building a good society requires individuals to cultivate characteristics that transcend self-gratification (cf. Bellah et al. 1991). And as wisdom researchers argue, because wise people embrace complexity, we should not expect wisdom to be related necessarily to either positive or negative feelings (e.g., Kunzmann and Baltes 2005). Our findings suggest that the same caution applies to spiritual seeking.

Given that life satisfaction and depression may not be the best criteria to use in assessing the links between spiritual seeking and positive aging, we wondered whether spiritual seekers might be protected against adversity by maintaining a sense of control over their lives. We reasoned that, even if spiritual seekers were to use physical illness as an opportunity to take stock of their lives, this should nonetheless preserve their perception that what happens in life is within their control. In support of this conjecture, we found that spiritual seekers who were in poor physical health maintained the same sense of personal control as their healthy peers. The same pattern emerged for religiousness. It is interesting, however, that among both spiritual seekers and our highly religious participants, the buffering effect on the sense of control in individuals who were in poor physical health was present in women but not men.[9]

When our findings on sense of control are combined with those for depression and life satisfaction, the overall picture suggests that religiousness has a broader buffering effect than spiritual seeking against adversity stemming from poor physical health. Thus, highly religious women not only preserve their sense of control but also tend to maintain high levels of life satisfaction and to ward off feelings of depression in the face of poor health. The fact that highly religious women who are in poor health maintain their feelings of control, life satisfaction, and happiness indicates that they deal with adversity in ways different from spiritual seeking women who are in poor health. Church-centered religiousness provides these women with contentment and satisfaction, and this in turn may enhance and reinforce their sense of control (cf. Shapiro, Schwartz, and Astin 1996). Highly religious women, therefore, are able to assimilate illness and personal adversity in their lives in a relatively seamless manner.

Spiritual seeking women, by contrast, preserve their sense of control in the face of adversity despite not being buffered against depression and a decline in life satisfaction. How is this possible? Because these women tend to be open to experience and to reflect about their lives, they are likely to use physical illness as an opportunity to actively confront unresolved personal and emotional issues and, in the process, attain new levels of self-understanding and, perhaps, control over their lives. As a result, they are able to accommodate illness and adversity in their lives notwithstanding the occasional feelings of sadness and dissatisfaction that may shadow them.

The sense of personal control that high scorers on spiritual seeking can muster in the face of adversity, despite not being buffered against depressed and dissatisfied feelings, was illustrated by Diana Voss. When she was interviewed in late adulthood, Diana was living with her husband in a newly built house on the California coast that they themselves had helped design. Diana was an artist who mainly did calligraphy, silk screening, and gouache painting. She had commented in her early adulthood interview (in 1958) that her artwork kept her away from people, something she felt was not a good thing. She had, she said then, a "real inability to feel comfortable in social situations."

Diana had had an emotionally troubled life. She had suffered through an agonizing personal crisis in her late thirties and her forties. This stress had been exacerbated by the fact that three of her five children had gotten into serious difficulties with drugs in the 1970s. In late adulthood, Diana was suffering from heart problems and severe osteoporosis, which was at times physically disabling—but, an avid walker, she tried to maintain a regular exercise schedule. She was taking several medications and had endured multiple hip and knee surgeries. She was not complaining about her physical disabilities, however, and in fact took the attitude that other people she knew were more severely impaired. And while she was not dissatisfied with her life, she freely admitted that she still felt a great deal of sadness about earlier emotional entanglements. She had one of the highest scores in the study on our self-reported measure of depression.

Yet Diana felt very much in control of her life and "centered." She and her husband were planning a trip to Alaska, and rather than dwelling on the past, she said, she liked to "get on with her day"—taking coastal walks and playing the recorder, as well as working on her art projects. Spiritual activities were also a centering part of Diana's day. She became an Episcopalian after she met her husband, who was an active church member. Nonetheless, Diana was also deeply attracted to Catholicism and found its mysticism particularly appealing, especially in times of personal conflict and trouble. Though she fully identified as a Christian who believed in God, she explained that she had "a pantheistic view of God—I just love the beauty in the world. I know that God has made it." Diana was attending the Episcopal Church every week and also participating in a women's weekly spiritual growth group. This group and her many years of active membership in Alcoholics Anonymous were greatly important to her. Additionally, she regarded her painting and music as ways to maintain "spiritual depth" and her emotional connection to God's pantheistic presence.

Her earlier personal struggles with relationships, Diana reflected, had made it difficult for her "to love, to be a loving person," something that she had long wanted to be. She was now feeling "a peace and a serenity"—something, she said, she always considered to be an achievement. This new acceptance, she said, derived from her "spiritual growth." Along with her love of nature and her painting, it gave her a serenity that "freed" her to be more loving and compassionate toward others. When asked about what held her up when things were difficult, Diana responded, "I think this is a time when I just ask God to help me. Not that I have some great idea of God. Except more and more, I'm able to see that God could be a person. I've always had trouble thinking of God as a person, but I no longer find that so unbelievable." She also spoke of the focus she found in painting: "My general approach for years has been one of wanting simplicity in my work and trying to find the essence of whatever the thing is. . . . I focus on the present moment. I really do live right where I am. . . . I consider my painting and my music to be prayerful things."

In sum, despite her depressed feelings and her willingness to acknowledge an ongoing sadness about her earlier personal and family problems, Diana, like other spiritual-seeking and religious women in our study, maintained a strong sense of personal control over her life in late adulthood despite the physical health problems she confronted daily.

GENDER, RELIGION, AND POSITIVE AGING

Our results indicating gender differences in personal control suggest that, among highly religious and spiritual seeking individuals, women and men cope differently with adversity. This finding points to the larger issue of gender differences and religion. It is well established that women involve themselves in religion more than men do (see, e.g., Cornwall 1989), and our study participants too demonstrated this reality: more women than men scored high on religiousness (see chapter 5) and on spiritual seeking (see chapter 7). The greater presence of religiousness and spiritual seeking in women's than in men's lives is sociologically interesting in itself. Yet surprisingly little research has been conducted on whether women's greater religious and spiritual engagement leads to noticeable gender differences in everyday social and psychological functioning.[10] As noted by Rodney Stark (2002), the fact that women are more religious is so obvious that there has been virtually no study of this phenomenon.

But although women are more religious than men, it may still be the case that religiousness and spiritual seeking have the same implications for men's as for women's everyday functioning. As we have discussed (chapters 6 and 7), mean group differences are independent of individual variability. In other words, women's higher levels of participation in church and non-church-centered religion tell us nothing about whether the relations among religiousness, spiritual seeking, and everyday functioning are influenced by gender.

Overall, our data revealed very few gender differences among high scorers on religiousness or on spiritual seeking. The main gender difference, not surprisingly, was in the implications of religiousness for social relationships, an area of everyday life to which, as is well documented, women assign greater priority (e.g., Edgell 2006; Gilligan 1982; Putnam 2000). For women, religiousness was positively correlated with everyday engagement in social activities like visiting family, friends, and neighbors; deriving a sense of well-being from positive relations with others; and maintaining broad social networks. By contrast, these correlations were not significant for men. The only correlation significant for men and not for women was between religiousness and marital satisfaction. Moreover, when we compared women and men who scored high on religiousness, we found that highly religious women scored significantly higher than men on positive relations with others and on everyday social engagement. And we found a similar pattern of gender differences in agreeableness. But in other areas of functioning—including generativity, community involvement, and authoritarianism—and in examining the buffering effect of religiousness on life satisfaction and depression in response to adversity, there were no gender differences among our highly religious participants. The only gender difference that emerged among our spiritual seekers was that women were more involved than men in knowledge-building activities. Otherwise, the positive associations between spiritual seeking and engagement in everyday creativity, well-being from personal growth, and openness to experience, as well as the negative relation between spiritual seeking and authoritarianism, were unrelated to gender.

In sum, our data suggest that the marked gender differences in different types of religious engagement have fewer implications for everyday life than might otherwise be expected. Nevertheless, it is time that we move beyond using gender as merely a control variable in statistical models—similar to how many researchers still tend to use social class and denomination—and, instead focus on how its interplay with religiousness and spiritual seeking affects everyday behavior. This should provide us with firmer ground in our attempt to understand why, across generations, women display a greater preference than men for religious and spiritual engagement (cf. Stark 2002).

FEAR OF DEATH

As Ruth Manning recognized, many Americans find hope through religion. Belief in an afterlife, a core aspect of Christian faith, has been a source of comfort and hope for generations of Americans. Yet, underscoring Americans' autonomy regarding religion, many profess a belief in an afterlife without feeling compelled to complement this belief with church attendance. Well over three-quarters of Americans say they believe in an afterlife (more than 80 percent, Greeley and Hout 1999), yet fewer than half (approximately 44 percent; Gallup and Lindsay 1999) report attending church on a regular basis. Paralleling these national figures, in late adulthood 79 percent of our study participants reported some belief in an afterlife, but fewer than half our participants indicated that they regularly attended church. Does this disjuncture between religious belief and practice have an effect on individuals' fear of death? After all, religion offers the tantalizing possibility of immortality while at the same time raising the specter of eternal damnation.

Not unexpectedly, both religiousness and spiritual seeking were positively related to belief in an afterlife.[11] However, among our study participants, neither church-centered religiousness, spiritual seeking, nor belief in an afterlife correlated with the fear of death.[12] This was true of both men and women. There was a denominational difference, however. Surprisingly, Catholics were more afraid of death than their mainline and nonmainline Protestant counterparts.[13] One might have expected that the rich sacramental rituals Catholics have surrounding death would make death a less threatening specter. On the other hand, perhaps Catholics' greater fear reflects a lingering effect of socialization into a specifically judgmental Catholic theology: as noted in chapter 3, in adolescence Catholics were more likely than others to endorse a view that hell is torturous. Yet there was no denominational variation among the study participants in late adulthood in regard to belief in a rewarding afterlife. Moreover, mainline and nonmainline Protestants did not differ on fear of death. Taken as a whole then, these findings suggest that something more general about socialization into pre–World War II Catholicism may have a sleeper effect, producing Catholics' greater fear of death close to sixty years later.

But did religiousness protect any of the study participants against the fear of death? In support of other research (see, e.g., Downey 1984; Smith, Nehemkis, and Charter 1983–84), our data showed that individuals who were somewhat religious were the most afraid of death, and those who scored either high or low on religiousness were the least afraid (see figure 9). There was no parallel relationship evident between spiritual seeking and the fear of death. Of further significance, we found that individuals who scored high on church-centered religiousness and who believed in an afterlife feared death the least, whereas individuals whose practices did not match their beliefs—those in our study who scored low on religiousness but believed in an afterlife—feared death the most (Wink and Scott 2005). The study participants who were rated low on religiousness and who did not believe in an afterlife feared death less than those who, though scoring low on religiousness, believed in an afterlife. Because our measure of religiousness is strongly intertwined with church attendance, we interpret our results to support

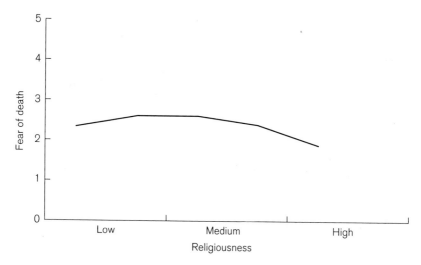

Figure 9. Fear of death by religiousness in late adulthood. Redrawn with permission from Paul Wink and Julia Scott, 2005, "Does Religiousness Buffer against the Fear of Death and Dying in Late Adulthood?" *Journal of Gerontology: Psychological Sciences* 60B: 211, figure 1. Copyright The Gerontological Society of America.

the idea that the fear of death in old age is most characteristic of individuals who show an inconsistency between their belief in the afterlife and their church practices. Conversely, fear of death is least characteristic of those who show consistency between belief in an afterlife and religiousness. In short, consistency between religious beliefs and practices pays off, at least when it comes to thoughts of the Grim Reaper, a finding that confirms the wisdom in American everyday culture that it is practices, not beliefs alone, that matter.

It is easy to understand why our highly religious participants were not afraid of death: church-centered religiousness provides them with many evocative reminders of the spiritual joys of heaven, and it sustains the hope that they, because of their church commitment, will attain salvation and meet their loved ones in the afterlife. The greater fear of death among those who express a belief in an afterlife, but who in daily life give short shrift to church, likely derives from the absence in their lives of regular reminders of salvation, both its promises and its demands. Individuals who believe in an afterlife but do not participate in church practices may feel uncertain about their own afterlife status, notwithstanding their hope of or belief in an afterlife. This uncertainty, and the specter of punishment after death for not attending church, may increase their fear of death (see, e.g., Leming 1979–80; Nelson and Cantrell 1980).

But what might account for the low fear of death among our non-religious participants? From an existential perspective, it is assumed that, irrespective of religion, individuals are motivated to pursue personal meaning that can buffer them against fear and anomie (see, e.g., Wong 2000). Although religiousness provides definite answers to the dilemma of human existence and offers individuals a sense of control over their lives, the same can be true of secular worldviews and everyday strategies that assume the finality of life. What unites individuals who scored either high or low on religiousness may be a strong sense of self and a consistent outlook on the eventualities of both life and death. For this reason, Jack Adams and David Allen were as well buffered as Barbara Shaw and Jay Campbell against the fear of death.

Once again, as with the other aspects of social and psychological functioning documented in these chapters, the patterns regarding religiousness and fear of death in late adulthood also held in relation to the person's religiousness in middle adulthood (an interval of twenty-five years). This means that study participants rated high or low in religiousness in their forties tended to be less afraid of death in their late sixties and their seventies than those who were moderately religious in their forties. Knowing a person's level of religiousness in middle adulthood was thus as good a predictor of fear of death in late adulthood as was his or her level of religiousness in late adulthood.

The protective effect of consistency between an individual's religious beliefs and church-centered practices in staving off fear of death was well illustrated by the answers our study participants gave during the late-adulthood interview in response to the questions "What does death mean to you?" and "What becomes of us when we die?" Barbara Shaw, our socially outgoing Texas Baptist introduced in chapter 1, responded, "I know God; I know Jesus. And I totally expect to be with him for all eternity. . . . I don't fear death because of where I'm going." Another woman, who attended a Baptist church every week and participated in a weekly Bible study class, said, "I believe what the Bible says. Jesus has gone and prepared a place for us that we can't even imagine, it is so wonderful. So I thought about that too when my mother died. She is gone; she is in another realm or whatever. Where it is, I don't know. There is no time there, no sorrow. You just can't imagine. . . . I am not afraid."

Ted McRae, a born-again Christian who also was unafraid of death, commented,

> Well, now, you've got to realize that both my wife and I and most of our family are all born-again Christians. So we're of the Christian faith. Not the Christian religion, the Christian faith, which says that you're going to die physically, but your soul doesn't die, and someday we'll be united with our Lord, and he's going to return. That's what we believe in. . . . I've got to go strictly by the book, what happens in the Bible. . . . I don't have any doubts. I have no doubt.

Similarly, Jay Campbell, the lifelong highly religious Presbyterian (see chapter 5), simply said, "Religiously, I go to heaven. That should be better than here. There won't be any questions that I can't answer. Philosophically, that's what I believe." Another Presbyterian man in the study who wasn't afraid of death explained his belief: "We believe— and I get this from the Bible—that we are spirits living in an animal, or human, body. When I'm talking to you and you're talking to me, what animates you is your spirit, which we believe is eternal. It comes from God. So I believe that, when a person dies, the spirit has left the body and has gone to be with God."

An absence of the fear of death was also evident in the responses provided by our study participants who were neither religious nor spiritual and who believed that nothing happens after death. Jack Adams, the lifelong atheist discussed in chapter 5, said, "I just go back to dirt, like a rotten pear or a rotten peach laying on the ground." Jack was not afraid of death; his main concern was that the government would tax his assets after his death, a scenario he had eliminated by setting up a trust for his family to ensure that that would not happen. Another man, a successful business executive who was also nonreligious throughout his life, and who had a "zero" fear of death, said, "You get burned up, that's it. Nothing happens. . . . There is no such thing as an afterlife." A nonreligious woman who was similarly unafraid of death stated, "To tell you the truth, I haven't even thought about it [death or afterlife]. I said that I wanted to be cremated, and that they could do whatever they want with the ashes." Similarly, David Allen commented that, when we die, "I think life is terminated at that point, just like all the other creatures that live and die on a routine basis. . . . Our mythology of heaven and hell is just a way that more primitive people were able to face the realities of living long or short lives." David said he doesn't think about death at all, although he had set up a living trust for his family, and that he was "not at all" afraid of death.

The comparatively greater fear of death experienced by the study participants who believed in an afterlife, but who were otherwise not religious, seemed to come from the fact that they did not engage in prayer or the church habits that would have affirmed the existence of salvation after death. One Catholic man, for example, had a definite belief in an afterlife. He explained, "According to our religion, most of your soul is supposed to depart your body, and if there's a heaven, you go up there, or you go the other way. . . . It's hard to visualize. . . . It's beyond my comprehension, that's for sure." This man, however, did not pray or attend church, and he rated his fear of death at six on a seven-point scale. A woman who was brought up as a Christian Scientist said, "I don't know. I hope we have a second chance so that we all meet each other somewhere. I just hope and pray that that's the way it is. I don't know. I've never had a firm conviction of anything—if there is an afterlife, if there is an anything, I guess." Yet despite her hopes for an afterlife, she too did not attend any church services, and she was among those in our study who were most afraid of death.

Another nonchurchgoing woman, who in early adulthood had been an active Episcopalian and whose teenage son had died tragically in a car accident, spoke of her belief in an afterlife, saying, "I guess I can't help but feel there is more than what we're experiencing right now. And that when our physical bodies leave the earth, or cease to function, there is a spark or a spirit or an essence of ourselves that still exists. I'm not really sure in what form or how, but it's out there, somewhere. And there's never any end to that. There's a place and a space for all of us." Once again, however, belief in an afterlife without the concomitant habit of church participation was not sufficient to buffer this woman who, in late adulthood, ranked her fear of death as high.

The fact that spiritual seeking and fear of death were not related either positively or negatively may stem from the fact that belief in an afterlife, whether understood in traditional (e.g., heaven) or less conventional terms (e.g., reincarnation), is not as central to the worldview of spiritual seekers as it is to a church-centered religious theology—especially Christianity. Moreover, as noted earlier in this chapter, it may also be true that, just as spiritual seekers are open to both negative and positive feelings associated with personal illness and adversity, they may be similarly open to the ambiguities of death, and therefore some may fear death more than others do. Kate Ward's comments about her understanding of death help to illuminate this point. When asked

"What does death mean to you? What becomes of us when we die?" she responded,

> I believe—now, I don't know whether I believe completely, or whether I think; I feel more comfortable with the phrase "I think"—that when our bodies are dead, our spirit and consciousness continue to exist in some form. How, I don't know . . . but I like to believe this. I don't know if this is the way it really works—and nobody does—but it encourages me. I would hate to think that I just bumbled though this physical world, and that was it. I would like to think, and I do believe, that I'm part of the universe. And that I get returned somehow—my spirit or my conscious-ness—to something that is, hopefully, more worthwhile than this.

Later in the interview, when Kate was asked about her fear of death, she commented, "Seeing as how I believe in a life beyond [laughs], I would like to say that I don't really fear death. I think that I really don't want to die—I mean, I think I have quite a few years left to enjoy life and, hopefully, make some kind of contribution. But I can't stave off death. I might do as much as I can for myself physically, but 'Que sera, sera.'" Nevertheless, reflecting her uncertainty, Kate rated her fear of death higher than most others in the study.

Peter Jones, on the other hand, a nature-centered spiritual seeker (discussed in chapter 7), responded to the questions on death by stating, "I don't know. I don't have any definite ideas. . . . I definitely feel that my body should go back to nature, if at all possible. I'd prefer to be bur-ied right here on this piece of property in an old box (or maybe no box at all) that would rot. Then I would decompose and go back. . . . I feel it's part of a natural cycle of life to go back to the earth. . . . I don't fear death at all . . . with burial on the land. . . . I don't see any fear." Jane Bell (see chapter 1) talked about death similarly, saying, "All I can say is, who knows [what becomes of us when we die]? It's a great mystery. But I know it's not to be feared. I don't fear death. I have been close to it [when my husband was dying], and there's nothing to fear. . . . And the mystery of it—there's something very wonderful, expansive, and beautiful about it."

SUCCESSFUL AGING

The overall findings on the social and psychological functioning of our study participants in late adulthood support the emerging view of the postretirement period (from individuals' midsixties to late seven-ties) as a positive time in the life course. As noted, most of our study participants were in good physical health and highly satisfied with their lives, few were depressed, and most had minimal concerns about their impending mortality.

Despite the fact that most of the study participants enjoyed excellent social and economic circumstances in late adulthood, our findings pointed to the positive role of religiousness in their lives. Those who were religious showed higher levels of life satisfaction than their non-religious or spiritual seeking peers. In other areas of functioning—depression, sense of control, and fear of death—our data showed a more specific role for religiousness. In particular, among those who were in poor health, religiousness emerged as a strong buffer against depression and the loss of life satisfaction and personal control. These findings strongly support the common assumption that religious involvement helps individuals cope with adversity, a point reiterated across these pages by many of our participants (and by their parents too).

Although spiritual seeking did not provide the same protective buffer as religiousness and did not increase or preserve individual happiness during stressful times, life satisfaction and happiness in themselves are not the only criteria by which to judge positive aging. The ability to engage in life review and to accept and integrate the unpleasant emotional issues it may uncover is also adaptive for some older individuals. This seems especially true for spiritual seekers, who, notably, maintained their sense of personal control notwithstanding depression and adversity. By the same token, the low fear of death equally characteristic of the study participants who were either high or low in religiousness, and our more general findings that older individuals in good health do not need religion in order to have a purposeful and satisfying life, underscores the fact that, while religious engagement clearly enhances everyday existence, it is not always necessary to the crafting of a meaningful life.

11

American Lived Religion

In America, "the spirit of religion and the spirit of freedom . . . are intimately united and . . . reign in common," as Alexis de Tocqueville observed in the early nineteenth century (1835/1946: 308). We strongly concur with Tocqueville's perceptive assessment of American religion, and we argue that it applies equally well now as in the mid-1800s. One would be hard pressed to find in Europe, the ancestral home of almost all our study participants, anyplace, before or after the 1960s, that would have offered its residents the range of churches available to the families of our study participants in the 1930s and 1940s—despite the fact that our study participants were living in one of the less churched regions of America. Their neighborhoods provided diverse religious choices, options that undoubtedly contributed to the vibrancy of the church for so many of these people during the formative years of their adolescence, and for their parents too. As our findings revealed, long before the dawning of the 1960s, many of our study participants were generally free to choose which church or Sunday school or religious youth group to attend, and some even crossed Protestant-Catholic lines in doing so.

Access to diverse denominational traditions in America has long been matched with an everyday vocabulary of religious choice. Again, our findings indicated that many ordinary Americans in the decades preceding the 1960s readily invoked a language of individual autonomy in talking about church and their own religious habits. This autonomy enabled them to selectively arbitrate among churches and denominations, to invoke a morality not explicitly tied to theology, and to appreciate the sacred whether churched or not. This same autonomy has allowed variation within American families, both between parents and among parents and children, in their church habits. And beyond the family, the tug of religious autonomy allowed individuals to drift in and out of church as they negotiated their own life transitions and social roles as well as the larger culture, a context that, at any given time, may or may not be conducive to religious or spiritual investment. Although religious practices have certainly become more varied since the 1960s, the language of personal autonomy and choice in which they are framed has continuity with the remarkable religious independence of earlier generations of Americans.

The localized congregational basis of so much of American religion both today and in the past (see, e.g., Warner 1993), the doctrinal variation that can characterize two neighboring churches of the same denomination, and the doctrinal and political variation that exists among members of the same church (see, e.g., D'Antonio et al. 2001) all attest to one of the deep sociological truths about America: Americans are a religious people, but whether in church or beyond church walls, they believe that their choices and opinions are their own business, and they are not easily swayed by the opinions of others. Regardless of what their parents or peers may believe, and regardless of the pronouncements of religious and secular elites, Americans tend, like Michael Perry's grandfather (see chapter 4, page 60), to make up their own minds about things.

Importantly, making up one's own mind does not breed agnosticism among Americans, nor has it brought about the demise of religion. On the contrary, this autonomy appears to accentuate religion's vitality. A modern-day Tocqueville might be surprised to find that the decline in religiousness experienced in many western European countries (see, e.g., Davie 1994) has not affected America. She might be even more surprised by the debates in America over whether creationism should be taught in schools alongside, or even instead of, the theory of evolution—a debate hard to imagine in any western European country—and by the cultural legitimacy allowed to "intelligent design" arguments for the existence of God.[1] Yet on reflection, these differences between

America and western Europe are a direct corollary of America's emphasis on individual autonomy, an ethos institutionalized in its laws and public policies and embedded in everyday language (see, e.g., Glendon 1987; Bellah et al. 1985). The cross-Atlantic religious and cultural differences we see today, therefore, should not be that surprising. After all, the privileging of personal preference in choosing a place of worship implies also a primacy of personal experience in the evaluation of evidence concerning the origins of the world and the demarcation between biblical truth and scientific fact. Unlike many Europeans, many Americans are not easily swayed by intellectual elites and by obtuse scientific theories that, like Darwinism, for example, challenge the evidence of our senses and deep-seated intuitions about "the order of things," to use Foucault's term (1974). (See Eurobarometer 2005.)

We should also not forget that, in many places around the world where people once lacked religious autonomy, a newfound individualism, largely motivated by economic and political change, is easily expressed in rebelliousness against a dominant state-protected or culturally imposed religion. Again, this trend is evident in many European societies where the increasingly pervasive impulse is to discard the yoke of a previously strong religious identity, an action recently crystallized in the European Parliament's eschewal of any recognition of Europe's Christian history in the formulation of a constitution for the European Union. In short, many Europeans show their new autonomy by not going to church and by rejecting religion, rather than by exercising choice within the vast religious and spiritual marketplace as Americans do.

The pragmatic autonomy Americans exercise toward church also maps well onto its social function. After all, a highly mobile and individualistic society, one that from the early seventeenth century has been driven by the "gospel of mobility" and opportunity (Thernstrom 1984: 221)—an ideology affirmed by both later-generation Puritans and the transcendentalists alike—needs a common glue. And the American religious marketplace, with its plethora of welcoming churches, provides a perfect avenue for establishing and sustaining common bonds. It is perhaps the unforgiving rationality in American society, with its strong emphasis on the economic bottom line and the maximizing of personal rewards and benefits, that feeds religion's persistence rather than its decay. This is the same rationality that Weber (1904–05/1976) thought would drive religion away and make it irrelevant in modern times. Conversely, however, the instrumentality and utilitarianism of everyday American life appear to maintain, if not strengthen, the social and psychological need for church in contemporary American society, because church provides a place where emotions, nonmaterial values, and bonds of friendship can flourish.

The social programming institutionalized in many churches today provides a remarkable array of nonreligious activities, and many churches adapt their programs to changing demographic and cultural trends (see, e.g., Ammerman 2005; Chaves 2004: Edgell 2006; Smith and Denton 2005). Yet, again, this social programming, though its content varies, has a long history. Our data from across the decades captured the clearly acknowledged importance Americans have long seen in the social and socializing opportunities church provides children and adolescents in particular, but also parents and older Americans. Church involvement is certainly about worship and prayer, and it offers a larger sense of meaning and purpose with which to frame the mundane reality of everyday life. Moreover, notwithstanding the distinctively American attitude that children's religious decisions are up to them, parents across the generations expose their children to formalized religious training. But church involvement is also thoroughly social, a social activity in its own right and the conduit to other opportunities for social interaction. The social aspects of church do not necessarily detract from its liturgical and worship aspects. It would be surprising if churches and congregations did not prioritize worship as their central purpose (see, e.g., Chaves 2004: 127). But, when we listen to how ordinary people talk about church, it is also apparent that religious habits are frequently shaped by social considerations rather than by family history or theological motivation. In a culture of dislocation, whose effects are exacerbated by the rootlessness demanded by the globalized Internet age (cf. Giddens 1991), churches and spiritual groups provide a centering place for individuals in motion. As such, the opportunity for social interaction that church allows and, in fact, encourages adds to the pragmatism and autonomy with which so many Americans approach religion. Their decisions about church—whether to attend, where to attend, how frequently to go, or how great a commitment to make—can be heavily influenced by the social opportunities a particular church offers at a given time.

The pragmatic autonomy that enables Americans to be religious also enables those who are religious to stay religious to various degrees; as our findings showed, there was remarkable continuity in our study participants' levels of religious involvement over time, notwithstanding the multiple life course and sociocultural changes encountered. Clearly, the constellation of changes in individuals' social roles and experiences (e.g., marriage, parenthood, empty nest, postretirement, divorce, illness), in tandem with historical, cultural, and institutional changes, affects people's religious and spiritual commitments; we saw these dynamics in the ebb and flow of the participants' religiousness across the life course and in the increase in spiritual seeking in the postmidlife and post-1970s period. Yet the fact that the study participants' levels of religiousness in late adulthood essentially paralleled their levels in early adulthood, and the fact that spiritual seeking in late adulthood was preceded by religiousness in adolescence and early adulthood, gives pause to the assumption that changes in religious involvement, whether driven by biographical or cultural events, are invariably dramatic or irreversible. Indeed, one of the great ironies of American religion is that, despite the highly autonomous way in which Americans construe religious beliefs, preferences, and practices, there is an enormous amount of stability in their respect for religious socialization and in their religious beliefs and behavior, and this stability coexists alongside the currents of change.

American societal trends in religion suggest a similarly dynamic mix of stability and change. On the one hand, over the last several decades there has been a lot of stability evident in Americans' self-reported beliefs in God and the afterlife and in church attendance habits. This stability coexists, however, alongside a small but steady increase in the proportion who identify as born-again Christians (Winseman 2005) and, conversely, alongside a recently observed and significant twofold increase in the proportion of American adults who report no religious preference (from 1991 to 1998; Hout and Fischer 2002). An interesting task for the future will be to monitor whether the trend toward religious disaffiliation continues to increase, and whether it persists in characterizing all cohorts or, over time, some cohorts become more likely to reaffiliate. In other words, only over the long term will we discover whether this newly observed increase in unchurched Americans heralds a decline in American institutionalized religion or presents yet another historical disruption in the long ebb and flow of American religion.

In any event, although social change occurs, it is easy to make distorting inferences about religion when the focus is confined to the short term and not the longer historical context. Just as a snapshot of Americans on election day in 2004, when pollsters discovered that "moral values" informed the electoral decisions of many voters,[2] might lead some to believe that religion's importance is on the rise in America, an inference contradicted by long-term trend data, so too would it have been easy to infer that the general increase in religiousness among the IHD study participants from late-middle adulthood (age fifties) to late adulthood (age late sixties, and seventies), or between 1982 and 2000, was a result of aging, or the cultural upswing of religion in the 1980s, or both. Yet our longer-term data demonstrated that this was not the case. The study participants resumed their religious involvement in the 1990s after a hiatus observed in 1970 and 1982, an interval in which religious decline coincided with a shift in the study participants' family roles and, more broadly, with cultural upheaval and, for Catholics, acute conflict in the church.

The overall stability observed in individuals' religious involvement does not mean, of course, that all Americans are, or in any given historical period were, uniformly involved in religion. Quite the contrary. As our data highlighted, religion invariably appeals to some individuals and not to others. In this sense, religious involvement can be thought of as a bell-shaped, normally distributed characteristic, with relatively few individuals at either tail of the distribution and most with varying degrees of moderate involvement (cf. Stark and Finke 2000: 196–97). The fact that a solid proportion of our study participants (and of their parents), as well as a solid proportion of Americans more generally, keep a good distance from church at any given time suggests that the appeal of religion is rarely, if ever, all-encompassing.

It is evident, therefore, that whether one focuses on individual lives or broader societal trends, a long-term perspective, rather than a truncated one, guarantees a more nuanced assessment of the dynamics of religion, one that can pick up the continuities in religious attitudes and habits as well as the dips and surges in religion's relevance to individuals and society. New trends do not appear out of the blue. Of course, to detect religious and cultural continuities requires, as Philip Gorski (2003) argues, a long-term perspective on history. It also needs a deep perspective like the one provided by our extensive interview data. In sum, we advocate studying religion with both a long-range telescope and a high-powered microscope, which allow one to take in both the long vista of the sociohistorical and cultural landscape and the minutiae of everyday life.

RELIGIOUSNESS AND SPIRITUAL SEEKING

The last several years have seen much debate about the upsurge in spiritual seeking in America, and its intensity suggests that it touches a raw cultural nerve. Since the 1960s, an increasing number of Americans have described themselves as having spiritual interests and experiences that have little to do with denominations or churches (Hout and Fischer 2002; Roof 1999). What is contested is the interpretation of this trend, its fit with the historical narrative of American religion, and, even more sharply drawn, the implications of these newer, more individualized forms of spirituality for social participation, civic involvement, and seekers' personal relationships.

We believe it is time to move beyond the essentializing presumption inherent in the historical metanarrative of American religion, the view that Jonathan Edwards is more culturally authentic than Ralph Emerson or the transcendentalists. Yes, Edwards by birth date preceded Emerson, and no one can challenge his huge imprint on the evolution of American Protestantism and culture. History, however, is not a competition. One of its purposes, rather, is to flesh out the many various strands that have interacted with and energized one another over time, and that have generated new and mutated strands in the process. Comparing the theological and cultural legacies of Edwards and Emerson is certainly a worthwhile endeavor. But much of the recent debate over spiritual seeking has, by and large, centered on pitting one against the other, an exercise that simply has a polarizing rather than an enlightening effect. Thus Edwards gets associated with "socially responsible" individualism, and Whitman and Emerson with a socially unresponsive "expressive individualism" (Bellah et al. 1985). And alternatively, in an effort to redress the theological and historical narrowness behind the demonization of contemporary spirituality (Schmidt 2005), the critics of Emerson (such as Bellah) are portrayed as having a judgmental and aggressive moral conservatism, while Emerson is celebrated as the inspiration of the "Spiritual Left" (Schmidt 2005).[3]

Religiousness and spiritual seeking have long coexisted in America. What has changed is that the presence of a greatly expanded spiritual marketplace since the 1960s has made it easier for Americans to engage in a range of spiritual practices and beliefs. Given our research findings, we argue that American society not only includes, but benefits from having, dwellers and seekers, or conservers and explorers. Religiousness and spiritual seeking, though their boundaries are not always sharply drawn in individual lives, essentially reflect two alternative social traditions and personal ways of being. Our findings indicated that both religiousness and spiritual seeking, though varied in many of their implications, are good for the individual and for society.

At the individual level, both church-centered religiousness and a more individually negotiated spiritual seeking are different but equally adaptive ways of engaging with the sacred and of functioning in everyday life (see also Helson and Cate 2007). At the broader societal level, both are related to social responsibility and caring for a larger common good. Certainly, the interests and activities and attitudes of highly religious and spiritual seeking individuals differ. But these differences are not antithetical; in most domains of functioning, they reflect a difference in emphasis rather than a polarization.

The only area of polarization that emerged in our data pertained to social attitudes. Here, our data strongly affirmed the well-documented links between religiousness and authoritarianism. Given such findings, it is understandable how the perception that leftist egalitarian politics are fueled by spiritual seeking, rather than by church-centered religiousness, has taken root (cf. Schmidt 2005). The general thrust of our results on authoritarianism is that religiousness does not necessarily promote authoritarianism, but neither does it encourage antiauthoritarianism. It is interesting that church-centered religiousness produces attitudes that contravene, however passively, the Christian ethos to love one's neighbor, and that it did so in our study notwithstanding the mainline Protestant backgrounds and high levels of education that characterized our participants as a whole. Our findings may reflect cohort and age effects: the fact that our study participants were born in the 1920s, an era when social and communal liberalism was less salient than in the postwar decades (e.g., Putnam 2000: 355–57), and the fact that we assessed their authoritarianism in late adulthood, a time in the life course when individuals tend to be more rigid in their opinions than at earlier phases (e.g., Labouvie-Vief and Diehl 1999).

Nevertheless, from a cultural perspective it is interesting that, although Americans are highly autonomous in choosing whether and how to be religious, their religiousness still encourages "obedience to authority" rather than an antiauthoritarian stance. Given that almost all our highly religious study participants were involved in local congregations, the tie between religiousness and authoritarianism suggests that we need more research investigating why membership in a congregation—which can do so many good things in American life—fails to actively prevent members from assuming authoritarian views.

Notwithstanding the polarization between religiousness and spiritual seeking that emerged in our findings on authoritarianism, one should keep in mind that our findings on the study participants' everyday lives as a whole suggest that highly religious and spiritual-seeking individuals would find they have much in common if they were to sit at a common dinner table. In short, as we try to assess the meaning and implications of the changing religious and spiritual landscape in America, we should not fall into the trap of making invidious comparisons—we already know from the debates surrounding gender, race, and sexuality that such comparisons tend to privilege one type of difference over another rather than acknowledging differences as constitutive of social life. Our findings suggest that advancing the common good is neither the prerogative nor the historical legacy of any one religious or spiritual strand.

In our opinion, a well-functioning and vitalized society requires both religious conservers who uphold existing traditions and preserve the social order and religious seekers who challenge the existing order and inject novelty. In other words, a society without spiritual seekers is threatened by stagnation, and one without religious dwellers is in danger of disequilibrium. The strength of the current American religious marketplace is that it allows a relatively free interplay between these two venerable cultural traditions as well as providing opportunities for individuals to find their preferred mode of worship.

We do not expect our findings on religiousness and spiritual seeking to put an end to the debate over whether church-centered religiousness or spiritual seeking has greater cultural authenticity and greater personal and social value. We do hope, however, that the overall lack of polarization we have revealed between these two ways of connecting with the sacred will give pause to critics of all stripes who are tempted to demonize either church and organized religion or non-church-based spirituality. Moreover, in view of the likelihood that unchurched forms of spirituality are going to increase in salience for Americans, especially with the aging of the populous baby boomers, we hope that social scientists and cultural critics alike will be rigorous in how they set about assessing spirituality. Throughout our research, we have been particularly careful to investigate both types of religious orientation in an evenhanded and systematic manner. We were fortunate, not only in that we could compare religiousness and spiritual seeking among the same group of people (and over time), but also in that we were able to develop behavioral measures of both constructs. While it is common in the social and health sciences to comment on the difficulty of measuring spirituality, with some individuals even asking whether it can be measured, we believe that spirituality, like religiousness, can be scientifically investigated. In this it is worth recalling that, for many decades, several serious social scientists dismissed the idea that religion could be scientifically measured and thus ignored religion as a social phenomenon.

In view of the increased prevalence of unchurched spirituality in everyday life, we believe that the various expressions of contemporary spirituality cannot be ignored and that they require systematic analysis. Our research suggests it is possible to operationalize and scientifically study spiritual seeking. Given the many meanings and definitions of spirituality in circulation, there is, of course, no one definition that captures all its implications or satisfies everyone (cf. Moberg 2002). We nonetheless believe that scientific and cultural discourse is better served when behavioral indicators of religiousness (most typically, the individual's frequency of church attendance) are compared with behavioral indicators of spirituality rather than with self-reported personal descriptors (such as "I consider myself a spiritual person"). Such comparability is all the more critical given the fraught evaluative debate on the social consequences of religiousness and spiritual seeking. Many Americans might easily call themselves spiritual without engaging in the spiritual practices that are necessary to maintaining connection with the sacred. Yet the people who intentionally practice spirituality likely differ in important ways from those who simply think of themselves as spiritual.

RELIGION AND AGING

At this time in America, there is much anticipation of the postretirement years of the baby boomers. As many of us are aware, the over-sixty-five population is expected to almost double by 2030, when Americans age sixty-five and older are anticipated to constitute more than a fifth of the nation's adult population (see, e.g., Sorensen 2007). The likely place of religion in this changing demographic picture has not received much attention to date. Our findings on the aging of the parents of the baby boomers do, however, offer some useful clues about the successful aging of the boomers themselves.

Most critically, our study provides strong support for the assumption that religious engagement, whether characterized by a church-centered religiousness or spiritual seeking, aids and abets the everyday functioning of individuals in late adulthood. Religious or spiritual individuals in our study participated in a greater range of social activities and personal hobbies and did so more frequently than those who were neither religious nor spiritual. While we recognize that there are many ways of crafting a purposeful old age, our data underscore the fact that, as in adolescence and in early adulthood, religious engagement can signal a general sense of agency and purpose among older individuals. The ties between religion and positive functioning are all the more apparent during times of personal adversity. There is something about church-centered religiousness in particular that cushions people against dissatisfaction and despair in the face of bad health, the bane of old age. And although spiritual seekers respond to adversity differently, they too are buffered against the loss of a sense of personal control over their lives. The bottom line is that religious or spiritual engagement provides added value to an already enriched life.

The value that religion has contributed to the positive aging of our study participants could not be reduced to or explained away by individual differences in other personal and social characteristics. As we noted, the positive association between religiousness or spiritual seeking and everyday purposeful activities was independent of good physical and mental health; similarly, the buffering effect of religiousness on life satisfaction and depression among those in poor physical health was not attributable to the strength of their social network. Although we found that religion had a unique effect on the texture of everyday life and on life outcomes, the nature of this effect varied by type of religious involvement and, to some extent too, by denomination. Taken as a whole, our data suggest that the relevance of religion, and its influence on lives over time, is best understood by focusing on how different religious orientations relate to personal experiences, family history, and cultural mood—and how in turn these are seen through the different lenses provided by gender and denominational characteristics—rather than by searching for the meaning of a universal religious factor.

Our findings on the positive role of religion in late adulthood take on added significance for several reasons. Most striking, our findings come from a community sample of Americans for whom religion had an important role in their lives but not one that overwhelmed all other activities. Most of our study participants came from mainstream religious denominations that are not overly demanding in their expectations for their adherents. And further, as noted throughout the book, many of our religious and spiritual participants were autonomous in expressing their beliefs and church commitments. Even so, religion was positively associated with several dimensions of everyday functioning, with concern for the welfare of others and a commitment to the social good, with life satisfaction, and with cushioning against some of the adversity and loss associated with old age. These robust results emerged, moreover, notwithstanding our study participants' positive social and economic living circumstances, their generally good health, and their high levels of energy and life satisfaction. In other words, if religion can have such a strong relation to positive functioning among religiously mainstream and high-functioning older adults, might it yield even greater benefits to those who are affiliated with stricter religious denominations and whose socioeconomic and living situations are less advantaged than those of our study participants?

The current expectation is that, as a result of a general increase in the quality of health care and nutrition, aging baby boomers will encounter less physically incapacitating illness than their parents' generation. It is still good to know that religiousness acts as a buffer against declining mental health in response to stress and adversity, whether derived from illness or from some of the other challenges of aging and everyday life. After all, even the healthy baby boomers will ultimately have to confront the inevitable physical decline and personal losses that come with old age.

The positive relation among religiousness, spiritual seeking, and social and psychological functioning in late adulthood focuses attention too on the possible psychological mechanism that helps to account for our findings. Our focus on a practice-based engagement with the sacred, whether through a church-centered religiousness or a more individualized spiritual seeking, ensured that the study participants who scored high on either religiousness or spiritual seeking would share a history of sustained engagement in disciplined practices aimed at integrating the sacred into their identity. Such a commitment, clearly, requires personal strength and psychological resources, what is often referred to as ego strength. As we saw, our religious and spiritual individuals oriented their ego strength in different ways, not only in regard to the sacred but also with respect to many aspects of everyday life. Our highly religious participants can be described as the "trusting faithful," insofar as they largely accepted the existing traditions: they ordained an inherited religious faith and the institutional accretions that had developed for its expression. Their sense of trust was part of a larger basic trust that, irrespective of whether an individual is religious or not, promotes self-integrity and reciprocity in social relations. Spiritual seekers, by contrast, are more like intrepid mariners ready to sail the open seas in search of new lands, driven by their own curiosity and propelled by the need to overcome personal adversity. This too requires strength and trust, but it is a trust in the bounty yielded by openness to new experiences rather than in the certainties of old. It is a journey, moreover, whose success is not assured but requires the psychological strength and ability to mold the dross of adversity into spiritual gold.

We certainly recognize that the different generational experiences of the baby boomers may give their religious beliefs and practices in old age a different valence than we found for those of their parents. Yet our findings, which indicate that disciplined spiritual seekers are vitally involved in everyday life and engaged in socially responsive and generative activities, provide solid grounds for the optimistic view that—even with the passing of the pre–World War II generation of civic-minded Americans, and the rise in a non-church-based spirituality—the social fabric of America is unlikely to unravel. The changing of the guard will undoubtedly change the tapestry of American religion and society, but it will remain patterned on at least some of the old cloth.

It is poignant that our study's portrait of the rich and variegated ways in which religion gives texture and meaning to everyday life comes largely from a slice of American religion that has declined. The decline of the mainline, the decreasing numerical strength of mainline Protestants and their displacement by more evangelical-oriented Protestants, is uncontested. A complex mix of theological, organizational, political, and cultural factors has undoubtedly contributed to the mainline's decline. Perhaps there is a certain inevitability that a tradition which celebrates individual religious autonomy and expects the church to support the individual's social and civic commitments will run afoul of the individual's exercise of this autonomy in a more complicated religious and social landscape in which—as Ian Logan, our Methodist engineer, commented—it is no longer so clear what is right and, even if one knows what is right, how to get at it.

Although a comparison of mainline and nonmainline Protestants was not our central aim in this book, we cannot but notice the self-emphasis apparent among the nonmainline participants in our study. This self-investment was evident in the nonmainline participants' stronger emphasis on private religious activities such as prayer and Bible reading; their comparatively lower levels of altruism, givingness, and concern for others; and their stronger tendency to express authoritarian attitudes and to make clear in-group/out-group distinctions. Clearly, our findings regarding nonmainline Protestants have to be interpreted cautiously because of their very small number in our study. Nonetheless, our data suggest that commentators who criticize the self-absorption and diminished commitment to the common good apparent among baby boomers and their children (Generation X) should focus their attention not only on the spiritual seekers in our midst but also on evangelical Christians. Of course, evangelicalism itself is not monolithic; and notwithstanding its strict image, it too has been cited for its theological lightness and permissive therapeutic messages (e.g., Roof 1999; Schmidt 2005).[4] It is not accidental that spiritual seeking and evangelicalism, both of which have eroded the mainline Protestant majority, share a strong focus on the self and a more person-centered approach to religious practices, although, as we have argued, self-investment does not necessarily have to be antithetical to an ethic of concern for others.

Going far beyond the denominations represented in our study, we can say that all religious traditions face the challenge of intergenerational transmission of religious and spiritual beliefs and practices. This charge has never been easy, but it is especially unwieldy in today's globalized world, where social relationships, identities, and institutions are increasingly disembedded from the localized interactions that have hitherto defined everyday life (see, e.g., Giddens 1991). The religious atmosphere so critically conveyed in the family home must increasingly accommodate the alternative worldviews, traditions, and ways of being that the globalized network of electronic media provide without pause. As we discovered in our research with the IHD study participants, ordinary lives produce extraordinary accomplishments and achievements, and people are remarkably resilient in adapting to personal loss and tragedy. But individuals can carve out purposeful lives only if they have the economic, social, and cultural resources that allow them to fully engage with others and, in the process, fully realize the promise of the self. Religion provides one such resource. The challenge for future research is to determine how varied religious and spiritual practices bear fruit across the expanding religious, ethnic, and cultural diversity currently transforming America.

Methodological Appendix
Measuring Religiousness and Spiritual
Seeking in the IHD Longitudinal Study

DATA ON RELIGION

It was our good fortune that, during the interviews conducted at each of the five assessments spanning adolescence and late adulthood, the IHD participants were asked specific questions about their religious beliefs, attitudes, and practices. In personal interviews in 1934, the older cohort (approximately age fourteen) were asked whether they went to church or Sunday school, where they went, how frequently, and whether they liked it. They were also shown, among other images, a painting of the Last Supper and asked whether they could identify it, whether they had ever seen it previously, and if so, where they had seen it. In separate interviews, they completed self-report closed-response questions on their then-current religious practices and beliefs: whether they prayed and for what purpose; how they thought of God and of what God does; the source of their ideas about God; how they thought of Jesus, the Bible, after-death, and hell; how they felt about religious organizations; which activities they liked to do on Sundays; how frequently they went to church and Sunday school and how frequently they did so when younger; how frequently their parents attended church; what church and Sunday school they attended; and whether they participated in a range of church and other social groups. The middle-aged parents of the older cohort were also interviewed in 1934, and in self-reported questionnaires they were asked about their involvement in church and church-related social groups, their denominational affiliations, and how frequently they attended church.

In personal interviews in 1943, the younger cohort, who were then age fourteen or fifteen, were asked open-ended questions about whether they attended church, Sunday school, and other church-related groups, meetings, and activities; the denomination of the churches and groups they attended; how frequently they participated in these activities; and what they thought about their various church-related activities. In follow-up interviews conducted three years later, in 1946, these participants were asked again about their religious interests and whether these were similar to, or different from, those of their parents. In-depth interviews were also conducted during the 1940s with the parents of members of the younger cohort. During separate interviews, each parent was asked to talk specifically about the meaning of religion to him or her personally, to his or her spouse, and to the children, including the study participant. Each parent was also asked about the place of religion in the lives of his or her own mother and father and of his or her spouse's mother and father.

At the time of the first follow-up assessment in adulthood, conducted in 1958 (early adulthood), the two original cohort studies were managed independently, and each used a different interview format and questions. During a series of lengthy personal interviews conducted over several days, the older cohort were asked open-ended questions about their religious beliefs and habits: whether they believed in God; what they thought of organized religion; whether, where, and how frequently they went to church and engaged in church activities; whether their religious beliefs and habits had changed; whether their spouses shared their religious beliefs; and whether they came from religious families. There were also asked about their "philosophy of life." Members of the younger cohort and their spouses were asked open-ended questions during separate personal interviews about the religious histories of their families and about their own beliefs and affiliation, whether and how frequently they attended church, and whether they sent their children to church and to Sunday school.

The two studies were merged in the 1960s (Block 1971), and consequently all the participants were asked a similar set of open-ended questions about religion at each subsequent assessment. In 1970 (middle adulthood), the participants were asked about their moral philosophy, whether they were church members and whether they attended church regularly, what religion meant to them, whether they believed in God, whether they thought of God as a personal or impersonal God, and whether they believed in an afterlife. During the third adult follow-up assessment, conducted in 1982 (late-middle adulthood), personal interviews with the participants included open-ended questions about whether they currently belonged to a church or to any organizations and social groups (such as a church choir, the Parent-Teacher Association, or the Masons), and whether religious activities were part of their general social routine. In self-reported questionnaires completed at this time, the participants indicated the frequency of their church attendance, their denomination, and their level of activity in church and church-related groups.

During the fourth and last follow-up assessment in late adulthood (interviews conducted from 1997 to 2000), we included several questions on religion. In the in-depth interviews, the participants were asked to talk about the beliefs and values that guided their daily lives; whether and how frequently they went to church; which church they belonged to; how active they were in its activities; whether their frequency and level of involvement had changed over the preceding ten years; whether they thought of themselves as religious; how they thought about the place of religion or the sacred in their daily lives; whether they had had any personally significant religious or spiritual experiences; and whether they believed in, and how they envisaged, life after death. The self-report questionnaires that the participants completed at this time included questions on church attendance, spiritual well-being, and the personal importance of religion, and the questions from the Religion Index for Psychiatric Research (Koenig, Parkerson, and Meador 1997).

RATING STRATEGY

The IHD study, therefore, contains a lot of detail about the religious beliefs, attitudes, and activities of the study participants and their parents. Typical, however, of the lack of question standardization generally found in longitudinal studies (see, e.g., Pearce and Axinn 1998), some of the specific questions asked or the exact wording of the questions about religion varied across the different interview times, and at any given time some of the interviewees were not as extensively probed as other interviewees. We dealt with this methodological problem by using the recasting method recommended for coding longitudinal data that is not directly comparable (Elder, Pavalko, and Clipp 1993; McCullough et al. 2005). Therefore, rather than relying solely on answers to the question asked about frequency of church attendance, for example—a question which, for various reasons, might be lacking data for some individuals for one or another interview time—we instead developed a single standardized metric of religious activity that took account of the person's answers to all the religion questions asked. We thus treated the individual's combined answers to the set of religion questions asked at each interview as a single *religion narrative* for each individual for each time period. Therefore, we had a total of five religion narratives for each participant—for adolescence (interviews conducted either in the 1930s or the 1940s), early adulthood (interviews conducted in 1958), middle adulthood (interviews conducted in 1970), late-middle adulthood (interviews conducted in 1982), and late adulthood (interviews conducted in 1997–2000). We also had a parental religion narrative for the middle-aged parents, obtained when the participants were adolescents.

In accordance with the cultural changes in American religion since the 1960s, we defined *religiousness* in terms of institutionalized or church-centered religious beliefs and practices, and we defined *spiritual seeking* in terms of noninstitutionalized or non-church-centered religious beliefs and practices (see, e.g., Roof 1999; Wuthnow 1998). This distinction follows Wuthnow's metaphor of religious dwelling and spiritual seeking; importantly, the distinction between institutionalized and noninstitutionalized religious beliefs and practices does not follow a public/private axis—for example, a woman who does not attend church but who privately reads the Episcopal Book of Common Prayer would, by our definition, still be participating in institutionalized religion; she would be a "dweller" rather than a "seeker."

We assessed the study participants' *religiousness* and *spiritual seeking* using two separate five-point rating scales based on the details contained in their religion narratives. Thus, we treated religiousness and spiritual seeking as different, but overlapping, variables for which each individual received a score for each interview time, as opposed to classifying each participant as either religious or spiritual or neither. Consequently, in our study an individual could score high on either religiousness or spiritual seeking, or on both constructs, or on neither (for any given interview time).

The main advantage of using the participants' religion narratives as the basis for our ratings was that it allowed us to assess the religiousness or spiritual seeking of individuals in a meaningful way when one of their respective indicators was missing, or when a particular indicator alone (e.g., frequency of church attendance) might not have fully captured the respective importance in the study participant's life. One woman, for example, in late adulthood was not able to attend church as often as she liked, because she was caring for her husband, who had Alzheimer's disease. Prayer, however, and reading the Psalms were important parts of her daily routine, and she had a strong faith in God. This woman, therefore, received a high score on our religiousness scale but would not have, had we confined our assessment to church attendance alone. The main drawback of our rating strategy is that, in the case of religiousness in particular, it does not allow us to differentiate between the private (e.g., prayer) and public (e.g., church attendance) aspects of institutionalized religious involvement. Although this distinction is theoretically important, in practice these two aspects of religiousness tend to be closely related (see, e.g., Myers 1996; Wilson and Musick 1997).

For the assessment in adolescence (when the interviewees were ages fourteen to eighteen) and for all four assessments conducted in adulthood, two independent raters coded the interview narratives on religion (composed of the interviewees' answers to the structured open-ended questions on religion) for evidence of religiousness. Spiritual seeking was coded for the four assessments in adulthood, but not for adolescence; there was insufficient variation in the adolescent religion narratives to code it in a meaningful way. In addition, the raters coded evidence of parental religiousness based on the interviews conducted with the parents (when their children were adolescents). Parental spiritual seeking was not coded, because of insufficient variation in the parents' religion narratives. The transcripts from all the interviews were coded after the personal interviews in late adulthood were completed. Our decision to use the same raters to code data from different time periods was based on a concern that, if we used multiple panels of raters, this might undermine the comparability of the ratings.

Although the use of the same raters circumvented this problem, it raised the issue of lack of independence between the ratings, as well as the possibility that ratings for one time period would be contaminated by information from another time period. We decided that the likelihood of this confound being present in our study was minimal, because it was highly unlikely that the raters would remember and match responses of anonymous participants across a pool of 1,340 religion narratives: $N = 242$ parental narratives; $N = 246$ adolescent (interviews conducted in the 1930s with members of the older cohort, born 1920–21, and interviews conducted in the 1940s with members of the younger cohort, born 1928–29); $N = 216$ early adulthood (interviews from 1958); $N = 226$ middle adulthood (interviews from 1970); $N = 226$ late-middle adulthood (interviews from 1982); $N = 184$ late adulthood (interviews from 1997 to 2000). The transcripts were randomized within each time period for the adolescent, the four adulthood, and the parent interviews.

RATING OF RELIGIOUSNESS

We rated the study participants' religiousness on a five-point rating scale assessing the extent to which institutionalized or church-centered religious beliefs and practices (e.g., church attendance and private prayer) were important in their everyday lives. This rating took into account whether and how frequently the interviewees attended church, whether and to what extent they believed in God and an afterlife, and how frequently they prayed and read the Bible; and the rating generally assessed the importance of religion in the participant's daily life.

A score of five on our five-point religiousness scale indicated that church-centered or institutionalized religious beliefs and practices played a *central* role in the respondent's life denoted by belief in God, heaven, and prayer, and/or frequent (once a week or more) attendance at a traditional place of worship. A score of four indicated that church-centered religion played an *important* role in the individual's life. The person typically believed in God and an afterlife and attended a place of worship on a weekly or almost weekly basis. A score of three indicated that church-centered religion had *some* importance in the individual's life: there was some uncertainty about belief in God and an afterlife, and church attendance tended to be infrequent (e.g., monthly). A score of two indicated that church-centered religion played a *peripheral* role in the individual's life, as reflected in uncertainty about the existence of God or an afterlife, as well as in sporadic attendance at a place of worship and sporadic prayer. A score of one indicated that institutionalized religion played *no* part in the life of the individual, as reflected in an explicitly stated lack of belief in God, an afterlife, or prayer, as well as in the absence of attendance at a place of worship.

The Kappa coefficient of reliability between the two raters for religiousness was .71 (late adulthood), .67 (late-middle adulthood), .66 (middle adulthood), .61 (early adulthood), .64 (adolescence), and .69 (parental religiousness); ($p < .00$ at each interview time). Given the high inter-rater reliability, the two coders' ratings were averaged into a single score on religiousness for each interviewee at each interview time.

Our interview-based ratings of the study participants' religiousness in late adulthood correlated highly with their own self-reported ratings of church attendance, private prayer, and intrinsic religiousness. We validated our interview-based ratings of religiousness against Koenig, Parkerson, and Meador's self-reported Religion Index for Psychiatric Research (1997), which was included in our late-adulthood self-report questionnaire ($N = 154$). The five-item index by Koenig and colleagues assesses three dimensions of religion: involvement in organizational (i.e., frequency of church attendance) and in nonorganizational (i.e., time spent in private prayer/Bible study) religious activities, and intrinsic religiosity (i.e., religion as an end rather than a means). Our religiousness scale correlated .86, .67, and .75 with involvement in organizational and nonorganizational religion and intrinsic religiosity, respectively (all $ps < .00$). Additionally, our interview-based religiousness scale correlated .75 ($p < .00$) with the interviewees' self-reported ratings of the personal importance of religion. These findings thus strengthen our confidence in the validity of our interview-based measure of religiousness.

RATING OF SPIRITUAL SEEKING

Similar to the method we used to rate religiousness, our method of rating spiritual seeking was based on the study participants' religion narratives—that is, their answers to the set of questions asked about religious beliefs, attitudes, and practices at each interview time. Our five-point rating of spiritual seeking assessed the extent to which non-institutionalized or non-church-centered religious beliefs and practices were important in the participants' lives. In order to be assigned a moderate or high score on spiritual seeking in our study, the individual had, among other core criteria, to express a strong interest in spiritual questions that, while focused on the transcendent or sacred nature of being, could include, but went beyond, the more conventional beliefs associated with institutionalized religion. These beliefs typically involved an emphasis on the sacredness of ordinary objects and the importance of experiencing sacred connections in everyday life, either with God, a Higher Power, or nature (see, e.g., Underwood 1999: 12).

Such beliefs and experiences alone, however, were not sufficient for the individual to receive a moderate or high score on our scale. Spiritual practices were also a critical element in our assessment of spiritual seeking. To attain a high score on spiritual seeking, the study participant had to report a systematic engagement in practices specifically aimed at incorporating a spiritual dimension in their everyday lives. In other words, simply being aware of spiritual feelings was not sufficient. Such awareness had to be accompanied by intentional spiritual practices such as meditation, for example. These spiritual practices could occur within established sacred places (such as churches) and could use prayers and other resources from within institutionalized religious traditions, or they could be independent of such institutionalized places and resources. In sum, although spirituality is frequently invoked in popular culture in a superficial way, for our study participants to receive a high score on spiritual seeking it was not sufficient for them to express a vague interest in spirituality, or to simply describe themselves as spiritual, or to indicate that they dabbled from time to time in meditation, yoga, or other unchurched religious practices. Rather, they had to regularly engage in disciplined spiritual practices, such as meditation, that intentionally enabled them to experience a transcendent or sacred Other.

A score of five on our five-point spiritual seeking scale indicated that non-church-centered or nontraditional religious beliefs and practices played a *central* role in the life of the individual. The person typically reported an awareness of a sense of connectedness with a sacred Other (e.g., God, a Higher Power, or nature) and systematically engaged in spiritual practices on a regular basis (e.g., meditating, participating in experiential or spiritual groups, Celtic nature-centered rituals, and undertaking a shamanic journey). A score of four indicated that spiritual seeking was *important* in the daily life of the individual: the individual reported a sense of sacred connectedness, and he or she regularly engaged in spiritual practices (but they were not as central in the life of this person as in that of an individual who received a score of five). A score of three indicated that spiritual seeking had *some* importance in the life of the individual: the individual reported having spiritual experiences, and she or he engaged in occasional spiritual practices. A score of two indicated that the individual expressed a *marginal* interest in spiritual issues (e.g., reported a vague sense of continuity between self and nature) or reported some spiritual experiences (e.g., an oceanic feeling when contemplating nature), but she or he did not engage in any spiritual practices. A score of one indicated that the individual reported *no* interest in spiritual matters. The Kappa coefficient of reliability between the two raters for spiritual seeking was .63 (late adulthood), .56

(late-middle adulthood), .55 (middle adulthood), and .71 (early adulthood); (p < .00 at each interview time). Given the high inter-rater reliability, the two coders' ratings were averaged into a single score on spiritual seeking for each interviewee at each interview time.

We want to underscore that, as should be clear by now, our ratings of spiritual seeking (and of religiousness) emphasize the importance of intentional and systematic practices. We believe that spiritual seeking cannot be considered simply a transitory feeling as is sometimes suggested by its invocation in popular culture. Similarly, we believe that self-report questions asking survey respondents whether they consider themselves spiritual (as, for example, in the General Social Survey) do not sufficiently reveal whether individuals are serious or disciplined about their spirituality. Rather, just as social scientists have traditionally and almost invariably linked religiousness to behavioral indicators such as church attendance, so too we believe that the measurement of spiritual seeking should be linked to intentional behavioral practices. Thus, in our ratings, we assessed whether there was evidence that individuals intentionally worked at maintaining their spiritual commitment and engaged in practices that would nurture the initial experience of the transcendent that sparked their spiritual awareness (cf. Neuman 1982).

We did not have a validated self-reported measure of spirituality or of spiritual seeking against which we could validate our rating of spiritual seeking. As we did for religiousness (see above), however, we validated our interview-based ratings of spiritual seeking against Koenig, Parkerson, and Meador's Religion Index for Psychiatric Research (1997), which was included in our late-adulthood self-report questionnaire (N = 154). Whereas religiousness showed a stronger relation with involvement in organizational than nonorganizational religious activities, a reverse pattern was found for spiritual seeking. It correlated .30 with involvement in organizational religious activities, .35 with involvement in nonorganizational religious activities, and .40 with intrinsic religiosity (all ps < .00). Additionally, our spiritual seeking scale correlated .33 (p < .00) with a self-reported rating of the personal importance of religion. Although our measure of spiritual seeking correlated higher with participation in privatized religious activities than with participation in public religious activities, this correlation was only moderate in magnitude. This was the case because, as we have indicated, an emphasis on the privatized aspects of faith is not central to our definition of spiritual seeking.

RELATION BETWEEN RATINGS OF RELIGIOUSNESS AND SPIRITUAL SEEKING

Although we defined religiousness and spiritual seeking as two distinct orientations toward religion, the two measures correlated positively with each other: .26 in early adulthood, .26 in middle adulthood, .34 in late-middle adulthood, and .36 in late adulthood ($p < .01$ at each interview time). These correlations reflect the fact that, as indicated above in the section on rating strategy, seeking and dwelling are different but overlapping approaches to religion; one does not preclude the other. An individual can be committed to church-centered religious beliefs and practices and at the same time be a highly active spiritual seeker engaged in intentional practices that negotiate among a range of religious and spiritual resources. This means that a small number of individuals scored high on both religiousness and spiritual seeking, but this was not true of the majority of the interviewees. In late adulthood, for example, the correlation between religiousness and spiritual seeking was much lower than that found in surveys using self-report questions asking respondents whether they consider themselves religious and/or spiritual, where the correlations typically exceed .70 (e.g., Roof 1999; Zinnbauer et al. 1997).

ELUCIDATION OF OUR RATINGS THROUGH THE USE OF PARTICIPANTS' QUOTES

The following brief quotes taken from transcripts of interviews conducted with the participants in late adulthood help to concretize the differences between religiousness and spiritual seeking as defined in our study. In interviewees' remarks about their everyday beliefs and values, religiousness would be associated with a statement such as "I believe totally in scripture. I think we can always learn from it. I think there is a lot there to give us hope and peace and love for this life and beyond." Spiritual seeking would be better captured with a response such as "I have a very close connection to nature, . . . and God or spirit is not something out there. It is mine, . . . and I'm cocreator of the spirit. . . . We are all one." Similarly, when participants were asked how they construed the afterlife, religiousness would be typified by a statement such as "When death comes, the last breath, my security is in my firm belief in what Jesus taught in the Bible, and that I am immediately with Him in Paradise, Heaven." The response to the same question by a person whom we would characterize as a spiritual seeker would more likely be: "I do believe that I'm part of the universe, and that I get returned somehow—my spirit or my consciousness—to something that is, hopefully, more worthwhile, at a higher level." With regard to religious and spiritual practices, a woman who scored high on religiousness said, "I attend religious services usually every Sunday, but during the year we also have Bible study," whereas a woman who received a moderate score on spiritual seeking said, "If one believes in the universal spirit, 'Our Father in Heaven' doesn't work too well. So I've been introduced to a centering prayer that is an old revival of a Catholic contemplative prayer—not too distant from Transcendental Meditation."

Notes

1. THE VIBRANCY OF AMERICAN RELIGION

1. The names of, and other personally identifying information about, the study participants quoted throughout the book have been changed to protect their anonymity. The quotations from interviews conducted with the study participants during adolescence and in 1958, 1970, 1982, and 1997–2000 are taken from their interview transcripts. Additionally, because previous IHD researchers and interviewers frequently wrote summary comments about interviewees' personalities and other characteristics, we occasionally quote their comments, taken from the IHD archives.

2. The IHD was then called the Institute of Child Welfare. A grant from the Laura Spellman Rockefeller Foundation helped to establish the institute and was the main source of support for the Berkeley Guidance Study for twenty years (Eichorn 1981). The study used a sample of infants born in Berkeley between January 1, 1928, and June 30, 1929 (choosing every third birth). Macfarlane's study was called a guidance study because of her interest in assessing personality development and behavior and the impact of parental guidance from the professional staff. The GS assessed the infants' health and their physical, motor, personality, and social development at regular intervals in infancy and, as the study continued, made regular assessments throughout the participants' early childhood and into adolescence. The mothers were also interviewed periodically. Home and family observation visits were another feature of this study, and as a result of these various data-gathering processes, extensive socioeconomic, cultural, and other background data were obtained about each child's family (Eichorn 1981).

3. A unique feature of the OGS was that the institute provided the participants with their own clubhouse near the junior high school that most of them attended, and here they participated in a host of informal club activities—such as chatting and listening to records—after school and on the weekends. Later

in high school, the study participants were taken on skiing and other group trips. The OGS participants thus constituted a highly cohesive group with close ties to one another and to the institute and its core researchers (Eichorn 1981). The OGS, and subsequently the GS too, received funding from various private foundations, including the Ford Foundation, the W. T. Grant Foundation, the Spencer Foundation, and the MacArthur Foundation, as well as from the federal government: the National Institute of Mental Health, the National Institute of Child Health and Human Development, the National Institute of Aging, and the National Science Foundation (Clausen 1993). As we have noted in the preface, the extensive follow-up study in late adulthood (1997–2000) was funded by a Soros Foundation grant awarded to Paul Wink.

4. The greatest attrition in the IHD study occurred during childhood and adolescence, because families who moved out of the Berkeley and Oakland school area were dropped from the study. As a result, the initial number of 467 participants at recruitment declined to 319 by the end of high school (Clausen 1993). A total of 303 individuals participated in at least one of the first three follow-up studies in adulthood, with the number of participants ranging from 233 to 240 (not necessarily the same individuals). The number dropped to 184 in late adulthood, primarily because of increased rates of mortality among the older participants (those born in 1920–21). In sum, 91 percent of participants known to be alive were interviewed in late adulthood.

The remaining 9 percent were not contactable or they declined to participate. Analyses of the overall attrition patterns show a slightly greater tendency for men from working-class families and with troubled family backgrounds and lower IQ not to participate as regularly as other study members (Eichorn 1981: 41). Other studies similarly find that attrition is greatest in families in which the husband or father does not have a college education (e.g., Myers 1996). Comparing the personality and social background data of individuals who participated in the late-adulthood assessment with those who participated in late-middle adulthood, but who declined to be interviewed in late adulthood, showed few differences. In late-middle adulthood, the two groups did not differ in level of education or intelligence, in acceptance of social norms, or in self-reported levels of well-being, health, and energy. Those who participated in 1982 but not in the 1997–2000 phase were, however, significantly more introverted and less comfortable in social situations (Wink and Dillon 2002). The study participants' fathers (28 percent) were more likely than mothers (19 percent) to be college graduates. Most of the mothers (76 percent) were not employed outside the home. The occupational status, educational level, and social class of mothers and fathers, as well as of the study participants, were measured using the Hollingshead Occupation Scale, the Hollingshead Education Scale, and the Hollingshead Social Class Index, respectively (see Hollingshead and Redlich 1958).

5. An interval of eight years may not seem like too great a difference in terms of age. Yet, from a life course perspective, the timing of important historical events and their coinciding with different developmental phases in the lives of members of these two cohorts make for substantial differences in each cohort's particular experiences (cf. Elder 1998).

6. Putnam refers to Americans born between 1910 and 1940 as representing a "long civic generation" and defines those born between 1925 and 1930 as its core cohort. This "exceptionally civic" generation—with a record of "voting more, joining more, reading more, trusting more, giving more"—is "substantially more engaged in community affairs and more trusting that those younger than they" (2000: 254).

7. Many sociologists discuss the "decline of the mainline." See especially Finke and Stark 1992; and Roof and McKinney 1987. Finke and Stark show that, between 1940 and 1985, evangelical churches made substantial gains in their share of religious adherents: Southern Baptists increased their membership by 32 percent, Assemblies of God by 37 percent, and Church of the Nazarene by 42 percent. Among the mainline, however, Methodists experienced a decline of 48 percent, Presbyterians 49 percent, Episcopalians 38 percent, and Congregationalists 56 percent during the same period (1992: 248). More recent data shows that, whereas 30 percent of Americans identified as either Methodist, Lutheran, Presbyterian, or Episcopalian in 1967, this figure declined to 18 percent by 2004 (Lyons 2005: 111).

The nationwide decline in the proportion of followers of mainline denominations was reflected in our study. Most of the study participants who were not church members or who did not actively identify with a denomination in late adulthood (1997–2000) had grown up in mainline Protestant families. Although some of the study participants who grew up Catholic left the Catholic Church in early adulthood or later, they were replaced by others who joined the church in early adulthood (usually upon marriage) or later in life. Therefore, despite individual change, the proportion of Catholics in the original sample and in late adulthood was approximately the same (16 percent). Similarly, some of the participants who came from nonmainline families (e.g., Christian Scientist or Seventh-day Adventist) were, in late adulthood, not church members or did not indicate any active attachment to their denomination of origin. Conversely, some of the study participants who came from nonreligious families or who were Catholics or mainline Protestants embraced evangelicalism in middle life. In our late-adulthood analyses of the relations between religiousness and social and psychological functioning (chapters 8, 9, and 10), our nonmainline group is largely composed of evangelical Christians.

8. See Roof and McKinney 1987; and Thuesen 2002. Peter Thuesen argues that "the mainline's unique gifts to the American religious mixture lie in the logic of mainline churchliness," which he summarizes in terms of (1) a tolerance of ethical differences and diversity; (2) an ecumenical concern with identifying points of agreement among denominations; (3) a corporate emphasis on the church as the Body of Christ; and (4) a universal reality that mystically encompasses the nation, a trait that, as Thuesen notes, is close to Catholicism but, he argues, "without the more autocratic dimensions of Catholic polity" (48–49).

9. In 1998, 90 percent of Americans in the age category sixty-five to seventy-four said that religion was important in their lives (Gallup and Lindsay 1999: 10). In the Pacific region (California, Nevada, and Hawaii), 51 percent of mainline Protestants identify as Republican, 36 percent as Democrat, and 18 percent as independent; 38 percent of Catholics identify as Republican, 33 percent as

Democrat, and 16 percent as independent. Nationally, 49 percent of mainline Protestants identify as Republican and 33 percent as Democrat; and 38 percent of Catholics identify as Republican and 44 percent as Democrat. These percentages are based on survey data collected by the Bliss Institute at the University of Akron from 1992 to 2000 and were made available to Dillon as part of the Religion by Region Project sponsored by the Leonard Greenberg Center for the Study of Religion in Public Life, Trinity College, Hartford, Connecticut.

10. Several scholars document the transformative effect of the 1960s on American religion (see, e.g., Ahlstrom 1972; Glock and Bellah 1976; Porterfield 2001; Roof and McKinney 1987). While noting continuities with earlier generations, Wade Clark Roof nonetheless argues that the baby boom generation "redefined the nation's religious norms, beliefs and practices" (1999: 53). But as Robert Wuthnow suggests, religion switching in the 1950s "paved the way" for the quest culture associated with later cohorts and their greater tendency to explore spirituality independent of church. The ability to switch denominations or religions raised the prospect that it was also possible to do without religion entirely (1998: 56). Ellwood (1997) also notes the continuities between American religion in the 1950s and the spiritual turn associated with the 1960s.

11. From as early as the beginning of the twentieth century, sociologists have assumed that the wide-ranging changes associated with the ever-increasing modernization of society would bring about a linear decline in the significance of religion. Most famously, this was the prediction of social theorist Max Weber, one of the founding fathers of sociology. Commenting more than one hundred years ago on the ever-increasing rationality of industrialization and capitalism, he observed, "The modern man is in general, even with the best will, unable to give religious ideas a significance for culture and national character which they deserve" (1904–05/1976: 181–83). There is an extensive literature assessing the secularization thesis. See, among others, Chaves 1994; and Gorski 2003.

12. Our definitions of religiousness and spiritual seeking parallel the contrasting metaphors of religious dwelling and spiritual seeking introduced by Wuthnow (1998). We discuss the questions about religion asked of the study participants at each interview time, and we explain our operationalization and measurement of religiousness and spiritual seeking, in the methodological appendix.

2. MEET THE PARENTS

1. Source: *Statistical Abstract of the United States* 1929. Berkeley's population more than doubled between 1890 and 1900, growing from 5,101 to 13,214, and Oakland's increased from 48,682 to 66,960 in the same period. Both experienced rapid growth thereafter (*Statistical Abstract of the United States* 1954: 25).

2. Source: Workers of the Writers' Program of the Work Projects Administration in Northern California 1940.

3. In the IHD study, 43 percent of paternal grandfathers, 35 percent of paternal grandmothers, 40 percent of maternal grandfathers, and 38 percent of maternal grandmothers were born outside the United States.

4. California's first missionaries were the Franciscans, a Catholic order who established the attractive—and still-standing—churches and missions along much of the California coast in the eighteenth century (see, e.g., Ahlstrom 1972: 44–46). For an interesting discussion of the mutual suspicion in the relationships between the early Spanish missionary settlers and California Indians, see Hurtado 1999: 1–19.

5. Using census data from 1850, Finke and Stark show that frontier states, including Iowa, Arkansas, Michigan, and Texas, had the lowest rates of religious adherents in 1850, compared to Maryland, Ohio, and Indiana, which had the highest rates, and, less so, New England (1992: 68).

In the late 1990s, almost one in ten individuals (9 percent) in the West expressed no religious preference, more than double the proportion of religiously nonaffiliated individuals in the South (Gallup and Lindsay 1999: 17). Additionally, more individuals in the Pacific region (California, Hawaii, and Nevada) identified as "secularists" than in any other region of the United States. Twenty-three percent of individuals in the Pacific region, compared to 20 percent in New England, 17 percent in the Midwest, and 13 percent in the South, identified as "secularists." These figures are derived from survey data collected by the Bliss Institute at the University of Akron, 1992–2000, made available to Dillon as part of the Religion by Region Project sponsored by the Leonard Greenberg Center for the Study of Religion in Public Life, Trinity College, Hartford, Connecticut.

6. Berkeley's population in 1930 was 82,109, a figure that increased to 85,547 by 1940. The population of Oakland was 216,261 people in 1920, and it increased to 302,163 in 1940 (*Statistical Abstract of the United States* 1954: 25). The proportion of Blacks in California increased from 1.4 percent to 4.7 percent, and both Berkeley and Oakland experienced about an 8 percent increase in their Black populations during this period (*Statistical Abstract of the United States* 1954: 38).

7. This historical assumption is largely a reflection of the strong effect that Tocqueville's observations from his travels in the eastern part of America in the 1830s have had on the American cultural and scholarly imagination. Tocqueville wrote:

> In the United States on the seventh day of every week the tradition and working life of the nation seems suspended; all noises cease; a deep tranquility, say rather the solemn calm of meditation, succeeds the turmoil of the week, and the soul resumes possession and contemplation of itself. On this day, the marts of traffic are deserted; every member of the community, accompanied by his children, goes to church, where he listens to strange language which would seem unsuited to his ear. . . . On his return home he does not turn to the ledgers of business, but he opens the book of Holy Scripture; there he meets with sublime and affecting descriptions of the greatness and goodness of the Creator, of the infinite magnificence of the handiwork of God, and of the lofty destinies of man, his duties, and his immortal privileges. (Tocqueville 1840/1946: vol. 2, p. 143)

But see Lynd and Lynd 1929, 1937; Fichter 1954; and Finke and Stark 1992 for historical evidence against the uniform appeal of religion in the United States.

8. The percentages for parental religiousness are derived from our interview-based ratings of parental religiousness, as described in the methodological appendix.

9. The mean difference in religiousness between Catholics and mainline Protestants was significant: $t(49,132) = 2.60$, $p = 01$; and between nonmainline and mainline Protestants, it was significant at a trend level: $t(29,132) = 1.68$, $p = .09$.

10. Among Catholics, the significant correlation between mother's and father's self-reported religious involvement was $r(29) = .83$, $p = .00$, and among Protestants, the significant correlation between the mother's and father's religious involvement was $r(129) = .90$, $p = .00$. These data are for the parents of the older cohort only, who in 1934 provided self-reported assessments of their religious involvement. The quotations from parents used in this chapter are taken from the transcripts of the in-depth interviews conducted with the parents of the younger cohort.

11. Taking an even longer historical perspective on the coexistence of religious commitment and indifference, in John Winthrop's New England, clergy and elders at the Boston Formal Synod in 1679 lamented, among other failings, the "much visible decay of godliness, contentiousness in the churches, and violation of the Sabbath" (Miller 1956/1964: 5–6).

12. In 1934, 33 percent of mothers and 45 percent of fathers of the older cohort were not attending church services, as indicated by their responses to a specific question on church attendance asked only of older-cohort parents. Forty-seven percent of Catholic mothers and 38 percent of Protestant mothers had similarly high levels of self-reported religious involvement during their children's adolescence ($x^2 = 4.5$, $df4$, $n.s.$). Catholic fathers (74 percent) were more frequent churchgoers than Protestant fathers (41 percent) (based on self-reported data for the older cohort, collected in 1934), and Catholic fathers (43 percent) were more religiously involved overall than Protestant fathers (26 percent), a difference reflecting the church-attendance component of religious involvement. The difference between Catholic and Protestant fathers in overall religious involvement was statistically significant ($x^2 = 10.50$, $df4$, $p < .03$).

13. Among Protestants, the mother's self-reported religious involvement was significantly related to the father's education ($r(68) = .29$, $p < .01$) and was related at a trend level to the mother's education ($r(67) = .22$, $p = .07$). Among Catholics, the mother's religious involvement was not significantly related to the mother's ($r(19) = .17$, $n.s.$) or the father's education ($r(19) = .19$, $n.s.$). Among Catholics and Protestants, the correlation between the mother's religious involvement and the economic deprivation felt due to the Depression was ($r(92) = -.07$, $n.s.$). These data are for parents of the older cohort.

14. Among the parents of the younger cohort (of study participants born in 1928–29), 27 percent of either fathers or mothers spontaneously recounted, when interviewed in depth in the 1940s, that they themselves rejected religion as young adults precisely because of their negative experiences while growing up in rigidly religious families. Parents' accounts of religious strictness were not confined to any particular denominational theology but, as illustrated by the quotes we have included, referred to a range of religious traditions and to religious proscriptions applied in their families.

15. Roof found that life in authoritarian families "produced a deeply felt ambivalence resulting in two, quite alternative paths"—one path is a "strong

affirmation of those values . . . [and the alternate is] a break with that past."
He argues that for some individuals a strict upbringing can be "a mechanism of
cultural and religious continuity[,] . . . but for others it can be heavy baggage
resulting in resistance, if not outright rejection" (1999: 231–32).

16. The historian Mark Noll describes the Puritans' intergenerational
challenge:

> As the 1640s gave way to the 1650s, more and more children of the earliest settlers
> failed to experience God's grace in the same fashion as their parents, and hence
> they did not seek full membership in the churches. The problem became acute when
> these children began to marry and have children of their own. Under the Puritans'
> Reformed theology, converted people had the privilege of bringing their infant chil-
> dren to be baptized as a seal of God's covenant grace. Now however many of those
> who had been baptized as infants were not stepping forth on their own to confess
> Christ. Yet they wanted to have their children baptized. The Puritan dilemma was
> delicate: leaders wished to preserve the church for genuine believers, but they also
> wanted to keep as many as possible under the influence of the church. Their solution
> was to propose a "halfway" covenant whereby second-generation New Englanders
> could bring their third-generation children for baptism and a halfway membership.
> Participation in the Lord's Supper remained a privilege for those who could testify to
> a specific work of God's grace in their lives. (1992: 48)

17. Gallup poll data indicate that 89 percent of Americans affirm that they
would want a child of theirs to receive religious training. Closely similar proportions characterize women (90 percent) and men (86 percent), Protestants (93
percent) and Catholics (94 percent), and all age groups. However, understand-
ably—because they may not have yet given this much thought—fewer younger
adults (83 percent of those age eighteen to twenty-nine) affirm this view than
older Americans (91 percent). See Gallup and Lindsay 1999: 63.

3. ADOLESCENT RELIGION IN THE 1930s AND 1940s

1. Based on answers to a series of closed-response questions asked of the
older cohort (born in 1920–21) in 1934, 88 percent went ice-skating and to
movies and 40 percent to dances and ball games.

2. These percentages are based on our five-point religiousness ratings of the
adolescents' interview transcripts. See the methodological appendix for details
of the religion questions asked and the coding and rating procedures we used.
High scorers on religiousness received a score of 4, 4.5, or 5; the moderately
religious received a score of 2.5 to 3.5; the somewhat religious, a score of 1.5 or
2; and those not at all religious, a score of 1. The percentages we derived from
our interview-based ratings of religiousness closely parallel a rating completed
by the IHD staff indicating that 56 percent of the study participants attended
church services on a regular basis in childhood, with another 33 percent reporting sporadic church attendance.

3. The data reported in this section are based on answers to open-ended
questions about church and Sunday school asked of the younger cohort (born
in 1928–29). Sixty-one percent explicitly indicated that they liked church or
that it was all right. There were no denominational differences apparent in adolescents' attitudes toward religious activities, but there was gender variation:

girls (66 percent) were more likely than boys (54 percent) to say that they liked church or Sunday school.

4. Smith and Denton found that today 40 percent of Catholics and 39 percent of mainline Protestants attend religious services at least once a week (2005: 37).

5. Smith and Denton show, for example, that today 55 percent of conservative White Protestants and 71 percent of Mormons attend religious services at least weekly, compared to 39 percent of mainline Protestants (2005: 37).

6. For example, Roof and McKinney argue that the new religious individualism associated with the baby boom generation means that intrafamily, "individually based differences in beliefs and values now operate more freely in religion" (1987: 69). Our data provide evidence that this ethos was not completely absent in earlier decades.

7. The correlation between adolescent religiousness and parental religiousness was $r = .69, p < .001$.

8. Based on a separate, discrete measure of childhood church attendance, 59 percent of girls compared to 51 percent of boys were regular churchgoers ($x^2 = 5.18, df 2, p < .07$). A two-way analysis of variance (ANOVA) with our interview-based measure of adolescent religiousness as the dependent variable, and gender and denomination as the independent factors, indicated a significant main effect of gender ($F(1,207) = 5.56, p < .05$). The main effect of denomination and the gender-by-denomination interaction were not significant. An ANOVA is a statistical procedure that establishes whether scores on a given measure (e.g., religiousness) are significantly predicted by group membership (e.g., being male or female, Catholic or Protestant). In addition to testing for the main effects of group membership, a two-way ANOVA allows for the detection of an interaction—that is, the significant effect of simultaneous membership in two groups (e.g., being a male Protestant or a female Catholic)—on a given measure (e.g., religiousness).

9. Among mainline Protestants, nonmainline Protestants, and Catholics, adolescent religiousness was not significantly related to the mother's or father's education or to the father's occupation, or to the Depression.

10. These figures, based on the older cohort's self-reported answers, triangulate with our interview-based ratings of adolescent religiousness indicating that 13 percent of the study participants as a whole (both cohorts combined) were not exposed to religion while growing up.

11. In 1934, members of the older cohort (born in 1920–21) were given a set of nine sentence stems and questions (e.g., "I pray in order to . . . ," "I think of God as . . . ," "I think of Jesus as . . . ," and "From where did you get your idea of God?") accompanied by a list of options in which participants could check all that were applicable to them. The percentages in this section are from this subsample of participants. The quoted comments are from the younger cohort's adolescent interviews.

12. The numbers for the older cohort subsample are small, and thus it does not make great sense to assess statistical significance in terms of denominational variation. Nonetheless, 54 percent of Catholics within this cohort (7 of 13) compared to 15 percent of mainline (9 of 57) and 9 percent of nonmainline

(1 of 11) Protestant adolescents endorsed the idea of hell as a place of torture and where people pay for the bad they have done. It is interesting to note that, in a survey of adults in the 1950s reported by Herberg, although 73 percent "believed in an afterlife, with God as Judge . . . only 5 percent [had] any fear . . . of Hell" (1955: 85–86).

13. Based on answers to open-ended questions about church and Sunday school asked of the younger cohort (born in 1928–29), approximately 40 percent spoke of their interest in the spiritual or intellectual aspects of church.

14. The data reported in this section are based on answers to open-ended questions about church and Sunday school asked of the younger cohort (born in 1928–29).

15. The percentages reported here are derived from answers to the sentence-stem question "I feel that religious organizations . . ." asked of the older cohort in 1934 (see note 11 above).

16. Gallup and Lindsay (1999) use data comparing teenagers' religious beliefs and church attendance in 1959–61, the end of the decade of historically high church attendance in America, with those of 1988–93.

17. Although Smith and Denton acknowledge that instrumental religion is not a teenage invention and is embraced by many adults, they do not say when it was invented. In any case, they are unequivocal that it is qualitatively deficient compared to its precursor (2005: 154).

4. THE IMPRINT OF INDIVIDUAL AUTONOMY ON EVERYDAY RELIGION IN THE 1950s

1. See also Pritchard 1976; Douglas 1982; and Hall 1997 for a reminder of the historical continuities in American religion.

2. Gallup poll data show, for example, that weekly church attendance was higher in 1958 (49 percent) than in 1939 (41 percent), 1975 (40 percent), 1989 (43 percent), 1994 (42 percent), and 1998 (40 percent; Gallup and Lindsay 1999: 15). See Herberg 1955 and Wuthnow 1988 for analyses of the public salience of religion in American society in the 1950s.

3. The *Saturday Evening Post,* April 4, 1953. See also *Walking to Church,* in *Norman Rockwell: Pictures for the American People* (Hennessey and Knutson 2000: 130, 140) and on display at the Norman Rockwell Museum in Stockbridge, Massachusetts.

4. By 1958, 91 percent of the study participants were married and 87 percent had one or more children.

5. Although the early adulthood interviews did not contain any specific questions on the topic of religious freedom or autonomy per se, two raters (one of whom was unaware of the source of the data and of the study's research questions) independently coded the study participants' early adulthood religion narratives (composed of their answers to structured, open-ended questions about their religious beliefs, attitudes, and habits) for explicit evidence of (1) autonomy in individual choice in regard to religion, (2) the relative independence of faith or religious belief from church participation, and (3) the relative independence of morality from sectarian theological creeds (1 = characteristic is present; 0 = characteristic is absent).

These three themes were not independent of one another, and consequently, in any one narrative there could be evidence of just one theme, a combination of any of the three themes, or no evidence of any of these themes. (The narratives were also coded for evidence of the social and faith aspects of religion, themes we discuss in chapter 6.) The narratives of all study participants for whom there was sufficient thematic detail in the religion section of the interview transcript, regardless of their level of religious involvement, were coded ($N = 129$ of the 184 study participants who were interviewed in both early and late adulthood). The Kappa coefficient of reliability for the two raters was .59 for choice, .40 for belief independent of church, and .68 for Golden Rule. The three themes were moderately interrelated: choice and Golden Rule, $r = .26$; choice and belief independent of church, $r = .27$; Golden Rule and belief independent of church, $r = .28$ ($N = 129$, $ps < .01$).

6. The Protestant/Catholic difference was significant: $x^2 = 5.09$, $df1$, $p < .05$. The gender, cohort, and social class differences were not statistically significant (using the chi-square test).

7. In 1958, 48 percent of our participants were moderately or highly religious, 26 percent were somewhat religious, and 26 percent were not religious. (See the methodological appendix for details about our religiousness rating.) Fifty-one percent of those who were moderately or highly religious in early adulthood (as rated from the 1958 interviews), 56 percent who were somewhat religious, and 58 percent who were not religious spoke of religion in terms of choice. Similarly, 51 percent of those who were moderately or highly religious in adolescence, 58 percent who were somewhat religious, and 59 percent of those who were not religious invoked choice in talking about their religious habits and attitudes in 1958. These differences were not statistically significant (using the chi-square test).

8. The historical importance of the appeal of local pastors in influencing religious choices was evident also in the recollections of some of the participants' parents. For example, in the early 1940s, one mother recalled that, although her paternal grandparents were "pillars of the church," her maternal grandparents "only went to church occasionally and only when they liked the minister."

9. In early adulthood, the view that religious belief was independent of church participation characterized 28 percent of men and 30 percent of women; 27 percent of high-social-status individuals versus 39 percent of low-social-status individuals; and 31 percent of Protestants and 17 percent of Catholics. Twenty-six percent of those who were moderately or highly religious compared to 39 percent who were somewhat religious and 25 percent who were not religious also expressed this view (all chi-squares not significant).

Members of the older cohort (56 percent), however, were more likely than the younger cohort (14 percent) to mention the independence of religious beliefs from church affiliation or attendance ($x^2 = 26.04$, $df1$, $p < .00$). This significant cohort difference may reflect the fact that in 1958 the younger cohort was asked fewer and less probing questions about religion than was the older cohort. If the cohort difference in regard to the independence of faith is a result of this discrepancy, the figure of 30 percent is likely to underestimate the number of participants who endorsed the theme of religious autonomy, because only one-third of the individuals included in this analysis came from the older age cohort.

10. Parsons (1967) extended the insights of the German social theorist Max Weber. Weber's famous essay *The Protestant Ethic and the Spirit of Capitalism* (1904–05/1976), first published at the turn of the twentieth century, discussed how the early Calvinists came to rationalize their religious beliefs about salvation by regarding everyday life as an opportunity in which to serve and glorify God. Thus the Calvinists took religion out of the churches and made it an integral part of their everyday routines involving hard work, frugality, and asceticism.

11. Erikson notes the Golden Rule's consistency with the Kantian imperative to see people as ends rather than means, and with the words of Abraham Lincoln stating that we should have "charity toward all and malice toward none. . . . As I would not be slave, I would not be master." Erikson also points out that its moral emphasis has an affinity with the Hindu idea of "maintenance of the world" and the principle of Karma (1964: 220–21). See also Dillon and Wink 2004. It is interesting to note that Norman Rockwell, who was a neighbor of Erikson's in Stockbridge in the 1950s, produced an illustration of the Golden Rule in 1961. Rockwell recognized the universality of the Golden Rule, having commented in regard to his painting: "I'd been reading up on comparative religion. The thing is that all major religions have the Golden Rule in common. 'Do unto others as you would have them do unto you.' Not always the same words but the same idea" (quoted in the *Norman Rockwell Album*, on display at the Norman Rockwell Museum, Stockbridge, Massachusetts).

12. The difference between Protestants and Catholics was statistically significant (x^2 = 3.97, df_1, p < .05). Similarly, the older participants (54 percent) invoked the Golden Rule more frequently than the younger participants (14 percent) (x^2 = 24.27, df_1, p < .001). This significant cohort difference is likely due to the fact that, during the 1958 interview, immediately before they were asked the questions about religious beliefs and habits, the members of the older cohort were asked, "Most of us don't stop to think about it, but most of us have a philosophy of life. What is yours?" The differences, however, between men (35 percent) and women (23 percent), and between participants of high (30 percent) and low (26 percent) socioeconomic status, were not statistically significant. Early adulthood religiousness was also unrelated to Golden Rule morality; 36 percent of the participants who were moderately or highly religious in 1958, 26 percent who were somewhat religious, and 21 percent who were not religious invoked the Golden Rule (these differences were not statistically significant).

13. Although some will argue that "talk is cheap," it is noteworthy that the individuals in our study who invoked the Golden Rule in early adulthood were also more likely than others to be described by clinical psychologists—who independently assessed their personalities—as having a personal functioning style that showed sensitivity to the needs of other individuals and groups.

14. Based on their study of baby boom Presbyterians, Hoge, Johnson, and Luidens state, "Everyone, regardless of their degree of church involvement, told us of their respect for a code of conduct that stresses honesty, fairness, not

hurting others. . . . This agreement is especially striking because we asked our interviewees no formal questions about this code" (1994: 111).

15. Boylan notes that, although the evangelizing content of Sunday school was seen as a necessary complement to the general moral education provided in the public schools, and though sectarian loyalties mattered, nonetheless, "apart from catechisms and lesson books, the children's literature published by the various denominational societies was hardly sectarian in content." She also points out that the uniform lesson plan adopted at the 1872 convention "represented a triumph for . . . interdenominationalism" (1988: 20, 80, 98). Although denominations continued to set the specific content of lessons, the convention established which, and in what sequence, scriptural passages would be uniformly studied by all Sunday school children. The effort to articulate a nonsectarian, transdenominational moral ethos was also driven by political efforts to foster national unity among Americans despite their varied differences, differences that were sharply apparent during the Civil War (McGreevy 2003: 115).

16. Additionally, in contrast to Protestantism, Catholicism has given significantly greater emphasis to obligatory rituals such as weekly mass attendance. The Second Vatican Council (1962–65) emphasized the importance of living the gospel in everyday life, thus stressing the continuities between individuals' Catholic and secular identities (Dillon 1999). But whatever the effect of this doctrinal reform, we would not expect to see evidence of it among Catholics until later in the century, and then perhaps only slightly, given that the Catholics in our study were socialized in the pre–Vatican II era.

5. THE EBB AND FLOW OF RELIGIOUSNESS ACROSS THE LIFE COURSE

1. Other than the IHD study, the long-term studies of the life course that have included questions on religion are the Terman Life Cycle Study of Children with High Ability, 1922–1986 (Holahan and Sears 1995), and Vaillant's 1977 study of Harvard male graduates. Vaillant's study and the Terman religion data do not, however, appear to have the breadth or the in-depth interview detail contained in the IHD study. The Terman data presented by Holahan and Sears (1995) for early and late-middle adulthood come from a single question asking about religious affiliation or interest in organized religion, and the older-adulthood data are based on the participants' retrospective assessments of whether their interest in religion had remained stable or changed since their middle years. Vaillant (2002) assesses religion retrospectively from late adulthood and makes only passing references to religion in his earlier reports on the study (1977: 34, 36; 1993).

2. Unless otherwise specified, the analyses presented in this section are based on a repeated measures ANOVA with five levels of religiousness (adolescence plus four time points in adulthood) as the within-subjects factor. The N consists of 133 participants for whom we have ratings on religiousness at all interview times. The $F(1,132)$ value for the quadratic effect was 30.91, $p < .001$. The F values for the decreases in religiousness from adolescence to early adulthood and from early to middle adulthood were 9.48 and 8.69, respectively, $p < .01$. The F value for the increase in religiousness from late-middle to late adulthood

was 15.99, $p < .001$. The magnitude of change for all significant effects did not exceed one-quarter of a standard deviation. The main disadvantage of a repeated ANOVA is that it eliminates from the analyses all subjects who do not have complete data for all time periods. We therefore replicated our analyses using growth curve analyses, which allowed for the estimation of missing data. The N in this new analysis increased from 133 to 245, but the result was the same, with the pattern of change best described as a quadratic, rather than a linear, function.

3. The t value for planned comparisons between religiousness in late adulthood and adolescence was $t(133) = -1.85$, $p = .07$, and between late and early adulthood was $t(133) = -.31$, *n.s.*

4. The decline from adolescence to early adulthood was a quarter of a standard deviation, and from adolescence to middle adulthood was just shy of one-half of a standard deviation. The increase from late-middle to late adulthood was less than one-quarter of a standard deviation. In psychological and medical research, a difference of one-half of a standard deviation is described as being clinically significant, because it results in observable differences in the individual's functioning (see Wink and Dillon 2001).

5. The details of various studies differ, but see Stolzenberg, Blair-Loy, and Waite 1995; Greeley 1980; Chaves 1991; Myers 1996; and Wilson and Sherkat 1994; and for a recent analysis of the responsiveness of churches to changes in family structure, see Edgell 2006.

6. The percentages for adolescence reported in this chapter are for those study participants for whom we have data on religiousness for all time periods (as represented in the analyses of change over time in figures 1 and 2), and hence the percentages reported for adolescence are slightly higher than those reported in chapter 3 (which included all the interviewees for whom we had data for adolescence, even though some subsequently dropped out of the study). We analyzed the effect of gender on change in religiousness over time by including it as a between-subjects factor in the repeated measures ANOVA. The overall age by gender interaction was marginally significant ($F(4,128) = 2.04$, $p = .09$). When we restricted our analyses to only two time periods (adolescence and early adulthood), there was a significant interaction between age and gender ($F(1,131) = 6.46$), reflecting the fact that during this time period men declined in religiousness, whereas women did not ($p \leq .01$).

7. Comparing Catholics and mainline Protestants, between middle and late adulthood there was a significant interaction between religiousness and denomination ($F(1,112) = 6.94$, $p = .01$). This was due to the sharp decrease among those brought up Catholic, whereas those who came from mainline Protestant families showed no change.

8. The three trajectories of change in religiousness over the life course were obtained using latent variable mixed-class growth models (see Muthén and Muthén 1998–2006). Unpublished data available from the authors.

6. INDIVIDUAL TRANSFORMATION IN RELIGIOUS COMMITMENT AND MEANING

1. The technical term for what we label as individual stability is "rank order stability." Rank order stability is calculated statistically using the correlation

coefficient and thus requires longitudinal data that have repeated measures of each variable for each person over time. This contrasts with group level stability, which is calculated by comparing group means for data collected at two different time periods. The two methods of calculating change are statistically independent because correlations are sensitive only to the rank ordering of individuals. Therefore, a perfect correlation of 1.0 is achieved even if the score of each individual in the study drops or increases, so long as the person who scored highest at time one continues to do so at time two and so forth. Nevertheless, it is feasible for a sample to have the same means at time one as time two, even if all group members change radically in their scores, so long as on the aggregate level all these changes cancel themselves out (i.e., for every individual who increases his or her score, there is someone else whose score declines by the same amount).

2. In the interview transcripts, systematic detail about the religious affiliation and involvement of the spouse prior to or in early adulthood was insufficient to make a meaningful determination about the influence of spouses on the study participants' religiousness. Indicative, however, of the religious gap that frequently characterizes married couples, in early adulthood approximately 9 percent of the study participants, but only 2 percent of spouses, had no religious affiliation. At least twelve Catholic and two Jewish study participants married Protestants, and four Protestant and one Jewish study participant married Catholics.

3. The typical way to estimate how much individual variability on a given variable X is accounted for by variable Y is to square the correlation between the two variables. In the case of religiousness, .74 squared equals .55. This means that, if our measure of religiousness was perfectly reliable (free of error in measurement), then on the average, religiousness at one point in adulthood would account for 55 percent of variability in religiousness at another point in time. This leaves a sizeable proportion of the variance—45 percent—unaccounted for and, therefore, presumably explained by factors other than antecedent levels of religiousness. However, because measurement in social science is prone to more error and thus does not achieve the same kind of reliability as in the natural sciences, this sets a ceiling on the magnitude of the correlation coefficient between any two psychosocial variables. As a result, in the case of religiousness an average correlation of .77 is likely to leave very little true unexplained variance once a correction is made for error of measurement.

4. See, for example, Beit-Hallahmi and Argyle 1997; and Stark and Finke 2000. Smith (2006) finds that early adulthood is the modal time for religious transformation.

5. These ideas are elaborated in Kohlberg 1981; Labouvie-Vief, DeVoe, and Bulka 1989; and Sinnott 1994.

6. This cohort difference was statistically significant: $x^2 = 5.11$, $df1$, $p < .02$.

7. In the religion section of the late-adulthood interview (1997–2000), study participants were asked, "What are the beliefs and values that guide your life?" In the early-adulthood interview (1958), the older cohort only were asked, "Most of us don't stop to think about it, but most of us have a philosophy of life. What is yours?"; the younger cohort were asked more generally about their beliefs.

8. Although the interviewers did not ask the study participants to specifically comment on the relevance or appeal of the social and faith aspects of religion to them, it was possible to code their responses to the structured open-ended questions asked about their religious beliefs, attitudes, and practices according to evidence of these dimensions. The study participants' religion narratives (composed of their answers to the questions asked about religious beliefs, attitudes, and practices) were coded reliably for evidence of the social and faith aspects of religion (1 = characteristic is present; 0 = characteristic is absent) by two raters, one of whom was unaware of the source of the data and of the study's research questions. These themes were not independent of each other, and consequently in any one narrative there could be evidence of one, both, or neither. The narratives of all study participants for whom there was sufficient detail in the religion section of the interview transcript, regardless of their level of religious involvement, were coded ($N = 129$ of the 184 study participants who were interviewed in both early and late adulthood).

7. SPIRITUAL SEEKING

1. According to Miller, "Emerson believed that every man has an inward and immediate access to that Being for whom he found the word 'God' inadequate and whom he preferred to designate as the 'Over-Soul.' He believed that this Over-Soul, this universal essence which is beauty, love, wisdom, and power all in one, is present in Nature and throughout Nature" (1956/1964: 185–86).

2. Among Roof's baby boomers, "79 percent of those who are religious also claim to be spiritual, but 54 percent of those who are not religious say they are spiritual as well" (1999: 173).

3. The uncoupling of religion and spirituality has raised concern among some psychologists about the negative consequences of such a split for the understanding of traditional religiousness. Because psychologists tend to place a premium on personal growth, some see the emergence of spirituality that is independent of religion as leading to a polarization between a "good," or dynamic, spirituality and a "bad," or static, religiousness (see Zinnbauer and Pargament 2005).

4. In keeping with evangelicals' tendency to prioritize a personal relationship with Jesus independent of denominational or church structures, among our study participants in late adulthood the nonmainline Protestants scored higher on a measure of involvement in nonorganizational religious activities (Koenig, Parkerson, and Meador 1997) than both mainline Protestants ($t(8,53) = 3.48$, $p < .01$) and Catholics ($t(7,16) = 3.38$, $p < .01$). In late adulthood, eight nonmainline Protestants who were interviewed in depth also completed the self-report questionnaire that included the measure of religious activities devised by Koenig, Parkerson, and Meador (1997). Of the eight, six were evangelical.

5. Figure 4 presents findings for the total sample and for men and women. For statistical details and for data on cohort and denomination, see Wink and Dillon 2002. For the life course pattern of change, the three-way interaction between age, gender, and cohort was not significant ($F(3,136) = 1.01$, n.s.). This

means that, although with age women increased more than men in spiritual seeking, this pattern of change was characteristic of both younger and older women. Equally, cohort did not influence the pattern of change for men.

6. The gender differences in religiousness ($t(89,96) = 3.89$, $p < .01$) and spiritual seeking ($t(89,96) = 3.61$, $p < .01$) were statistically significant, as was the gender by cohort interaction for spiritual seeking ($F(1,181) = 3.66$, $p = .05$). The significant positive correlation between spiritual seeking and the mother's education was $r(157) = .23$, $p < .01$. For spiritual seeking, the differences in denominational background were statistically significant, $x^2 = 6.99$, $df 2$, $p < .05$. In late adulthood, Catholics continued to score lower on spiritual seeking than mainline Protestants ($t(23,58) = 2.41$, $p < .05$).

7. The increase in spiritual seeking from late-middle to late adulthood was more than one-half of a standard deviation, whereas the increase in religiousness during this interval was only one-quarter of a standard deviation. See Wink and Dillon 2002 for more detailed statistical analyses of spiritual development in adulthood.

8. Clearly, the low individual (rank order) stability of spiritual seeking in the first half of adulthood is in part due to the small number of study participants who were spiritual seekers in 1958 and 1970. However, in further support of the maturational thesis that spiritual seeking tends to emerge in the second half of adulthood, a recent study of contemporary American teenagers found very little evidence that they were interested in spiritual seeking (Smith and Denton 2005), notwithstanding the post-1960s cultural changes. Smith and Denton comment that, when they asked their interviewees questions about being "spiritual but not religious," in fact "most teens literally did not understand what it was we were talking about" (78). Adult development scholars would not be surprised by this; they do not expect spiritual seeking to be a phenomenon of youth.

9. Identity exploration was assessed using a measure developed by Marcia and colleagues (1993). In middle adulthood (in 1970), the mean difference between the score of the younger cohort and that of the older cohort was ($t(136,97) = 2.00$, $p < .05$). The intercohort mean difference in 1958 was ($t(138,99) = 1.39$, $n.s.$).

10. Adolescent religiousness ($r = .24$, $p < .02$, $N = 164$) and early adulthood religiousness ($r = .40$, $p < .00$, $N = 153$) correlated positively with spiritual seeking in late adulthood. Religiousness and introspection in early adulthood and negative life events occurring in early (age thirties) and middle adulthood (age forties) were significant predictors of spiritual seeking in late adulthood, accounting for 38 percent of the cumulative variance in the sample (see Wink and Dillon 2002 for the statistical details).

8. THE ACTIVITIES, PERSONALITY, AND SOCIAL ATTITUDES OF RELIGIOUS AND SPIRITUAL INDIVIDUALS IN LATE ADULTHOOD

1. Individuals age sixty-five and over currently constitute over 12 percent of the U.S. population, and demographers project that this figure will increase to approximately 20 percent by the year 2030. See U.S. Administration on Aging 2002.

2. In their landmark study, Rowe and Kahn give only scant attention to the significance of religion for "successful aging." They note, however, that participation in religious groups (among other organizations and social networks) enhances the health of older persons. They find that "those who actually attend religious meetings do better than those who simply say they are religious. Active participation does a person more good than mere attendance" (1998: 163–64). See Kahn 2002 and Strawbridge et al. 2002 on successful aging.

Although there is a burgeoning literature on religion in old age (see, e.g., Eisenhandler 2003; Koenig, McCullough, and Larson 2001; McFadden, Brennan, and Patrick 2003; Schaie, Krause, and Booth 2004), few studies differentiate between the young-old and the old-old. Because we gathered extensive data from our study participants at their most recent assessment (1997–2000), when they were in their late sixties and their seventies, our study is especially well suited to helping us understand the role of religiousness and spiritual seeking in the postretirement period, when everyday functioning is still relatively unimpeded by physical decline, bereavement, and other losses, and understand how late adulthood is affected by religious and other aspects of our participants' lives as recorded in the data gathered from them at earlier times in the life course.

3. Because of the eight-year age difference between participants in the two original samples (Berkeley Guidance Study and OGS), it was not surprising that, by late adulthood, the older OGS group had a higher mortality rate (40 percent) than the younger Guidance Study cohort (approximately 10 percent). Similarly, given gender differences in mortality, slightly more women (53 percent) than men (47 percent) were interviewed in late adulthood. These percentages are based on a sample size of 157. In this and the next two chapters, the percentages we discuss in regard to the relation between our measures of religiousness, spiritual seeking, and psychosocial functioning in late adulthood come primarily from responses to self-report questionnaires. Of the 184 participants interviewed in late adulthood, 157 also provided self-reported questionnaire data. On religiousness, spiritual seeking, and other sociodemographic characteristics, the study participants for whom we have both interview and self-reported data do not differ from those who were interviewed in-depth but who did not complete the self-report questionnaire (see Wink and Dillon 2003).

4. Only 49 percent of older-age married households nationwide have an annual income over forty thousand dollars (Smith 2003: 3–4). Women in our study reported lower household income than men; $F(1,147) = 7.74, p < .01$.

5. Four percent of the sample never married. The overall divorce rate for the original sample was 18 percent, but it was only 9 percent among those who survived into late adulthood. IHD women were significantly more likely than men to live alone; $x^2 (1,182) = 8.78, p < .01$. Among older-age Americans nationwide, 77 percent of men and 53 percent of women live with their spouse (Smith 2003: 3). There were no cohort differences among our study participants in regard to who lived alone ($x^2 = (1,175) = 1.85, n.s.$).

6. The gender difference in marital satisfaction was statistically significant: $F(1,134) = 4.93, p < .05$. The overall relation between religiousness and marital satisfaction was significant at a trend level ($r(138) = .14, p = .10$), and was significant for men ($r(73) = .25, p < .05$) but not women ($r(65) = .17, n.s.$).

7. These differences were significant: for children, the mean was 3.46 versus 2.90; $t(61,117) = 2.25$, $p < .05$. For grandchildren, the mean was 6.37 versus 4.12; $t(50,115) = 3.69$, $p < .01$.

8. A two-way ANOVA with frequency of divorce as the dependent variable, and gender and a dichotomized rating of spiritual seeking as the independent factor, resulted in a significant gender-by-spiritual-seeking interaction ($F(1,153) = 3.75$, $p < .05$). The interaction resulted from the fact that spiritual seeking women were more likely than anyone else to divorce. For a more detailed description of the study participants' living circumstances in late adulthood, see Wink 2007.

9. We investigated the everyday purposefulness of our study participants in late adulthood using the self-reported Life Task Participation Scale (Harlow and Cantor 1996). This scale assesses the frequency of an individual's participation across twenty-six different activities.

10. We used four of eight scales from the Life Task Participation Scale (Harlow and Cantor 1996). The Social Life Tasks Scale consisted of four items using a four-point Likert scale to assess how much an individual was involved in visiting and communicating with relatives, friends, and neighbors (two items), entertaining, and going to concerts, plays, lectures, or museums (two items). The Community Service Life Tasks Scale consisted of three items measuring the extent of an individual's involvement in community service done with a group or performed at home, and helping friends or neighbors. The Creative Life Tasks Scale consisted of three items assessing how much an individual was involved in playing an instrument, creative writing, painting, sculpture, dramatics, and singing with a group. The Knowledge Building Life Tasks Scale consisted of a single item measuring the frequency of participation in tasks aimed at increasing knowledge or skills. See Wink and Dillon 2003.

Because of the moderate positive correlation between our ratings of religiousness and spiritual seeking, we used two different types of statistical analyses to investigate the relations among religiousness, spiritual seeking, and other variables discussed in this and subsequent chapters. In one set of analyses, we *correlated* religiousness and spiritual seeking with the measures of interest. These findings provide an index of the relation between religiousness and spiritual seeking as manifested in the "real lives" of our participants (i.e., without controlling for or partialing out the overlap between religiousness and spiritual seeking). The second set of findings is based on partial correlations; this is a statistical procedure that allows the estimation of the relation between various characteristics and religiousness and spiritual seeking while statistically controlling for the overlap between both measures. While more artificial, partial correlations have the advantage of sharpening the contrast between religiousness and spiritual seeking and, thus, further illuminating the meanings of religiousness and spirituality in their "pure" form as two statistically independent measures of two different religious orientations. In table 4 (and in subsequent tables) the p value indicates the likelihood of obtaining the result by chance. A p value of .05 means that the probability of obtaining the effect by chance is one in twenty, or 5 percent. A p value of .01 means that the likelihood of capitalizing on chance is one in a hundred.

11. We assessed the well-being of our study participants in late adulthood using two of Ryff's Scales of Psychological Well-Being (1989). The Well-Being from Positive Relations with Others Scale assessed the degree to which an individual derived a sense of well-being from having warm, satisfying, and trusting relationships with others and had the capacity to maintain a strong sense of affection and intimacy (as contrasted with feelings of isolation and mistrust). The Well-Being from Personal Growth Scale assessed the extent to which an individual derived a sense of well-being from experiences of the self as growing, expanding, and continuing to develop (as contrasted with a sense of personal isolation). We discuss these results further in Wink and Dillon 2003.

12. All these characteristics are components of secure attachment (Bartholomew and Horowitz 1991). The partial correlation between religiousness and secure attachment was $r(115) = .28, p < .01$, and between spiritual seeking and secure attachment was $r(115) = 12, n.s.$ The relation between religiousness and secure attachment was significant for both men $(r(56) = .30, p < .05)$ and women $(r(62) = .23, p < .07)$.

13. The analyses were performed using a t-test for independent samples. The N for the religious-spiritual group was 85 and for the nonreligious-nonspiritual group was 72. Although the mean differences between the two groups were statistically significant for each category of everyday activities (all p values < .05), the effects were small—typically less than half a standard deviation.

14. The participants' overall involvement in everyday activities was measured by a summary index of engagement across twenty-six different life tasks on the Harlow and Cantor Life Task Participation Scale (1996). The findings described in this paragraph are based on a multiple regression, with overall life-task involvement as the dependent variable and interview-based health ratings, religiousness, spiritual seeking, and self-reported depression as the predictor variables.

15. In assessing personality in late adulthood, we used expert ratings of the "Big Five" personality characteristics (McCrae and Costa 2003) derived from raters' assessments of personality based on the study participants' interview transcripts in late adulthood. The Big Five assesses five dimensions of personality: agreeableness, conscientiousness, openness to experience, extroversion, and neuroticism. The expert ratings of the Big Five were obtained using the California Adult Q-sort (Block 1971, 1989). The Q-sort is a measure with a list of one hundred personality descriptors used to describe an individual. The one hundred characteristics are sorted into nine fixed categories that describe the individual being assessed, ranging from "extremely characteristic" to "extremely uncharacteristic." Each member of a panel of three raters independently characterizes the individual's personality, and the panel's individual ratings are subsequently averaged into a single composite score.

In our study, the expert observers watched the videotaped in-depth interviews conducted with the participants in late adulthood and made their assessment by drawing on the extensive information contained in the interview, during which the participants discussed all the major aspects of their lives, including family relations, work, leisure, religious and political activities, their health, and their views on aging and on life in general. We used the California

Adult Q-sort scores to derive measures of the Big Five personality dimensions. Importantly, the raters who assessed the personality characteristics of the study participants were unaware of the scores the participants received on religiousness and spiritual seeking, and thus their ratings were not influenced by their presuppositions or biases about the likely personality traits of religious and spiritual individuals.

16. It is interesting to note the denominational differences that emerged in regard to personality. On agreeableness, Catholics scored significantly higher than nonmainline Protestants ($t(20,8) = 2.04$, $p = .05$); on openness to experience, mainline Protestants scored significantly higher than both Catholics ($t(57,23) = 2.79$, $p < .01$) and nonmainline Protestants ($t(57,11) = 2.34$, $p < .05$).

17. These findings are based on an analysis using a structural equation-modeling framework to estimate cross-lagged and autoregressive effects in a two-wave panel design predicting religiousness and personality in late adulthood (see Wink, Ciciolla, Dillon, and Tracy in press).

18. In the case of agreeableness for women, the diagonal path from adolescent agreeableness to religiousness in late adulthood was significant. There was also a significant path from adolescent religiousness to agreeableness in late adulthood. This pattern differentiates agreeableness from conscientiousness, where, as shown in figure 5, only one of the diagonal paths was significant (see Wink, Ciciolla, Dillon, and Tracy in press).

19. For openness to experience, the paths from both adolescent openness and religiousness to spiritual seeking in late adulthood, and from openness in adolescence to openness in late adulthood, were all significant. The standardized regression coefficient for the relation between the mother's education and spiritual seeking in late adulthood was significant at a trend level (see Wink, Ciciolla, Dillon, and Tracy in press).

20. The association between religious involvement and authoritarianism dates back to pioneering research in the aftermath of World War II by Theodor Adorno et al. (1950) and Allport (1954). For a review of the literature on religion, authoritarianism, and prejudice, see Spilka et al. 2003. For a broader discussion of religion, politics, and culture wars, see, for example, Williams 1997; and Frank 2004.

21. We assessed authoritarianism in late adulthood with Altemeyer's Right-Wing Authoritarianism Scale (1996), a self-report measure that consists of three dimensions, which assess (1) submission to established authority, (2) hostility and aggression against individuals who oppose established authority, and (3) adherence to social conventions sanctioned by established authorities. On the Right-Wing Authoritarianism Scale, submission to authority is indicated by endorsing statements such as "The real key to the 'good life' is obedience, discipline, and sticking to the straight and narrow"; hostility and aggression are indicated by agreement with statements such as "There are many radical, immoral people in our country today, who are trying to ruin it for their own godless purposes, whom the authorities should put out of action"; and adherence to social conventions is indicated by disagreement with such statements as "Homosexuals and feminists should be praised for being brave enough to defy 'traditional family values.'" Previous research shows that the Right-Wing

Authoritarianism Scale has a very high level of internal consistency, meaning that its three dimensions are strongly intercorrelated. In other words, if a respondent endorses one of the items in the keyed direction, he or she tends to endorse all the other items in the same direction, irrespective of which of the three domains of authoritarianism is being assessed (Altemeyer 1996).

In our study, the positive correlation between religiousness and authoritarianism was $r(156) = .42$, $p < .01$, and the negative correlation between spiritual seeking and authoritarianism was $r(156) = -22$; $p < .01$ (see Wink, Dillon, and Prettyman in press b). Spiritual seeking correlated negatively with the submission ($r = -.27$, $p < .01$) and aggression ($r = -.22$, $p < .01$) subscales of the Right-Wing Authoritarianism Scale, but was unrelated to the conventionality subscale ($r = -.14$, *n.s.*). Religiousness correlated positively with all three subscales of the Right-Wing Authoritarianism Scale, .27, .28, and .45, respectively; all ps < .01. There was no relation between party affiliation (Democrat or Republican) and religiousness ($t(76,47) = .93$, *n.s.*) or spiritual seeking ($t(76,47) = -1.76$, *n.s.*). A note on regression analysis (cf. table 6 and subsequent tables): Multiple regression controls statistically for the overlap between several predictor variables. This allows for the assessment of the variables' independent effects on a given outcome variable. In this sense, a multiple regression is similar to partial correlation, except it allows the inclusion of more than one predictor in the model.

22. Although we know of no research on the relation between authoritarianism and spiritual seeking, Batson and his collaborators (Batson, Schoenrade, and Ventis 1993; Batson et al. 2001) found that a questing type of religious orientation (characterized by openness, flexibility, and the tendency to confront existential questions without relying on clear-cut answers) is not conducive to authoritarianism. Schmidt (2005) distinguishes between the authoritarianism associated with church-centered religiousness and the social tolerance associated with a seeker spirituality.

23. A one-way ANOVA indicated that the three denominational groups differed from each other on authoritarianism ($F(2,75) = 6.85$, $p < .01$) with non-mainline Protestants scoring higher than mainline Protestants ($p < .01$) and Catholics ($p < .05$).

24. These personality characteristics were assessed using the California Psychological Inventory Flexibility Scale (Gough and Bradley 1996). Flexibility correlated $-.46$ with authoritarianism ($p < .01$), $-.28$ with religiousness ($p < .01$), and .23 with spiritual seeking ($p < .05$), $N = 122$.

25. Research findings indicate the need to differentiate among the types of prejudice associated with religion. Church attendance has been found to be a consistent predictor of negative attitudes about gays and, to a lesser extent, feminists, but not about racial minorities and other groups not condemned by church teachings. See Spilka et al. 2004 for a review of findings on the association between religion and church-proscribed and nonproscribed prejudice. See Boyer 2006 for a review of the controversy in the Episcopal Church fueled by the election of Gene Robinson, an openly gay man, as bishop of New Hampshire, and Burns 2005 for an analysis of the complex public framing of religious and moral issues in American culture.

26. The groups listed included homosexuals, feminists, racial minorities, immigrants, labor unions, and older people. This list is derived from the research of Gurin, Miller, and Gurin (1980) on power discontent and class consciousness. See also Duncan 1999.

27. Studies (e.g., Stewart and Healy 1986; Alwin, Cohen, and Newcomb 1991) suggest that individuals' social and political values tend to form when individuals are in their twenties and thirties.

28. Our two scales showed adequate levels of alpha reliability, meaning that the opinion statements included in each scale were positively related to one another. The items in the scale measuring the perception that gays and feminists have too much power had an alpha reliability of .74, and the alpha reliability for the items in the scale measuring perceptions of the power of other groups was .68 ($N = 117$).

9. SPIRITUAL SEEKING, THERAPEUTIC CULTURE, AND CONCERN FOR OTHERS

1. The contrasting views of spiritual individualism espoused by cultural critics and humanist psychologists are not new. In political theory they are reflected, for example, in the contrasting writings of Thomas Hobbes (1651/1996), who saw human nature as basically brutish and therefore in need of the moral and behavioral constraints provided by a strong ruler and government; those of John Locke (1690/1975), who saw the individual at birth as a blank slate to be shaped for good or evil; and Jean-Jacques Rousseau (1782/1968), who advocated a more decentralized and democratic social order based on his view of human nature as predisposed to goodness.

2. In the clinical psychological literature, there is a well-established distinction between pathological and normal or healthy narcissism (e.g., see Cooper 2000; and Stone 2000, for reviews). Hypersensitive (covert) and willful (overt) narcissism are two types of pathological narcissism, and a third type, autonomous narcissism, is considered healthy. We discuss the different types of narcissism in Wink, Dillon, and Fay 2005. Three types of narcissism (autonomous, hypersensitive, and willful) were assessed with scales developed by Wink (1992) for the California Adult Q-sort (CAQ; Block 1971, 1978). The CAQ Autonomy Scale assessed autonomous (healthy) narcissism and consisted of eleven items, including "values own independence and autonomy" and "has high aspiration for self." The CAQ Hypersensitivity Scale measured covert pathological narcissism and consisted of twelve items, including "is thin skinned and sensitive to slight" and "has hostility toward others." The CAQ Willfulness Scale measured overt pathological narcissism and consisted of ten items, including "is self-indulgent" and "shows condescending behavior toward others."

3. We did so using a path analytical statistical procedure. We used measures of narcissism from early adulthood, because personality tends not to stabilize until after adolescence (see, e.g., McCrae and Costa 2003). We present and discuss the statistical details of our path analytical models in Wink, Dillon, and Fay 2005. "Involvement in psychotherapy" was coded on a three-point scale independently by two raters using answers to open-ended questions asked of individuals in early and middle adulthood about the individual's involvement

in psychotherapy (e.g., psychoanalytic psychotherapy, and marriage and other forms of counseling) and the duration of involvement. Transcripts of interviews conducted with the participants (1) when they were in their thirties (1958 interviews) were used to code for "involvement in psychotherapy in early adulthood" during the preceding ten years; and (2) when they were in their forties and fifties (1970 and 1982 interviews) were used to code for "involvement in psychotherapy in middle adulthood." A score of three indicated that the individual had been in therapy during the specified interval for at least three consecutive sessions. A score of two indicated sporadic therapy involvement (e.g., fewer than three consecutive sessions). A score of one indicated that the individual had had no therapy. The Kappa coefficient of reliability for the two sets of ratings of therapy involvement was .91 for early adulthood and .97 for middle adulthood.

4. Data from the National Health Survey show that 20 percent of middle-aged Americans made office visits to psychiatrists in 1975–76 and 25 percent did so in 1980–81 (Gardocki 1988: 3).

5. As a point of information, early adulthood willful (overt) narcissism was unrelated to therapy in early or middle adulthood and to spiritual seeking in late adulthood.

6. We assessed the interview transcripts for evidence of generativity using the observer-based Q-sort measure of generativity developed by Peterson and Klohnen (1995). The interview-based ratings assess three dimensions that are at the core of generativity: (1) a *giving* orientation toward others, (2) the individual's ability to take a broad *social perspective* that facilitates awareness of the needs of other individuals and groups, and (3) the individual's *prosocial competence*. The first two dimensions assess the motivation for generative behavior that originates in feelings of warmth, sympathy, and protectiveness toward others, or that derives from an awareness of interpersonal cues and social problems that tends to sensitize the individual to human needs and social inequality. The third dimension assesses the ability of the individual to realize his or her generative impulses through dependable, responsible, and productive engagement in goal-directed behavior. (We explain the procedure for using the Q-sort methodology in chapter 8, note 15.) Additionally, we used the self-reported Loyola Generativity Scale (LGS; McAdams and de St. Aubin 1992), which we included in the late adulthood assessment. The LGS has four subscales that reflect the view that generative behavior can originate from a variety of sources. The LGS taps dimensions of generativity that include an *altruistic* need to help others, the desire to have an *impact on others,* the desire to *outlive the self* (i.e., to leave a material or symbolic legacy; see Kotre 1996), and the propensity to engage in *creative activities*. High scores on the LGS have been positively associated with scores on a behavior checklist of generative acts, including attendance at community or neighborhood meetings and teaching somebody a skill (McAdams and de St. Aubin 1992). We present some of the findings discussed here in Dillon, Wink, and Fay 2003; and Dillon and Wink 2004.

7. In view of the links we document between narcissism and spiritual seeking, it is noteworthy that autonomous narcissism (but not hypersensitive narcissism) was positively related to altruism in late adulthood.

8. Mainline Protestants scored higher than nonmainline Protestants on the overall CAQ Generativity Scale ($t(45,8)$ = 3.18, p < .01), the CAQ givingness subscale ($t(45,8)$ = 2.67, p < .05), and the altruism subscale of the LGS ($t(53,7)$ = 1.98, p < = .05). Mainline Protestants scored higher than Catholics on the overall CAQ Generativity Scale ($t(45,20)$ = 2.07, p < .05) and the altruism subscale of the LGS ($t(53,19)$ = 2.03, p < = .05), but not on the CAQ givingness subscale ($t(45,20)$ = .8, *n.s.*).

9. The highly reputable General Social Survey, for example, asks respondents, "To what extent do you consider yourself a spiritual person?" The closed-response options to the question are: Very spiritual, Moderately spiritual, Slightly spiritual, Not spiritual at all (as well as Don't know, No answer, and Not applicable). For evidence of the strong association between church-centered religiousness and social participation and volunteering, see, for example, Hout and Fischer 2002; Putnam 2000; Verba, Schlozman, and Brady 1995; and Wilson and Musick 1997.

10. THE BUFFERING ROLE OF RELIGION IN LATE ADULTHOOD

1. Erik Erikson (1951, 1982) argued that positive aging necessitated the acceptance of the inevitability of one's life as the only one that could have been lived. According to Robert Butler (1963), this task is aided by the process of life review, whereby individuals reconcile the past with the present and shed regrets over missed opportunities and misdeeds. Among our study participants, close to three-quarters did not engage in life review (see Wink and Schiff 2002). When David Allen was asked specifically about whether he engaged in life review, he answered with an emphatic "No, I don't think I do." A growing body of research indicates that the postretirement period, like any other expected life-course change, does not necessarily result in depression, anomie, and a decline in life satisfaction (see, e.g., Coleman 1986; James and Wink 2007; Midanik et al. 1995; Weiss and Bass 2002). Laslett (1991) argues that this shift is largely a function of the greatly improved socioeconomic conditions in the postindustrial world in recent decades. See also Wethington et al. 2004.

2. The health status ratings were done on a four-point scale adapted from Belloc, Breslow, and Hochstim (1971). A score of four indicated the presence of one or more chronic illnesses resulting in serious disability or a threat to life (e.g., congestive heart failure) or both; a score of one indicated no physical complaints. We assigned individuals in late adulthood, whose average score was higher than two, to the poor physical health category, and those whose score was two or lower to the good physical health category. The Kappa coefficient of reliability for the health ratings in late adulthood was .67. We discuss our findings on religion and health and provide statistical details in Wink and Dillon 2001; and Wink, Dillon, and Larsen 2005.

3. In late adulthood, the correlations between religiousness and spiritual seeking with our interview-based health status rating, as well as with the study participants' self-reported assessments of their general health and of physical functioning (MOS SF-36; Ware 1993), were statistically not significant. The same patterns held using early adulthood religiousness and spiritual seeking

ratings to predict physical health in late adulthood. See Wink, Dillon, and Larsen 2005; and Wink and Dillon 2001.

4. Life satisfaction was measured with the commonly used self-reported Satisfaction with Life Scale by Diener and colleagues (1985). Depression was assessed using the well-validated self-reported CES-D Scale that has been used with older populations (Radloff 1977; Radloff and Teri 1986).

5. In late adulthood, religiousness correlated .17 ($p < .05$) with life satisfaction and –.08 with depression (*n.s.*). A follow-up analysis indicated that the relation between life satisfaction and religiousness was significant for women ($r(82) = .25$, $p < .05$) but not men ($r(75) = .14$, *n.s.*). There was no significant relation between religiousness and depression for either men or women. It is also noteworthy that there was no denominational variation evident in regard to either life satisfaction or depression.

6. Concerning the buffering effect of religiousness on psychological health, we confined our longitudinal analyses to depression. For further procedural and statistical details, see Wink, Dillon, and Larsen 2005: 209–11.

7. In the research literature, this phenomenon is referred to as the selection hypothesis—the idea that individuals who experience adversity subsequently turn to religion as a coping resource. See George, Ellison, and Larson 2002.

8. High scorers on spiritual seeking were significantly more likely than high scorers on religiousness to engage in life review. These findings are based on two separate two-way ANOVAs. In the first ANOVA, life review was the dependent variable, and gender and a dichotomized rating of spiritual seeking were the independent factors. In the second ANOVA, we substituted a dichotomized rating of religiousness for spiritual seeking. The only significant finding in both ANOVAs was the main effect of spiritual seeking on life review ($F(1,175 = 37.10$, $p < .01$). The positive relation between life review and spiritual seeking held for both men and women. Ego development was assessed with the Sentence Completion Test developed by Loevinger (1976), a projective measure that asks respondents to complete sentence stems (e.g., "A woman . . ."), and responses are used to classify the individual on eight levels of ego development (Wink 2006).

9. We assessed the sense of control (personal mastery and perceived constraints) using Lachman and Weaver's Control Scale (1998). The pattern of relations among the sense of control, religiousness, and gender was virtually identical to that found for spiritual seeking (see Wink, Dillon, and Prettyman in press a). Recent research on divine-related control and well-being is reported by Krause (2005) and Schieman, Pudrovska, and Milkie (2005).

10. In the *Handbook of the Sociology of Religion* (2003), Neitz reviews the interesting feminist implications of women's greater presence in institutionalized religion. However, the *Handbook of the Psychology of Religion and Spirituality* (Paloutzian and Park 2005) gives scant attention to gender differences, and the main substantive finding on gender differences reported in the *Handbook of Religion and Health* (Koenig, McCullough, and Larson 2001) concerns the fact that religious women are more strongly buffered than men against alcohol and substance abuse.

11. In addition to our interview-based measures of religiousness and spiritual seeking, which were rated according to the study participants' religion

narratives—that is, participants' answers to structured, open-ended questions about their religious or spiritual beliefs (in God or a Higher Power and afterlife) and practices—we included a self-reported measure of belief in a rewarding afterlife (Gesser, Wong, and Reker 1987) in the late adulthood assessment. Religiousness correlated .70, and spiritual seeking .36, with belief in a rewarding afterlife ($N = 155$, $p < .01$). See Wink 2006.

12. Religiousness correlated –.06 (*n.s.*) and spiritual seeking –.10 (*n.s.*) with fear of death ($N = 155$). These findings contradict several studies that report a negative correlation between fear of death and belief in God and in a rewarding afterlife (e.g., Fortner and Neimeyer 1999; Cicirelli 2002), but support other research showing a more complex relation between religion and fear of death (e.g., Leming 1979–80; Nelson and Cantrell 1980; McMordie 1981).

In late adulthood only 23 percent of our study participants indicated unequivocally that they were afraid of death, a figure that reflects the well-established fact that death anxiety decreases with age (e.g., Tomer 2000). In contrast, 42 percent of the participants said they were afraid of the process of dying or of a painful death. There was a positive and statistically significant relation between fear of death and fear of dying ($r(156) = .39$, $p < .01$). Being born in the early 1920s as opposed to the late 1920s did not influence who was afraid of death, though the younger cohort was more likely than the older cohort to be afraid of the process of dying. Neither religiousness nor spiritual seeking were related to the fear of dying. There was a negative and nonsignificant correlation between age cohort and fear of death ($r = –.07$, *n.s.*), and a negative and statistically significant correlation between cohort and fear of dying ($r = –.17$, $p < .05$). Wink and Scott 2005 reviews the extensive research literature on the fear of death and presents the IHD study's empirical findings on the fear of death, some of which we draw on in this section.

13. Catholics differed significantly from mainline Protestants ($t(19,53) = 3.02$, $p < .01$) and from nonmainline Protestants ($t(19,8) = 2.14$. $p < .05$) on the fear of death.

11. AMERICAN LIVED RELIGION

1. Opinion poll data from the Pew Research Center for the People and the Press indicate that 48 percent of Americans believe that life on earth has evolved over time, and 42 percent believe that it has existed in its present form since the beginning of time; 64 percent of Americans support teaching creationism and evolution in public schools, and 38 percent say that creationism should be taught instead of evolution; and 33 percent of Americans believe that scientists do not agree about evolution (Kohut and Lugo 2005: 7, 9, 10). For a review of the public controversy over teaching evolution and intelligent design, see Talbot 2005.

2. Postelection polls conducted in November 2004 indicated that "moral values" mattered most to American voters and took priority over the situation in Iraq, the economy and jobs, and terrorism (Kohut 2004: 2). These results occasioned much media commentary on the rising importance of religion in American politics.

3. In his otherwise thoughtful critique of the cultural criticisms of spirituality, Schmidt, like many others (e.g., Roof 1999), takes issue with Bellah and his colleagues' discussion of Sheila Larson's "Sheilaism" (see our chapter 9). Schmidt states, "The Bellah group, made up of clearheaded academics of high repute, suddenly mutated into an ecclesial court, even closing the discussion of Larson with an over-the-top gesture of thinly veiled aggression." Schmidt further criticizes the analysis by Bellah and colleagues as culturally stunted and historically thin (Schmidt 2005: 270, 271).

4. Although 42 percent of Americans describe themselves as born-again Christians, only half that number (22 percent) endorse the evangelical beliefs and practices that are considered core to being born again (Winseman 2005: 118–19).

Bibliography

Adorno, Theodor, E. Frenkel-Brunswik, D.J. Levinson, and R.N. Sanford. 1950. *The Authoritarian Personality.* New York: Harper & Row.

Ahlstrom, Sydney. 1972. *A Religious History of the American People.* New Haven: Yale University Press.

Allport, Gordon. 1954. *The Nature of Prejudice.* Cambridge, MA: Addison-Wesley.

Altemeyer, Bob. 1996. *The Authoritarian Specter.* Cambridge, MA: Harvard University Press.

Alwin, Duane, Ronald Cohen, and Theodore Newcomb. 1991. *Political Attitudes over the Life-Span: The Bennington Women after Fifty Years.* Madison: University of Wisconsin Press.

Ammerman, Nancy. 1997. "Golden Rule Christianity: Lived Religion in the American Mainstream." In *Lived Religion in America,* ed. David Hall, pp. 196–216. Princeton: Princeton University Press.

———. 2005. *Pillars of Faith: American Congregations and Their Partners.* Berkeley: University of California Press.

Atchley, Robert. 1999. *Continuity and Adaptation in Aging: Creating Positive Experiences.* Baltimore, MD: Johns Hopkins University Press.

Baltes, Margaret, Alexandra M. Freund, and Ann L. Horgas. 1999. "Men and Women in the Berlin Aging Study." In *The Berlin Aging Study: Aging from 70 to 100,* ed. Paul Baltes and Karl Mayer, pp. 259–281. New York: Cambridge University Press.

Bartholomew, Kim, and Leonard Horowitz. 1991. "Attachment Styles among Young Adults: A Test of a Four-Category Model." *Journal of Personality and Social Psychology* 61: 226–44.

Batson, C. Daniel, S. Edelman, S. Higley, and S. Russell. 2001. "And Who Is My Neighbor? Quest Religion as a Source of Universal Compassion." *Journal for the Scientific Study of Religion* 40: 39–50.

Batson, C. Daniel, Patricia Schoenrade, and W. Larry Ventis. 1993. *Religion and the Individual.* New York: Oxford University Press.

Beit-Hallahmi, Benjamin. 1992. *Despair and Deliverance: Private Secularization in Contemporary Israel.* Albany: State University of New York Press.

Beit-Hallahmi, Benjamin, and Michael Argyle. 1997. *The Psychology of Religious Behavior, Belief, and Experience.* New York: Routledge.

Bellah, Robert, Richard Madsen, William Sullivan, Ann Swidler, and Steven Tipton. 1985. *Habits of the Heart: Individualism and Commitment in American Life.* Berkeley: University of California Press.

———. 1991. *The Good Society.* New York: Knopf.

Belloc, Nedra, Lester Breslow, and Joseph Hochstim. 1971. "Measurement of Physical Health in a General Population Survey." *American Journal of Epidemiology* 93: 328–36.

Bendroth, Margaret. 2002. *Growing Up Protestant: Parents, Children, and Mainline Churches.* New Brunswick, NJ: Rutgers University Press.

Bendroth, Margaret, and Virginia Lieson Brereton, eds. 2002. *Women and Twentieth Century Protestantism.* Urbana: University of Illinois Press.

Berger, Peter. 1961. *The Noise of Solemn Assemblies: Christian Commitment and the Religious Establishment in America.* Garden City, NY: Doubleday.

Beyerlein, Kraig. 2003. "Educational Elites and the Movement to Secularize Public Education." In *The Secular Revolution,* ed. Christian Smith, pp. 160–96. Berkeley: University of California Press.

Bianchi, Eugene. 1987. *Aging as a Spiritual Journey.* New York: Crossroad.

Block, Jack. 1971. *Lives through Time.* Berkeley, CA: Bancroft.

———. 1978. *The Q-Sort Method in Personality Assessment and Psychiatric Research.* Palo Alto, CA: Consulting Psychologists Press.

———. 1989. "Prototypes for the California Adult Q-Set." Manuscript. Department of Psychology, University of California, Berkeley.

Bourdieu, Pierre. 1984. *Distinction: A Social Critique of the Judgment of Taste.* Cambridge, MA: Harvard University Press.

Boyer, Peter. 2006. "A Church Asunder." *New Yorker* (April 17): 54–65.

Boylan, Anne. 1988. *Sunday School: The Formation of an American Institution, 1790–1880.* New Haven, CT: Yale University Press.

Braam, A., A. Beekman, D. Deeg, J. Smit, and W. van Tilburg. 1997. "Religiosity as a Protective or Prognostic Factor of Depression in Later Life." *Acta Psychiatrica Scandinavia* 96: 199–205.

Braam, A. W., P. van den Eaden, and M. J. Prince. 2001. "Religion as a Cross-Cultural Determinant of Depression in Elderly Europeans." *Psychological Medicine* 31: 803–14.

Brokaw, Tom. 1998. *The Greatest Generation.* New York: Random House.

Brooks, David. 2000. *Bobos in Paradise.* New York: Simon and Schuster.

Brown, Marianna. 1901. *Sunday-School Movements in America.* New York: Fleming H. Revell Company.

Burns, Gene. 2005. *The Moral Veto: Framing Contraception, Abortion, and Cultural Pluralism in the United States.* New York: Cambridge University Press.

Butler, Robert. 1963. "The Life Review: An Interpretation of Reminiscence in Old Age." *Psychiatry Journal for the Study of Interpersonal Processes* 26: 65–76.

Chaves, Mark. 1991. "Family Structure and Protestant Church Attendance: The Sociological Basis of Cohort and Age Effects." *Journal for the Scientific Study of Religion* 30: 501–14.

———. 1994. "Secularization as Declining Religious Authority." *Social Forces* 72: 749–74.

———. 2004. *Congregations in America.* Cambridge, MA: Harvard University Press.

Cicirelli, Victor. 2002. "Fear of Death in Older Adults." *Journal of Gerontology* 57B: 358–66.

Clausen, John. 1993. *American Lives: Looking Back at the Children of the Great Depression.* New York: Free Press.

Coble, Christopher. 2002. "The Role of Young People's Societies in the Training of Christian Womanhood (and Manhood), 1880–1910." In *Women and Twentieth-Century Protestantism,* ed. Margaret Lamberts Bendroth and Virginia Lieson Brereton, pp. 74–92. Urbana: University of Illinois Press.

Coleman, Peter. 1986. *Aging and Reminiscence Processes: Social and Clinical Implications.* Chichester, U.K.: Wiley.

Cooper, Arnold. 2000. "Further Developments in Clinical Diagnosis of Narcissistic Personality Disorder." In *Disorders of Narcissism,* ed. Elsa F. Ronningstam, pp. 53–74. Northvale, NJ: Jason Aronson.

Cornwall, Marie. 1989. "Faith Development of Men and Women over the Life Span." In *Aging and the Family,* ed. Stephen Bahr and Evan Peterson, pp. 115–39. New York: Lexington Books.

D'Antonio, William, James Davidson, Dean Hoge, and Katherine Meyer. 2001. *American Catholics: Gender, Generation, and Commitment.* Walnut Creek, CA: AltaMira Press.

Davie, Grace. 1994. *Religion in Britain since 1945: Believing without Belonging.* Oxford, UK: Blackwell.

Diener, Ed, Robert Emmons, Randy Larsen, and Sharon Griffin. 1985. "The Satisfaction with Life Scale." *Journal of Personality Assessment* 49: 71–75.

Dillon, Michele. 1995. "Religion and Culture in Tension: The Abortion Discourses of the U.S. Catholic Bishops and the Southern Baptist Convention." *Religion and American Culture: A Journal of Interpretation* 5: 159–80.

———. 1999. *Catholic Identity: Balancing Reason, Faith, and Power.* New York: Cambridge University Press.

Dillon, Michele, and Paul Wink. 2004. "Religion, Cultural Change, and Generativity in American Society." In *The Generative Society,* ed. Ed de St. Aubin and Dan P. McAdams, pp. 153–74. Washington, DC: American Psychological Association Press.

Dillon, Michele, Paul Wink, and Kristen Fay. 2003. "Is Spirituality Detrimental to Generativity?" *Journal for the Scientific Study of Religion* 42: 427–42.

Douglas, Ann. 1977. *The Feminization of American Culture.* New York: Doubleday.

Douglas, Mary. 1982. "The Effects of Modernization on Religious Change." In *Religion and America: Spiritual Life in a Secular Age,* ed. Mary Douglas and Steven Tipton, pp. 25–43. Boston: Beacon Press.

Downey, Ann. 1984. "Relationship of Religiousness to Death Anxiety of Middle-Aged Males." *Psychological Reports* 54: 811–22.

Duncan, Lauren. 1999. "Motivation for Collective Action: Group Consciousness as Mediator of Personality, Life Experience, and Women's Rights Activism." *Political Psychology* 20: 611–35.

Edgell, Penny. 2006. *Religion and Family in a Changing Society.* Princeton: Princeton University Press.

Eichorn, Dorothy. 1981. "Samples and Procedures." In *Present and Past in Middle Life,* ed. Dorothy Eichorn, John Clausen, Norma Haan, Marjorie Honzik, and Paul Mussen, pp. 33–51. New York: Academic Press.

Eichorn, Dorothy, John Clausen, Norma Haan, Marjorie Honzik, and Paul Mussen, eds. 1981. *Present and Past in Middle Age.* New York: Academic Press.

Eichorn, Dorothy, Paul Mussen, John Clausen, Norma Haan, and Marjorie Honzik. 1981. "Overview." In *Present and Past in Middle Age,* ed. Dorothy Eichorn, John Clausen, Norma Haan, Marjorie Honzik, and Paul Mussen, pp. 411–34. New York: Academic Press.

Eisenhandler, Susan. 2003. *Keeping the Faith in Late Life.* New York: Springer.

Elder, Glen. 1974. *Children of the Great Depression.* Chicago: University of Chicago Press.

———. 1981. "Social History and Life Experience." In *Present and Past in Middle Life,* ed. Dorothy Eichorn, John Clausen, Norma Haan, Marjorie Honzik, and Paul Mussen, pp. 3–31. New York: Academic Press.

———. 1998. "The Life Course as Developmental Theory." *Child Development* 69: 1–2.

Elder, Glen, Elizabeth Pavalko, and E. Clipp. 1993. *Working with Archival Data: Studying Lives.* Newbury Park, CA: Sage.

Ellison, Christopher G., and Linda George. 1994. "Religious Involvement, Social Ties, and Social Support in a Southeastern Community." *Journal for the Scientific Study of Religion* 33: 46–61.

Ellison, Christopher G., and Jeffrey Levin. 1998. "The Religion-Health Connection." *Health Education and Behavior* 25: 700–20.

Ellison, Christopher G., Marc A. Musick, Jeffrey S. Levin, Robert J. Taylor, and Linda M. Chatters. 1997. "The Effects of Religious Attendance, Guidance, and Support on Psychological Distress: Longitudinal Findings from the National Survey of Black Americans." Paper presented at the annual meeting of the Society for the Scientific Study of Religion, October, San Diego, CA.

Ellwood, Robert. 1997. *The Fifties Spiritual Marketplace: American Religion in a Decade of Conflict.* New Brunswick, NJ: Rutgers University Press.

Erikson, Erik. 1951. *Childhood and Society.* 2d ed. New York: Norton.

———. 1964. *Insight and Responsibility.* New York: Norton.

———. 1982. *The Life Cycle Competed.* New York: Norton.

Erikson, Erik, Joan Erikson, and Helen Kivnick. 1986. *Vital Involvement in Old Age.* New York: Norton.

Eurobarometer. 2005. *Europeans, Science and Technology.* European Commission.

Ferraro, Kenneth, and Jessica Kelley-Moore. 2000. "Religious Consolation among Men and Women: Do Health Problems Spur Seeking?" *Journal for the Scientific Study of Religion* 39: 220–34.

Fichter, Joseph. 1954. *Social Relations in the Urban Parish*. Chicago: University of Chicago Press.

Finke, Roger, and Rodney Stark. 1992. *The Churching of America, 1776–1990: Winners and Losers in Our Religious Economy*. New Brunswick, NJ: Rutgers University Press.

Fortner, Barry V., and Robert Neimeyer. 1999. "Death Anxiety in Older Adults: A Quantitative Review." *Death Studies* 23: 387–411.

Foucault, Michel. 1974. *The Order of Things: An Archaeology of the Human Sciences*. London: Tavistock.

Fowler, John. 1981. *Stages of Faith*. New York: Harper & Row.

Frank, Arthur. 2004. *What's the Matter with Kansas?: How Conservatives Won the Heart of America*. New York: Metropolitan Books.

Fromm, Erich. 1941/1965. *Escape from Freedom*. Repr. New York: Avon Books.

Fuller, Robert. 2001. *Spiritual, But Not Religious: Understanding Unchurched America*. New York: Oxford University Press.

Gallup, George, and D. Michael Lindsay. 1999. *Surveying the Religious Landscape: Trends in U.S. Beliefs*. Harrisburg, PA: Morehouse.

Gardocki, G. J. 1988. *Office Visits to Psychiatrists: United States, 1985*. National Center for Health Statistics: Vital and Health Statistics, series 13, no. 94. Washington, D.C.: Government Printing Office.

George, Linda K., Christopher G. Ellison, and David B. Larson. 2002. "Explaining the Relationship between Religious Involvement and Health." *Psychological Inquiry* 13: 190–200.

Gesser, Gina, Paul Wong, and Gary Reker. 1987. "Death Attitudes across the Life-Span: The Development and Validation of the Death Attitude Profile (DAP)." *Omega* 18: 109–24.

Giddens, Anthony. 1991. *Modernity and Self-Identity. Self and Society in the Late Modern Age*. Stanford: Stanford University Press.

Gilligan, Carol. 1982. *In a Different Voice*. Cambridge, MA: Harvard University Press.

Glendon, Mary Ann. 1987. *Abortion and Divorce in Western Law*. Cambridge, MA: Harvard University Press.

Glock, Charles, and Robert N. Bellah, eds. 1976. *The New Religious Consciousness*. Berkeley: University of California Press.

Gorski, Philip. 2003. "Historicizing the Secularization Debate: An Agenda for Research." In *Handbook of the Sociology of Religion*, ed. Michele Dillon, pp. 110–22. New York: Cambridge University Press.

Gough, Harrison G., and Pamela Bradley. 1996. *California Psychological Inventory Manual*. 3rd ed. Palo Alto, CA: California Psychologists Press.

Greeley, Andrew. 1977. *The American Catholic: A Social Portrait*. New York: Basic Books.

———. 1980. *The Young Catholic Family*. Chicago: Thomas More Press.

———. 1985. *American Catholics since the Council: An Unauthorized Report*. Chicago: Thomas More.

Greeley, Andrew, and Michael Hout. 1999. "Americans' Increasing Belief in Life after Death." *American Sociological Review* 64: 813–35.

Gurin, Patricia, A. Miller, and Gerard Gurin. 1980. "Stratum Identification and Consciousness." *Social Psychology Quarterly* 43: 30–47.

Hall, David, ed. 1997. *Lived Religion in America*. Princeton: Princeton University Press.

Harlow, Robert, and Nancy Cantor. 1996. "Still Participating after All These Years: A Study of Life Task Participation in Later Life." *Journal of Personality and Social Psychology* 71: 1235–49.

Hatch, Nathan. 1989. *The Democratization of American Christianity*. New Haven: Yale University Press.

Helson, Ravenna, and Rebecca Cate. 2007. "Late Middle Age: Transition to the Third Age." In *The Crown of Life: Dynamics of the Early Postretirement Period*, ed. Jacquelyn James and Paul Wink, pp. 83–101. New York: Springer.

Hennessey, Maureen Hart, and Anne Knutson. 2000. *Norman Rockwell: Pictures for the American People*. 2nd ed. Stockbridge, MA: Norman Rockwell Museum.

Herberg, Will. 1955. *Protestant-Catholic-Jew: An Essay in American Religious Sociology*. New York: Doubleday.

Hine, Thomas. 1999. *Populuxe*. New York: MJF Books.

Hobbes, Thomas. 1651/1996. *Leviathan*. New York: Cambridge University Press.

Hoge, Dean, Benton Johnson, and Donald Luidens. 1994. *Vanishing Boundaries: The Religion of Mainline Protestant Baby Boomers*. Louisville, KY: Westminster and John Knox Press.

Holahan, Carole, and Robert Sears. 1995. *The Gifted Group in Later Maturity*. Stanford: Stanford University Press.

Hollingshead, August B., and Frank Redlich. 1958. *Social Class and Mental Illness*. New York: Wiley.

Hout, Michael, and Clause Fischer. 2002. "Explaining the Rise of Americans with No Religious Preferences: Politics and Generations." *American Sociological Review* 67: 165–90.

Hout, Michael, and Andrew Greeley. 1987. "The Center Doesn't Hold: Church Attendance in the United States, 1940–1984." *American Sociological Review* 52: 325–45.

Hudnut-Buemler, James. 1994. *Looking for God in the Suburbs: The Religion of the American Dream and Its Critics, 1945–1965*. New Brunswick, NJ: Rutgers University Press.

Hunter, James Davison. 1991. *Culture Wars: The Struggle to Define America*. New York: Basic Books.

Hurtado, Albert. 1999. *Intimate Frontiers: Sex, Gender, and Culture in Old California*. Albuquerque: University of New Mexico Press.

Iannaccone, Laurence. 1990. "Religious Participation: A Human Capital Approach." *Journal for the Scientific Study of Religion* 29: 297–314.

Idler, Ellen L., and Stanislav V. Kasl. 1997. "Religion among Disabled and Nondisabled Persons. I: Cross-Sectional Patterns in Health Practices, Social Activities, and Well-Being." *Journal of Gerontology* 52B: S294–S305.

Ingersoll-Dayton, Berit, Neal Krause, and David Morgan. 2002. "Religious Trajectories and Transitions over the Life Course." *International Journal of Aging and Human Development* 55: 51–70.

Jacoby, Mario. 1990. *Individuation and Narcissism: The Psychology of Self in Jung and Kohut.* New York: Routledge.

James, Jacquelyn, and Paul Wink. 2007. *The Crown of Life: Dynamics of the Early Post-Retirement Period.* New York: Springer.

Joyce, James. 1916. *A Portrait of the Artist as a Young Man.* Harmondsworth, U.K.: Penguin.

Jung, Carl. 1953. "On the Psychology of the Unconscious." In *The Collected Works of C. G. Jung,* ed. H. Read, M. Fordham, and G. Adler, pp. 3–119. Princeton: Princeton University Press.

———. 1958. "Psychology and Religion: West and East." In *The Collected Works of C. G. Jung,* ed. H. Read, M. Fordham, and G. Adler. Vol. 11. Princeton: Princeton University Press.

Kahn, John, and Leonard Pearlin. 2006. "Financial Strain over the Life Course and Health among Older Adults." *Journal of Health and Social Behavior* 47: 17–31.

Kahn, Robert. 2002. "On Successful Aging and Well-Being: Self-Rated Compared with Rowe and Kahn." *Gerontologist* 42: 725–26.

Koenig, Harold G., Michael McCullough, and David Larson. 2001. *Handbook of Religion and Health.* New York: Oxford University Press.

Koenig, Harold G., George Parkerson, and Keith Meador. 1997. "Religion Index for Psychiatric Research." *American Journal of Psychiatry* 153: 885–86.

Kohlberg, Lawrence. 1981. *Essays on Moral Development.* Vol. 1, *The Philosophy of Moral Development.* New York: Harper & Row.

Kohut, Andrew. 2004. *Moral Values: How Important?* Washington, DC: Pew Center for the People and the Press.

Kohut, Andrew, and Luis Lugo. 2005. *Public Divided on Origins of Life.* Washington, DC: Pew Center for the People and the Press.

Kohut, Heinz. 1977. *The Restoration of the Self.* New York: International Universities Press.

Kotre, John. 1996. *Outliving the Self.* 2nd ed. New York: Norton.

Krause, Neal. 2005. "God-Mediated Control and Psychological Well-Being in Late Life." *Research on Aging* 27: 136–64.

Kunzmann, Uta, and Paul B. Baltes. 2005. "The Psychology of Wisdom: Theoretical and Empirical Challenges." In *A Handbook of Wisdom,* ed. Robert Sternberg and Jennifer Jordan, pp. 110–35. New York: Cambridge University Press.

Labouvie-Vief, Gisela, M. DeVoe, and D. Bulka. 1989. "Speaking about Feelings: Conception of Emotion across the Life Span." *Psychology and Aging* 33: 425–37.

Labouvie-Vief, Gisela, and Manfred Diehl. 1999. "Self and Personality Development." In *Gerontology: An Interdisciplinary Perspective,* ed. C. Cavanaugh and S. K. Whitbourne, pp. 238–68. Oxford: Oxford University Press.

Lachman, Margie, and Suzanne Weaver. 1998. "The Sense of Control as a Moderator of Social Class Differences in Health and Well-Being." *Journal of Personality and Social Psychology* 74: 763–73.

Lasch, Christopher. 1979. *The Culture of Narcissism.* New York: Norton.

Laslett, Peter. 1991. *A Fresh Map of Life: The Emergence of the Third Age.* Cambridge, MA: Harvard University Press.

Leming, M.R. 1979–80. "Religion and Death: A Test of Homans' Thesis." *Omega* 10: 347–64.

Levinson, Daniel. 1978. *The Seasons of a Man's Life.* New York: Ballantine.

Locke, John. 1690/1975. *An Essay Concerning Human Understanding.* Oxford: Clarendon Press.

Loevinger, Jane. 1976. *Ego Development.* San Francisco: Jossey-Bass.

Lorenz, Frederick, K.A.S. Wickrama, Rand Conger, and Glen Elder. 2006. "The Short-Term and Decade-Long Effects of Divorce on Women's Midlife Health." *Journal of Health and Social Behavior* 47: 111–25.

Lynd, Robert, and Helen Lynd. 1929. *Middletown: A Study in Contemporary American Culture.* New York: Harcourt, Brace.

———. 1937. *Middletown in Transition: A Study in Cultural Conflicts.* New York: Harcourt, Brace.

Lyons, Linda. 2005. (May 24). "Tracking U.S. Religious Preferences over the Decades." *The Gallup Poll Tuesday Briefing.* Washington, DC: Gallup Organization.

Marcia, James, A. Waterman, D. Matteson, S. Archer, and J. Orlofsky, eds. 1993. *Ego Identity: A Handbook for Psychosocial Research.* New York: Springer-Verlag.

Marty, Martin. 1993. "Where the Energies Go." *Annals, ASPSS* 527: 11–26.

———. 1996. *Modern American Religion.* Vol. 3, *Under God, Indivisible, 1941–1960.* Chicago: University of Chicago Press.

Maslow, Abraham. 1964. *Religions, Values, and Peak Experiences.* Columbus: Ohio State University Press.

McAdams, Dan P., and Ed de St. Aubin. 1992. "A Theory of Generativity and Its Assessment through Self-Report, Behavioral Acts, and Narrative Themes in Autobiography." *Journal of Personality and Social Psychology* 62: 1003–15.

McCrae, Robert, and Paul Costa. 2003. *Personality in Adulthood.* New York: Guilford.

McCullough, Michael, Craig Enders, Sharon Brion, and Andrea Jain. 2005. "The Varieties of Religious Development in Adulthood." *Journal of Personality and Social Psychology* 89: 78–89.

McCullough, Michael, and Timothy Smith. 2003. "Religion and Health: Depressive Symptoms and Mortality as Case Studies." In *Handbook of the Sociology of Religion,* ed. Michele Dillon, pp. 190–204. New York: Cambridge University Press.

McCullough, Michael, M.E. Tsang, and S. Brion. 2003. "Personality Traits in Adolescence as Predictors of Religiousness in Early Adulthood." *Personality and Social Psychology Bulletin* 29: 980–91.

McFadden, Susan. 1999. "Religion, Personality, and Aging: A Life Span Perspective." *Journal of Personality* 67: 1081–1104.

McFadden, Susan, Mark Brennan, and Julie Hicks Patrick, eds. 2003. *New Directions in the Study of Late Life Religiousness and Spirituality.* New York: Haworth.

McGreevy, John. 2003. *Catholicism and American Freedom: A History.* New York: Norton.

McMordie, W.R. 1981. "Religiosity and Fear of Death: Strength of the Belief System." *Psychological Reports* 49: 921–22.

Midanik, L.T., K. Soghikian, L. Ransom, and I. Tekawa. 1995. "The Effect of Retirement on Mental Health and Health Behaviors." *Journal of Gerontology: Social Sciences* 50B: S59–61.

Miller, Perry. 1956/1964. *Errand into the Wilderness.* Repr. Cambridge, MA: Harvard University Press.

Mirowsky, John, and Catherine Ross. 2003. *Education, Social Status, and Health.* New York: Aldine de Gruyter.

Moberg, David. 2002. "Assessing and Measuring Spirituality: Confronting Dilemmas of Universal and Particular Evaluative Criteria." *Journal of Adult Development* 9: 47–60.

Moon, Dawne. 2004. *God, Sex, and Politics.* Chicago: University of Chicago Press.

Musick, Marc A., Harold G. Koenig, Judith C. Hays, and Harvey Cohen. 1998. "Religious Activity and Depression among Community-Dwelling Elderly Persons with Cancer: The Moderating Effect of Race." *Journals of Gerontology, Series B: Psychological Sciences and Social Sciences* 53B: S218–27.

Muthén, L.K., and B.O. Muthén. 1998–2006. *Mplus User's Guide: Statistical Analysis with Latent Variables.* Los Angeles: Muthén & Muthén.

Myers, Scott. 1996. "Families and the Inheritance of Religiosity." *American Sociological Review* 61: 858–66.

Neitz, Mary Jo. 2003. "Dis/location: Engaging Feminist Inquiry in the Sociology of Religion." In *Handbook of the Sociology of Religion,* ed. Michele Dillon, pp. 276–93. New York: Cambridge University Press.

Nelson, L.D., and C.H. Cantrell. 1980. "Religiosity and Death Anxiety: A Multi-Dimensional Analysis." *Review of Religious Research* 21: 148–57.

Neuman, Mathias. 1982. "The Religious Structure of a Spirituality." *American Benedictine Review* 33: 115–48.

Noll, Mark. 1992. *A History of Christianity in the United States and Canada.* Grand Rapids, MI: Eerdmans.

Pagels, Elaine. 1979. *The Gnostic Gospels.* New York: Random House.

Paloutzian, Raymond, and Crystal Park, eds. 2005. *Handbook of the Psychology of Religion and Spirituality.* New York: Guilford.

Parsons, Talcott. 1967. "Christianity and Modern Industrial Society." In *Talcott Parsons: Sociological Theory and Modern Society,* ed. Edward Tiryakian, pp. 385–421. New York: Free Press.

Patrick, Ann. 1999. "Forum on American Spirituality." *Religion and American Culture* 9: 139–45.

Pearce, Lisa, and William Axinn. 1998. "Family Religious Life and the Mother-Child Relationship." *American Sociological Review* 63: 810–28.

Peterson, William, and Eva Klohnen. 1995. "Realization of Generativity in Two Samples of Women at Midlife." *Psychology and Aging* 10: 20–29.

Porterfield, Amanda. 2001. *The Transformation of American Religion.* New York: Oxford University Press.

Pritchard, Linda. 1976. "Religious Change in Nineteenth Century America." In *The New Religious Consciousness,* ed. Charles Glock and Robert Bellah, pp. 297–330. Berkeley: University of California Press.

Putnam, Robert. 2000. *Bowling Alone: The Collapse and Revival of American Community.* New York: Simon and Schuster.

Radloff, Lenore S. 1977. "The CES–D Scale: A Self-Report Depression Scale for Research in the General Population." *Applied Psychological Measurement* 1: 385–401.

Radloff, Lenore S., and L. Teri. 1986. "Use of the Center for Epidemiological Studies Depression Scale with Older Adults." *Clinical Gerontologist* 5: 119–36.

Reimer, Sam, and Jerry Park. 2001. "Tolerant (In)civility: A Longitudinal Analysis of White Conservative Protestants' Willingness to Grant Civil Liberties." *Journal for the Scientific Study of Religion* 40: 735–45.

Rieff, Philip. 1966. *The Triumph of the Therapeutic.* Harmondsworth: Penguin.

Roberts, Brent W., and Wendy DelVecchio. 2000. "The Rank-Order Consistency of Personality from Childhood to Old Age: A Quantitative Review of Longitudinal Studies." *Psychological Bulletin* 126: 3–25.

Rogers, Carl R. 1961. *On Becoming a Person.* Boston: Houghton Mifflin.

Roof, Wade Clark. 1993. *A Generation of Seekers: The Spiritual Journeys of the Baby Boom Generation.* San Francisco: Harper & Row.

———. 1999. *Spiritual Marketplace: Baby Boomers and the Remaking of American Religion.* Princeton: Princeton University Press.

Roof, Wade Clark, and William McKinney. 1987. *American Mainline Religion.* New Brunswick, NJ: Rutgers University Press.

Ross, Catherine, and John Mirowsky. 2002. "Family Relationships, Social Support, and Subjective Life Expectancy." *Journal of Health and Social Behavior* 43: 469–89.

Rossi, Alice, S. 2001. *Caring and Doing for Others.* Chicago: University of Chicago Press.

Roth, Philip. 2006. *Everyman.* Boston: Houghton Mifflin.

Rousseau, Jean, Jacques. 1782/1968. *The Social Contract.* Baltimore, MD: Penguin.

Rowe, John, and Robert Kahn. 1998. *Successful Aging.* New York: Pantheon.

Ryff, Carol. 1989. "Happiness Is Everything, or Is It?: Explorations on the Meaning of Psychological Well-Being." *Journal of Personality and Social Psychology* 57: 1069–81.

Safranski, Rudiger. 1990. *Schopenhauer and the Wild Years of Philosophy.* Cambridge, MA: Harvard University Press.

Saroglou, Vassilis. 2002. "Religion and the Five Factors of Personality: A Meta-Analytic Review." *Personality and Individual Differences* 32: 15–25.

Schaie, K. Warner, Neal Krause, and Alan Booth, eds. 2004. *Religious Influences on Health and Well-Being in the Elderly.* New York: Springer.

Schieman, Scott, Tetyana Pudrovska, and Melissa Milkie. 2005. "The Sense of Divine Control and the Self-Concept: A Study of Race Differences in Late Life." *Research on Aging* 27: 165–96.

Schmidt, Leigh. 2005. *Restless Souls: The Making of American Spirituality.* New York: HarperCollins.

Seidler, John, and Katherine Meyer. 1989. *Conflict and Change in the Catholic Church.* New Brunswick, NJ: Rutgers University Press.

Shand, Jack. 1990. "A Forty-Year Follow-Up of the Religious Beliefs and Attitudes of a Sample of Amherst College Grads." In *Research in the Social Scientific Study of Religion,* ed. M.L. Lynn and D.O. Moberg, pp. 117–36. Greenwich, CT: JAI Press.

Shapiro, D.H., Jr., E. Schwartz, and J. Astin. 1996. "Controlling Ourselves, Controlling Our World." *American Psychologist* 51: 1213–30.

Sherkat, Darren. 2003. "Religious Socialization: Sources of Influence and Influences of Agency." In *Handbook of the Sociology of Religion,* ed. Michele Dillon, pp. 151–63. New York: Cambridge University Press.

Sinnott, Jan. 1994. "Development and Yearning: Cognitive Aspects of Spiritual Development." *Journal of Adult Development* 1: 91–99.

Skolnick, Arlene. 1981. "Married Lives: Longitudinal Perspectives on Marriage." In *Present and Past in Middle Life,* ed. Dorothy Eichorn, John Clausen, Norma Haan, Marjorie Honzik, and Paul Mussen, pp. 269–98. New York: Academic Press.

———. 1991. *Embattled Paradise: The American Family in an Age of Uncertainty.* New York: Basic Books.

Smith, Christian, and Melinda Lundquist Denton. 2005. *Soul Searching: The Religious and Spiritual Lives of American Teenagers.* New York: Oxford University Press.

Smith, D.K., A.M. Nehemkis, and R.A. Charter. 1983–84. "Fear of Death, Death Attitudes, and Religious Conviction in the Terminally Ill." *International Journal of Psychiatry in Medicine* 13: 221–32.

Smith, Denise. 2003. *The Older Population in the United States: 2002.* Current Population Report P20–546. Washington, DC: U.S. Census Bureau.

Smith, Tom. 2002. "Religious Diversity in America." *Journal for the Scientific Study of Religion* 41: 577–85.

———. 2006. "The National Spiritual Transformation Study." *Journal for the Scientific Study of Religion* 45: 283–96.

Sorensen, Annemette. 2007. "The Demography of the Third Age." In *The Crown of Life: Dynamics of the Early Post-Retirement Period,* ed. Jacquelyn James and Paul Wink. New York: Springer.

Spilka, Bernard, Ralph Hood Jr., Bruce Hunsberger, and Richard Gorsuch. 2003. *The Psychology of Religion: An Empirical Approach.* 3rd ed. New York: Guilford.

Stark, Rodney. 2002. "Physiology and Faith: Addressing the 'Universal' Gender Difference in Religious Commitment." *Journal for the Scientific Study of Religion* 41: 495–507.

Stark, Rodney, and Roger Finke. 2000. *Acts of Faith: Exploring the Human Side of Religion.* Berkeley: University of California Press.

Starr, Kevin. 1973. *Americans and the California Dream, 1850–1915.* New York: Oxford University Press.

Stewart, Abigail, and Joseph Healy. 1986. "The Role of Personality Development and Experience in Shaping Political Commitment." *Journal of Social Issues* 42: 11–31.

Stokes, Kenneth. 1990. "Faith Development in the Adult Life Cycle." *Journal of Religious Gerontology* 7: 167–84.

Stolzenberg, Robert, Mary Blair-Loy, and Linda Waite. 1995. "Age and Family Life Cycle Effects on Church Membership." *American Sociological Review* 60: 84–103.

Stone, Michael. 2000. "Normal Narcissism: An Etiological and Ethological Perspective." In *Disorders of Narcissism,* ed. Elsa F. Ronningstam, pp. 7–28. Northvale, NJ: Jason Aronson.

Strawbridge, William, Margaret Wallhagen, and Richard Cohen. 2002. "Successful Aging and Well-Being: Self-Rated Compared with Rowe and Kahn." *Gerontologist* 42: 727–33.

Swidler, Ann. 2001. *Talk of Love: How Culture Matters.* Chicago: University of Chicago Press.

Talbot, Margaret. 2005. "Darwin in the Dock." *New Yorker* (December 5): 66–77.

Thernstrom, Stephan. 1984. *A History of the American People.* Vol. 1: *To 1877.* New York: Harcourt Brace Jovanovich.

Thuesen, Peter. 2002. "The Logic of Mainline Churchliness: Historical Background since the Reformation." In *The Quiet Hand of God,* ed. Robert Wuthnow and John Evans, pp. 27–53. Berkeley: University of California Press.

Tocqueville, Alexis de. 1835/1946. *Democracy in America.* Vol. 1. Introduction by Phillips Bradley. Repr. New York: Knopf.

———. 1840/1946. *Democracy in America.* Vol. 2. Introduction by Phillips Bradley. Repr. New York: Knopf.

Tomer, Adrian, ed. 2000. *Death Attitudes and the Older Adult.* Washington, DC: Taylor and Francis.

Tornstam, Lars. 1994. "Gero-Transcendence: A Theoretical and Empirical Exploration." In *Aging and the Religious Dimension,* ed. E. Thomas and S. Eisenhandler, pp. 203–25. Westport, CT: Auburn House.

———. 2005. *Gerotranscendence: A Developmental Theory of Positive Aging.* New York: Springer.

Umberson, Debra, Kristi Williams, Daniel Powers, Hui Liu, and Belinda Needham. 2006. "You Make Me Sick: Marital Quality and Health over the Life Course." *Journal of Health and Social Behavior* 47: 1–16.

Underwood, Lynn. 1999. "Daily Spiritual Experiences." In Multidimensional Measurement of Religiousness/Spirituality for Use in Health Research: A Report of the Fetzer Institute/National Institute on Aging Working Group, pp. 11–17. Kalamazoo, MI: John E. Fetzer Institute.

U.S. Administration on Aging. 2002. *A Profile of Older Americans.* Washington, DC: U.S. Bureau of the Census.

U.S. Census Bureau. *Statistical Abstract of the United States.* Select years. Washington, DC: Bureau of the Census.

Vaillant, George. 1977. *Adaptation to Life.* Boston: Little, Brown.

———. 2002. *Aging Well.* Boston: Little, Brown.

Verba, Sidney, Kay Schlozman, and Henry Brady. 1995. *Voice and Equality: Civic Voluntarism in American Politics.* Cambridge, MA: Harvard University Press.

Wallach, M.A., and L. Wallach. 1983. *Psychology's Sanction for Selfishness: The Error of Egoism in Theory and Practice.* San Francisco: W.H. Freeman.

Ware, J. 1993. *SF-36 Health Survey: Manual and Interpretation Guide.* Boston: New England Medical Center.

Warner, R. Stephen. 1993. "Work in Progress toward a New Paradigm for the Sociological Study of Religion in the United States." *American Journal of Sociology* 98: 1044–93.

Weber, Max. 1904–05/1976. *The Protestant Ethic and the Spirit of Capitalism.* Repr. London: Allen and Unwin.

Weiss, Robert, and Scott Bass, eds. 2002. *Challenges of the Third Age: Meanings and Purpose in Later Life.* New York: Oxford University Press.

Wethington, Elaine, Ronald Kessler, and Joy Pixley. 2004. "Turning Points in Adulthood." In *How Healthy Are We?: A National Study of Well-Being at Midlife,* ed. Orville Brim, Carol Ryff, and Ronald Kessler, pp. 586–613. Chicago: University of Chicago Press.

Whyte, William H. 1956. *The Organization Man.* New York: Simon and Schuster.

Williams, Rhys, ed. 1997. *Culture Wars in American Politics.* New York: Aldine de Gruyter.

Wilson, John, and Marc Musick. 1997. "Who Cares? Toward an Integrated Theory of Volunteer Work." *American Sociological Review* 62: 694–713.

Wilson, John, and Darren Sherkat. 1994. "Returning to the Fold." *Journal for the Scientific Study of Religion* 33: 148–61.

Wink, Paul. 1991a. "Self and Object-Directedness in Middle-Aged Women." *Journal of Personality* 59: 769–91.

———. 1991b. "Two Faces of Narcissism." *Journal of Personality and Social Psychology* 61: 590–97.

———. 1992. "Three Narcissism Scales for the California Q-Set." *Journal of Personality Assessment* 58: 51–66.

———. 2006. "Who Is Afraid of Death? Religiousness, Spirituality, and Death Anxiety in Late Adulthood." *Journal of Religion, Spirituality & Aging* 18: 93–110.

———. 2007. "Everyday Life in the Third Age." In *The Crown of Life: Dynamics of the Early Postretirement Period,* eds. Jacquelyn James and Paul Wink, pp. 243–61. New York: Springer.

Wink, Paul, Lucia Ciciolla, Michele Dillon, and Allison Tracy. In press. "Religiousness, Spiritual Seeking, and Personality: Findings from a Longitudinal Study." *Journal of Personality.*

Wink, Paul, and Michele Dillon. 2001. "Religious Involvement and Health Outcomes in Late Adulthood." In *Faith and Health,* ed. T. Plante and A. Sherman, pp. 75–106. New York: Guilford.

———. 2002. "Spiritual Development across the Adult Life Course: Findings from a Longitudinal Study." *Journal of Adult Development* 9: 79–94.

———. 2003. "Religiousness, Spirituality, and Psychosocial Functioning in Late Adulthood." *Psychology and Aging* 18: 916–24.

———. 2007. "Do Generative Adolescents Become Healthy Older Adults?" In *Altruism and Health,* ed. Stephen Post. New York: Oxford University Press.

Wink, Paul, Michele Dillon, and Kristen Fay. 2005. "Spiritual Seeking, Narcissism, and Psychotherapy: How Are They Related?" *Journal for the Scientific Study of Religion* 44: 143–58.

Wink, Paul, Michele Dillon, and Britta Larsen. 2005. "Religion as Moderator of the Depression-Health Connection." *Research on Aging* 27: 197–220.

Wink, Paul, Michele Dillon, and Adrienne Prettyman. In press a. "Religion as Moderator of the Sense of Control-Health Connection: Gender Differences." *Journal of Religion, Spirituality, and Aging.*

———. In press b. "Religiousness, Spiritual Seeking, and Authoritarianism." *Journal for the Scientific Study of Religion.*

Wink, Paul, and Ravenna Helson. 1997. "Practical and Transcendent Wisdom: Their Nature and Some Longitudinal Findings." *Journal of Adult Development* 4: 1–15.

Wink, Paul, and Brian Schiff. 2002. "To Review or Not to Review? The Role of Personality and Life Events in Life Review and Adaptation to Old Age." In *Critical Advances in Reminiscence Work,* ed. Jeffrey Webster and Barbara Haight, pp. 44–60. New York: Springer.

Wink, Paul, and Julia Scott. 2005. "Does Religiousness Buffer against the Fear of Death and Dying in Late Adulthood?" *Journal of Gerontology: Psychological Sciences* 60B: 207–14.

Winnicott, Donald W. 1965. *The Maturational Processes and the Facilitating Environment.* London: Hogarth Press.

Winseman, Albert. 2005. "U.S. Evangelicals: How Many Walk the Walk?" *Gallup Poll Tuesday Briefing* (May 31): 118–19.

Wolfe, Alan. 1998. *One Nation, After All.* New York: Penguin.

Wong, Paul. 2000. "Meaning of Life and Meaning of Death in Successful Aging." In *Death Attitudes and the Older Adult,* ed. Adrian Tomer, pp. 23–35. Washington, DC: Taylor and Francis.

Workers of the Writers' Program of the Work Projects Administration in Northern California, comp. 1940. *San Francisco: The Bay and Its Cities.* New York: Hastings House.

Wulff, David. 1997. *Psychology of Religion: Classical and Contemporary Views.* New York: Wiley.

Wuthnow, Robert. 1988. *The Restructuring of American Religion.* Princeton: Princeton University Press.

———. 1998. *After Heaven: Spirituality in America since the 1950s.* Berkeley: University of California Press.

———. 1999. *Growing Up Religious.* Boston: Beacon Press.

———. 2003. *All in Sync: How Music and Art Are Revitalizing American Religion.* Berkeley: University of California Press.

———. 2004. *Saving America? Faith-Based Services and the Future of Civil Society.* Princeton: Princeton University Press.

Wuthnow, Robert, and John Evans, eds. 2002. *The Quiet Hand of God: Faith-Based Activism and the Public Role of Mainline Protestantism.* Berkeley: University of California Press.

Zinnbauer, Brian, and Kenneth Pargament. 2005. "Religiousness and Spirituality." In *Handbook of the Psychology of Religion and Spirituality,* ed. Raymond Paloutzian and Crystal Park, pp. 21–42. New York: Guilford.

Zinnbauer, Brian, and Kenneth Pargament, B. Cole, M. Rye, E. Butter, T. Belavich, K. Hipp, A. Scott, and J. Kadar. 1997. "Religion and Spirituality: Unfuzzing the Fuzzy." *Journal for the Scientific Study of Religion* 36: 549–64.

Index

activism. *See* social activism

Adams, Jack, 92–94, 136, 201

adolescents, 40–41

adolescent religiousness, 2, 6, 8, 40–59, 65, 67, 85, 89, 92, 95, 102, 106, 127, 132, 146, 147, 170, 174, 175, 182; long-term predictive power of, 92, 102–5, 246n18, 250n18. *See also* social aspects of church

adversity as path to spiritual growth, 9–10, 94, 104–5, 131–36, 188–89, 195

afterlife, 28, 47–48, 197–99, 200–3, 238n12, 256nn11,12

age of IHD participants, 12–13, 137–38

aging, 182–204, 214–17, 246n1. *See also* late adulthood; positive aging

agnostics, 37, 60

agreeableness, 144, 146–47, 148, 197, 249n15, 250nn16,18

AIDS, 90, 167–68, 181

Alcoholics Anonymous, 195

alcohol use, 92, 95, 183, 185, 190–91, 255n10

Allen, David, 180–82, 183, 186, 201, 254n1

Altemeyer, Bob, 250–51n21

altruism, 105, 162, 166–68, 181, 253n7. *See also* generativity

Alzheimer's patients, 10, 223

ANOVA, explained, 238n8

apostasy, 104

archetypes, 176

arts. *See* creative activities

ashram, 9

Atchley, Robert, 98–99, 112

atheists, 92–94

attitudes. *See* authoritarianism; social attitudes

attrition, 232n4

authoritarianism, 148–52, 156, 176–77, 197, 212, 250n20, 250–51n21, 251n22

autonomy, 60–61, 79, 121–22, 159, 164, 206–8. *See also* choice in religion; freedom, religious

baby boomers, 34, 79, 137, 213, 214–17, 238n6, 241–42n14, 245n2

Baha'i, 129

Baptist Church (American), 24, 26, 31, 41, 51, 54, 65, 67, 70

Bell, Jane, 8–11, 34, 123, 128, 131, 141, 147, 159, 164, 179, 203